REFLECTIONS ON
THE CONCEPT OF LAW

REFLECTIONS ON *THE CONCEPT OF LAW*

AW BRIAN SIMPSON

OXFORD
UNIVERSITY PRESS

OXFORD
UNIVERSITY PRESS

Great Clarendon Street, Oxford OX2 6DP

Oxford University Press is a department of the University of Oxford.
It furthers the University's objective of excellence in research, scholarship,
and education by publishing worldwide in

Oxford New York

Auckland Cape Town Dar es Salaam Hong Kong Karachi
Kuala Lumpur Madrid Melbourne Mexico City Nairobi
New Delhi Shanghai Taipei Toronto

With offices in

Argentina Austria Brazil Chile Czech Republic France Greece
Guatemala Hungary Italy Japan Poland Portugal Singapore
South Korea Switzerland Thailand Turkey Ukraine Vietnam

Oxford is a registered trade mark of Oxford University Press
in the UK and in certain other countries

Published in the United States
by Oxford University Press Inc., New York

First published 2011

British Library Cataloguing in Publication Data
Data available

Library of Congress Cataloging in Publication Data
Library of Congress Control Number: 2011933725

Typeset by SPI Publisher Services, Pondichery, India
Printed in Great Britain
on acid-free paper by
CPI Group (UK) Ltd, Croydon, CRO 4YY

ISBN 978-0-19-969332-0

1 3 5 7 9 10 8 6 4 2

Foreword

I am delighted to have been asked to provide a Foreword to this, Brian Simpson's last book. Brian began his academic life as a legal historian of the common law—the body of law derived from the decisions and practice of the courts, as distinct from the laws imposed by statute. But he also played a significant part in debates about the method and scope of Oxford legal philosophy. Throughout his time at Oxford, he contributed to the informal jurisprudence discussion group organized by Professor Herbert Hart, and edited one of the influential sets of Oxford Essays in Jurisprudence. Particularly striking among Brian's several original—and sometimes devastating—contributions to legal theory was his 1973 essay 'The Common Law and Legal Theory', which is included in the second of this series.[1] But since then, whilst continuing to be interested and to read widely in the area, Brian's subsequent writings did not directly engage with Oxford analytical jurisprudence, until recently. *Reflections* revisits Brian's fascination with, and ambivalent respect for, Hart's *The Concept of Law* and analytical jurisprudence more generally (whether of the Oxford variety, or those originating elsewhere).[2]

There are several different ways of reading *Reflections*. At one level, it is an attempt to set out in some detail Brian's understanding of the historical and intellectual context in which *The Concept of Law*, first published in 1961, was written. Nicola Lacey's illuminating biography, *A Life of HLA Hart: The Nightmare and the Nobel Dream*,[3] has already laid bare much of Hart's life, but Brian is able to describe the academic environment from his own experiences as a young don in the Oxford of the 1950s and 1960s. Some of this material was published earlier in Brian's reviews of Lacey in the *TLS*[4] and in

1. In AWB Simpson (ed), *Oxford Essays in Jurisprudence* (2nd Series, OUP, 1973).
2. OUP, 1961; 2nd edn, 1994.
3. OUP, 2004.
4. AWB Simpson, 'Stag Hunter and Mole', *Times Literary Supplement*, February 11, 2005, 6–7.

the *Michigan Law Review*,[5] but in *Reflections* Brian draws out in a more sustained way the diverse, if flawed, jurisprudential traditions that preceded Hart, and the range of intellectual sources that appear to have influenced Hart when he was writing *The Concept of Law*, providing an important supplement to Lacey's account. This is intellectual history of the most engaging kind, not least because it is peppered with classic examples of Brian's famous wit. There is much pleasure to be gained from Brian's accounts of post war Oxford life, irrespective of the background they present to Hart's work; indeed, it is the autobiographical aspects of the book that provide some of the most illuminating and funny moments.

At another level, *Reflections* is an extended critique of Hart's book, elaborating and extending the range of Brian's reservations about the methodology and substantive argument of *The Concept of Law*. From his earlier writings, we know that Brian was critical of what he saw as Hart's lack of attention in *The Concept of Law* to the workings of the common law tradition. Hart's emphasis on law as a system of rules was, he thought, more appropriate for the analysis of continental civil law systems. For Brian, the English common law system 'consists of a body of practices observed and ideas received by a caste of lawyers'.[6] Historically, cohesion was produced through institutional arrangements, such as the way the legal profession is organized, rather than by way of rules, which only developed when the previous consensus based on tradition or custom broke down. For Simpson, legal history and legal anthropology were therefore central tools in coming to an understanding of what law is; he considered that, for Hart, they were irrelevant. This earlier critique is developed further in *Reflections*, leading to further criticisms of *The Concept of Law*. The formulation of the rule of recognition, the absence of comparative law analysis, the difficulties with Hart's approach to adjudication, and the book's omission of any sustained discussion of human rights, are all analysed and criticized.

At a third level, *Reflections* comes as close as Brian ever came to setting out his own 'anti-grand-theory' theory of legal scholarship. Brian's own most important contributions to legal scholarship were in the area of legal history. During his time at Kent, but increasingly after he went to the United States, he developed the original idea, as Joshua Getzler, the Oxford legal historian has pointed out, that the 'leading cases' of the common law deserved the

5. AWB Simpson, 'Herbert Hart Elucidated' (2006) 104 *Michigan Law Review* 1437.
6. Simpson (ed), *Oxford Essays in Jurisprudence*, above, 94.

fullest possible study in their historical context.[7] He made this approach his own special area, drawing out new facts, and emphasizing the contingency of these leading cases, and deepening our understanding of their particular meaning and significance. His study of *Dudley and Stephens* (the 19th Century case in which shipwrecked sailors were prosecuted for killing and eating a cabin boy) became an immediate classic on its publication in 1984, under the striking title of *Cannibalism and the Common Law: The Story of the Tragic Last Voyage of the Mignonette and the Strange Legal Proceedings to Which It Gave Rise.*[8] *Cannibalism* was followed by a flow of fascinating studies of other leading common law cases. His study of detention without trial in Second World War Britain, effectively an extended study of *Liversidge v Anderson*, was published in 1992 as *In the Highest Degree Odious.*[9] A collection of shorter studies of several other cases, *Leading Cases in the Common Law*, was published in 1995. This genre of scholarship is now commonly known, according to Richard Helmholz, his former colleague at the University of Chicago Law School, as 'doing a Simpson'.[10]

One of the noteworthy aspects of this body of scholarship is the determined way in which Brian avoided being drawn into any sustained discussion of abstract legal theory, preferring to allow the books' relevance for legal theory to be drawn out by readers themselves. We know that Brian had in mind a book-length treatment of the common law tradition, along the lines of Merryman's book on the civil law tradition,[11] and this book might have addressed more directly his own theoretical views, but sadly it was not completed by the time of his death. In *Reflections,* however, in setting out his analysis of where he and Hart differ, we begin to get a clearer idea of Brian's own approach to legal theory. Agreeing with William Twining's description of him,[12] drawing on Isaiah Berlin's famous distinction,[13] as a fox rather than a hedgehog, he makes clear that his approach to law is essentially fox-like. In contrast, he regards Hart as an exemplar of a

7. JS Getzler, 'A.W.B. Simpson, Leading Cases in the Common Law' (1997) 18 *Journal of Legal History* 116–118.
8. University of Chicago Press, 1985.
9. OUP, 1994.
10. RH Helmholz, 'Brian Simpson in the United States', in K O'Donovan and GR Rubin (eds), *Human Rights and Legal History: Essays in Honour of Brian Simpson* (OUP, 2001), 285, 288.
11. John Henry Merryman, *The Civil Law Tradition* (Stanford University Press, 1969).
12. William Twining, 'The *ratio decidendi* of the Case of the Prodigal Son', in O'Donovan and Rubin, above, 149, 150.
13. Isaiah Berlin, *The Hedgehog and the Fox: An Essay on Tolstoy's View of History* (Weidenfeld and Nicholson, 1953).

hedgehog's approach to law. For Brian, legal theorizing should derive from detailed empirical analysis of what happens in social practice. He is thus deeply sceptical of grand abstract theories that ignore the evidence of such practice. Not surprisingly, he considered that analytical jurisprudence should build from social practice, rather than seek to impose itself on social practice.

This is not the place to consider whether Brian's analysis of Hart is ultimately correct. There is no doubt that much of what he writes will create controversy, and attract debate. At least, I hope it does. He would have relished being once again an *enfant terrible*, of course, but he never courted controversy for its own sake. He was the ultimate scholar, in seeking to advance understanding about law through debate and contestation. He considered that those who espoused analytical jurisprudence had largely ignored the implications of his work and the challenges it posed for their work. In seeking to engage with *The Concept of Law, Reflections* not only pays Hart the ultimate compliment of treating him seriously, but also shines a clearer light than before on Brian's own intellectual development and scholarly approach.

Christopher McCrudden FBA
Oxford
July 2011

Contents

List of Abbreviations

AJCL	American Journal of Comparative law
BDCL	Biographical Dictionary of the Common Law
BYIL	British Yearbook of International law
CLJ	Cambridge Law Journal
DNB	Dictionary of National Biography
HFE	Hart-Fuller exchange
HLR	Harvard Law review
HREE	Human Rights and the End of Empire
JCLIL	Journal of Comparative Legislation and International Law
JLS	Journal of Legal Studies
JSPTL	Journal of the Society of Public Teachers of Law
Lacey	*A Life of H. L. A. Hart: The Nightmare and the Noble Dream* (OUP, 2004)
LQR	Law Quarterly Review
MichLR	Michigan Law review
MLR	Modern Law Review
ODNB	Oxford Dictionary of National Biography
OJLS	Oxford Journal of Legal Studies
PAS	Proceedings of the Aristotelian Society
PBA	Proceedings of the British Academy
UCLALR	University of California Los Angeles Law Review
UCLR	University of Chicago Law Review
UPLR	University of Pennsylvania Law Review
YLR	Yale Law Review

I

The Apology to the Reader

This book is about HLA Hart's *The Concept of Law*. I have called it *Reflections*, echoing the title used by WW Buckland in his *Some Reflections on Jurisprudence* (1949). The point is to indicate that this book is very much an egocentric piece of writing, devoted to explaining my personal relationship with a book which has fascinated me for some fifty years. *The Concept of Law* was first published in 1961, and is still in print in a second edition of 1994, in which the original text remains unchanged. It has sold over 150,000 copies. However success is properly to be judged, it has to be conceded that this book is the most successful work of analytical jurisprudence ever to appear in the common law world. John Austin's *The Province of Jurisprudence Determined* of 1832 has lasted longer, but is no longer widely read, if indeed it ever was. I have no idea how many copies were printed, but I should guess five hundred or so, and Hart's edition of 1954 might have run to a couple of thousand. Austin has ceased to function as the point of entry into the subject; it once did before Hart took it apart in *The Concept of Law*.

Going Back to Troy I

Readers of this book could be forgiven for reacting with some weariness at the prospect of yet another contribution to the abundant literature which has been developed around *The Concept of Law*, and the criticisms which have been levelled against it. There is certainly no shortage. Hart's successor in the Oxford chair, Ronald Dworkin, whose appointment was indeed engineered by Hart himself, established his credentials as a jurist in the manner of the opening pages of *The Golden Bough*,[1] where a candidate to become the priest of Diana in the grove of Nemi has first to slay the current priest, whilst realizing that in the end he would suffer the same fate. Dworkin launched a vigorous attack on Hart's supposed failure to appreciate the significance of principles, as contrasted with rules, in the process of adjudication.[2] Apparently similar arguments had been advanced against views set out by Hart in undergraduate lectures by Dworkin in his final examination in Oxford in 1955—*The Concept of Law* did not exist in 1955.[3] Dworkin's continuous modifications of his arguments induced Geoffrey Marshall to say that arguing with him was like attempting to frisk a wet seal, and no doubt he can be faulted for this. But Neil MacCormick, in correspondence with me shortly before his death, suggested a more sympathetic view, whereby Dworkin is a person who just lets his ideas run, and they run forward. The moving finger writes, and having writ, moves on . . . There is no looking back over the shoulder, if seals have a shoulder, which I think they do. Since 1961 the volume of critical and expository literature has grown and grown. I do not propose to provide a bibliography, but there have been notable contributions, some sympathetic, some less so, from Neil MacCormick,[4] Joseph Raz,[5] Nicola Lacey,[6] John Finnis,[7] Frederick Schauer,[8] Jules Coleman and other contributors to a collection of essays on Hart's 'Postscript', published in the second edition of *The Concept of Law*[9],

1. JG Fraser, *The Golden Bough: A Study in Magic and Religion* (1890).
2. The attack opened with 'The Model of Rules' (1967) UCLR 35:14. See RM Dworkin, *Taking Rights Seriously* (1977) Chapters 2–4. This edition makes some changes to the original versions of what started life as articles in the UCLR (Ch 2), the Yale LJ (Ch 3) and the HLR (Ch 4). Dworkin's later development of his theories and frequent changes of position can be followed, albeit with difficulty, in *A Matter of Principle* (1985) and then into the wildly romantic *Law's Empire* (1986), and most recently into *Justice in Robes* (2006) as well as in his many contributions to the *New York Review of Books*.
3. See Lacey 185–6. Dworkin cannot today recall details. Hart kept Dworkin's exam scripts and returned them to Dworkin at a dinner in Brasenose. They no longer exist.
4. *Jurists: Profiles in Legal Theory, HLA Hart* (2nd edn, 2008). The first edition was published in 1981. See also *Legal Reasoning and Legal Theory* (1978); *Institutions of Law: An Essay in Legal Theory* (2007); *Rhetoric and the Rule of Law: A Theory of Legal Reasoning* (2005).
5. See his *The Concept of a Legal System: An Introduction to the Theory of a Legal System* (1970); *Practical Reason and Norms* (1975); *The Authority of Law: Essays on Law and Morality* (1979); *Between Authority and Interpretation: On the Theory of Law and Practical Reason* (2009).
6. *A Life of HLA Hart: The Nightmare and the Noble Dream* (2004).
7. *Natural Law and Natural Rights* (1980).
8. See eg, '(Re)taking Hart' (2006) 119 *Harvard LR* 852.
9. Jules L Coleman (ed and contributor), *Hart's Postscript: Essays on the Postscript to the Concept of Law* (2001).

from Mathew H Kramer,[10] from contributors to a 2007 British Academy Symposium,[11] from DJ Galligan.[12] This list could easily be extended.[13] Inevitably over the course of the years what Hart wrote back in the 1960s has somewhat faded away. A cynic, which I am not, might compare its fate to that of Troy I, buried under layer upon layer of overburden and much rubbish, but with gold to be found if the archaeologist can make it to the site early in the morning before the labourers make off with it. Entirely new analytical concepts have been invented; in addition to positivism we now have 'positive positivism',[14] 'plain fact positivism',[15] 'presumptive positivism',[16] 'exclusive legal positivism', 'the semantic sting',[17] and so it goes on in a fever of creative labelling.

In this book, however, I do not propose to consider this literature except very exceptionally. Instead the plan is to go right back to Troy I, paying virtually no attention to Troy II, or the rest of the overburden: back to *The Concept of Law* as it was written back in the 1950s and 1960s, and to the intellectual context in which it was produced. To this end I shall consider a number of Hart's writings which date from around this time. There will be one major exception. David Sugarman, to whom we should all be extremely grateful, arranged to interview Hart in 1988, which may of course embody some *pensées d'escalier*. Most of the interview has been published.[18] Sugarman has kindly also provided copies of a Legal Education Questionnaire which Hart completed for him in 1988 before the interview took place, Hart's observations on Oxford Legal Education, which were not included in the interview as published, and an uncorrected text of the published interview, together with a copy of the tape recording. I shall not give detailed footnote references to this material, and it will be obvious what is being used.

10. *In Defense of Legal Positivism: Law Without Trimmings* (1999).
11. MH Kramer and others (eds), *The Legacy of HLA Hart: Legal, Political and Moral Philosophy* (2008).
12. *Law in Modern Society* (2007).
13. There is a bibliography in *The Legacy of HLA Hart* which lists around 450 items, but not all of these are post 1961. The Hart industry is not however remotely comparable to the Wittgenstein industry. For an extensive bibliography of a more wide ranging type see W Twining, *General Jurisprudence: Understanding Law from a Global Perspective* (2009).
14. Kramer, note 10 above, at 130–161.
15. Dworkin in *Law's Empire* at 33 and generally.
16. Schauer, *Playing by the Rules* (1991) 196–206.
17. Dworkin in *Law's Empire* 45 and ff.
18. 'Hart Interviewed: HLA Hart in Conversation with David Sugarman' (2005) *JLS* 32:267.

What will be involved will in a sense be a game of let's pretend; let's pretend we are reading the book in 1961, having never had the opportunity to read the doubts and criticisms which have deluged out since those far off days. For this plan I need to offer both an explanation and a justification.

An Autobiographical Explanation: The Hart Group

The explanation is autobiographical. I was an undergraduate at Queen's College Oxford when Hart was appointed. I can still recall the excitement which was generated by it, though I, like many in the law school, including some of the dons, had never heard of him before. In company with my legal history tutor, Derek Hall, I attended his inaugural lecture in May 1953, urged to do so by Hall. In 1954 Hart was one of my examiners, and I was delighted and flattered when he gave my jurisprudence paper the mark of α – ? – I should perhaps explain that the Oxford grading system allowed for considerable subtlety, and I myself once gave a candidate the grade $\alpha\ \beta\ \gamma\ \delta$.[19] Hart's grade indicated some doubt as to whether two minuses was fair, and this again pleased me. An indirect consequence of Hart's view of my papers was that he supported me as a candidate for a junior research fellowship at St Edmund Hall, and for the tutorial fellowship which I was invited to take up at Lincoln College in 1955. Apparently the only other person considered was Norman St John Stevas, later a prominent conservative politician. The position was not advertised. The fellows were under the misapprehension that I played bridge, and needed a fourth player. It also led to an invitation in 1955 to join the faculty discussion group which Hart had established soon after he took up the chair. This met on Monday afternoons in the rooms of Rupert Cross in Magdalen; Rupert was blind, and this arrangement was the most convenient for him.[20] Hart called this a 'class' which it was not, but the use of the term is significant. Hart viewed the function of the group as being the education of his intellectually deprived colleagues in the law faculty. In his 1988 interview he mentioned only three of those who attended—his

19. The person involved was impossible to classify, and in the end was given a second on a split vote, much to the fury of David Daube, who had a high opinion of his abilities. Shortly afterwards he was appointed to a chair of law.

20. He became Vinerian Professor in 1964; the other candidate was John Morris who had been so rude about All Souls College (to which the chair was attached) that it was hardly possible for him to consider taking the position.

co-author Tony Honoré, Rupert Cross, the only other member of the law faculty with whom he developed a collaborative relationship, and the philosopher Tony Woozley. Woozley no longer attended in my time, having left for St Andrews in 1954. Those who also regularly attended were Tony Guest, then a law fellow at University College; Patrick Fitzgerald, law fellow at Trinity (who had gained a first in Greats and taken the bar finals, but held no law degree); and Geoffrey Marshall, politics fellow at Queen's. From time to time others joined the group, for example Nigel Walker, John Eekelaar, and Colin Tapper, and sometimes guests were invited, for example Barbara Wootton and Arthur Goodhart. Proceedings were informal and anyone could suggest a topic for next week's discussion, but Hart was very much the presiding, though not overly dominating, member.

Although it was not the practice to read formal papers, members of the group came to collaborate in the publication of a series of papers in *Oxford Essays in Jurisprudence*. The first volume was edited by Tony Guest and was published in 1961; Hart read and commented on all the papers in this collection, so that it was in a sense a collaborative work. The second was edited by me and appeared in 1973; my recollection is that on this occasion Hart was not so heavily involved, and I sent out draft papers to various academics for advice and comment as seemed appropriate. From the list of contributors one can identify individuals who came to attend the group, if only occasionally, and by no means all the published papers originated out of topics discussed in it. The series continued to a fourth volume published in 2000. I continued to attend the group until I left Oxford in 1972, though its character changed in ways which I did not entirely like when Dworkin replaced Hart in 1969. Nevertheless during my time in Oxford the meetings of the group ranked for me as far and away the most interesting and valuable event of the week. And attendance meant that I came to know Hart well at a professional level, though I never became a close friend or collaborator.[21] As I have explained elsewhere I had no idea of the three sources of anxiety which dogged him: his lack of confidence in his abilities as a philosopher, his insecurity over his sexuality, and his unease as to what he should do with the fact (of which I was long unaware) that he was a Jew.[22] I was not a diligent

21. I did later collaborate in responding to various queries arising from his editorial work on the Bentham project.
22. See my 'Herbert Hart Elucidated' (2006) MichLR 104:1437.

attender of lectures, and I only went to a few of Hart's; I did not find him an inspiring lecturer. At this time it was in any event not a common practice for teaching faculty members to attend professor's lectures, one reason being that they had very little time to devote to this—I used to teach something like twenty hours a week. I did however attend a joint seminar he ran with Tony Honoré on causation,[23] which I found very interesting, and I have a memory of attending a seminar on criminal responsibility he ran with Rupert Cross.[24]

Sitting at the Feet of the Masters

During my early time as an Oxford don I very much sat at the feet of those I conceived of as masters: Derek Hall for legal history, Herbert Hart for legal philosophy. Tony Honoré had been ill when I worked on the jurisprudence syllabus, and although I was greatly impressed by his abilities I found him somewhat intimidating, and failed to establish a close relationship with him, which I regret.

Masters do not have to be saints—indeed some masters are extremely unpleasant people, such as was Sir Isaac Newton. Hart was not in any way an unpleasant person, he came with warts like the rest of us, but I only became aware of them later in my time in Oxford. Briefly they may be summarized as follows. He was, if ever there was one, a champagne socialist. He had a tendency to become morally worked up on trivial or misconceived issues. He endlessly meddled in appointments, and was a poor judge of the merits of candidates; he promoted a disastrous candidate for a readership in tort law, being over impressed by an article which he wrongly imagined presented original views on tort law, a subject about which Hart knew little. There was a much better local candidate in Robert Heuston; there was fury that he had been passed by, and Hart's protégé was in effect driven out of Oxford. He also promoted John Barton for a fellowship at Merton, for which that college never really forgave him, though to be fair Barton, though profoundly eccentric, was a person of considerable ability. Hart's conduct over the choice of his successor, which involved ditching

23. This would be in Trinity Term 1953.

24. Lacey 162–4. This seminar was first given in Hilary Term 1966 under the title 'Mental Conditions of Criminal Responsibility'.

Honoré, his obvious successor, was appalling, though Honoré, seems to have forgiven him. He lacked a critical attitude to his own professional conduct; he was not immune from hypocrisy. He was thus human like the rest of us, and, notwithstanding his faults, he was an agreeable person to know, and generous in making himself accessible to graduate and undergraduate students. In spite of his own insecurity, which he successfully concealed, the public impression he gave to me reflected the arrogant and inhibiting self-confidence of the Oxford philosophers; they were, so they thought, extremely clever. He was extremely well read in both philosophical and general English literature; he was not at all well read in legal scholarship, though it was some time before I realized this. He was lucid in discussion, always seeking to put forward his views clearly and accurately.

In my early years at Lincoln College in the company of well-known scholars such as Howard Florey, Edward Abrahams, Sir John Beazley, Walter Oakeshott, Wallace Robson, David Henderson, and now forgotten figures such as Donald Whitton, and Harold Cox, I was in general hugely impressed by the scope of their scholarship, and the breadth of their reading. I was very conscious of the fact that my education at Oakham School, though first class in modern history, for there was one outstanding teacher, Robert Duesbury, who was justly idolized by his pupils, was otherwise quite second rate. I had first specialized in classics; the sixth form classics teacher, one John Moore, was a kindly man, but a poor classicist except at a purely technical level. His teaching method was continuous shouting and his main interest cricket. The intellectual culture of the country vicarages in which I had been brought up had been narrow and impoverished, though my father was something of an antiquarian. Given this background it was natural that I viewed Hart with awe, and I remain extremely grateful to him for all I learnt at his feet. And it was Hart who encouraged in me an interest in philosophy, which, for better or worse, will be reflected in this book.

I do not recall the Hart group ever having a general discussion of the central features or Hart's theory of law: the concept or a social rule, the internal and external attitudes to rules, the classification of rules as primary and secondary rules, the rules of recognition, change and adjudication. We never discussed *The Concept of Law* systematically. From time to time however discussion would develop on issues which were fairly directly connected to Hart's legal theory. Thus on one occasion Arthur Goodhart attended for a discussion of his *English Law and the Moral Law* (1953), and the consensus was that he had not been unconvincing in his defence of his position against Hart.

It was at this time common for members of the group to view Goodhart's abilities as a jurist with some disdain, and nobody could confuse Goodhart with any kind of philosopher. My first venture into publication in jurisprudence involved an assault on a much read and cited article by him. I suppose I, like Dworkin, must have grasped the fact that the way to establish a reputation in the academy was to go for the jugular of the guru. Insofar as Goodhart had any claim to guru status this depended on his theory as to how you determined the *ratio decidendi* of a case; at this time this was standard reading in both England and the USA. So between 1957 and 1959 I became involved in a somewhat tedious controversy over the matter, which greatly irritated the unfortunate Goodhart, though, being a kindly person, he forgave me.[25] The group did not discuss this, and Hart, curiously as it seemed to me, showed not the least interest. There is no explicit reference to it in *The Concept of Law*,[26] nor even to Goodhart's original article.[27] As we shall see Hart never developed an interest in the detailed analysis of the conventions and practices of legal argument and reasoning.

Chinks in the Armour

Indeed in due course I began to understand that there were aspects of legal scholarship and issues of legal theory in which Hart was wholly uninterested, and indeed wholly uninformed. There was no consequential sense of the fallen idol, merely a growing awareness that the great man was not a legal polymath. So far as my legal history master was concerned I similarly came to be aware of his weaknesses too. He was supposed to supervise me for a D Phil on late mediaeval and early modern law reporting, and had not the least idea how to perform this function, having himself never written a book, as opposed to editing a text. For books an author has

25. See (1957) 20 MLR 413, (1958) 21 MLR 155, (1959) 22 MLR 492. When the Hambledon Press published my collected papers in 1986 I excluded these pieces which I had come to view as simplistic. It was Goodhart who secured for me a visiting appointment to teach jurisprudence, not legal history, at the Dalhousie Law School in 1964.
26. In CL the expression occurs once on 134.
27. AL Goodhart, 'Determining the *Ratio Decidendi* of a Case' (1931) 40 YLJ 161, reprinted in *Essays in Jurisprudence and the Common Law* (1931).

to establish a structure; an editor of a text is provided with one on a plate. So I abandoned the enterprise, but retained the highest respect for his skills as an editor, and his general incisiveness as a scholar.

Encouraged by membership of the Hart group I began to read a fair amount of philosophy, and soon began to have doubts over the Oxford linguistic analysis school to which Hart belonged. As we shall see Hart had collaborated with the philosopher JL Austin, and professed considerable admiration for his abilities. Along with Gilbert Ryle, Austin was a dominant member of the Oxford group which espoused the cause of linguistic analysis, or ordinary language analysis. In the immediate post war period, and indeed earlier, the emphasis in philosophical circles was on the analysis of forms of communication which were thought to express statements or descriptions, which could, arguably, be true or false. Austin however was in particular associated with work on what came to be called 'performative utterances'. The basic insight was that some forms of human communication, whether by the use of speech or texts, constitute actions, in contrast to the making of a statement, as when one drops a brick on one's toe and utters the 'f-word'. Swearing is surely an action. I was quite unable to see what was so path-breaking in JL Austin's work on performatives.[28] What on earth was so innovatory about it? In what weird world did the Oxford philosophers live in, which pointing out the obvious ranked as some kind of intellectual breakthrough? What sort of hole had they dug themselves into, and why? And his style of writing seemed to me to be pretentious and ugly, though this is at its worst in his reconstructed and posthumously published works. He was incapable of presenting his ideas in lucid English, or perhaps unwilling to do so.

At this time I naively imagined, as indeed did Wittgenstein after he published a work, written in German, known as the *Tractatus Logico-Philosophicus* in 1921,[29] that philosophers might sometimes solve problems. Indeed Wittgenstein thought he had solved the lot, and for some time gave the subject up. Later, around the period in which we are interested, the idea

28. A short version, originally a BBC talk, is 'Performative Utterances', reprinted in JL Austin, *Philosophical Papers* (3rd edn) at 233. The full version is JO Urmson (ed), *How to Do Things with Words: The William James Lectures delivered at Harvard University in 1955* (1962). Publication of the full text, which develops an excruciating jargon which elaborates on the basic idea, has not changed my view.

29. English version by CK Ogden (1922), coauthor of *The Meaning of Meaning: A Study of the Influence of Language upon Thought and of the Science of Symbolism* (1923).

was entertained both in Cambridge and Oxford that once certain 'puzzles' or 'conundrums', themselves the product of mistaken ideas invented by philosophers, were cleared out of the way it would turn out that there were in reality no serious philosophical problems left. I myself did not appreciate that in the main, except when they stated the obvious, as in the case of performatives, philosophers were in the business of either identifying or even generating problems. Nor did I then, or indeed now, have any clear idea of what counts as solving a philosophical problem. In this I am in good company.

Since I shall be making a fair amount of reference to philosophical ideas and writers, whilst this book is written primarily for those who have not studied the subject, I think it will be useful for me to suggest some intelligible further reading, through which it is possible to obtain a basic grasp of the ideas and theories which were out there back in the post war period. Here there is no problem whatever, for Bryan Magee's brilliantly lucid *Talking Philosophy: Dialogues with Fifteen Leading Philosophers* could hardly be improved upon for this purpose.[30] Magee contrived to sign up outstandingly able teachers of philosophy to engage in a modern revival of the literary form of the platonic dialogues, and the resulting text does not engage in any sort of dumbing down for the general reader. Also strongly to be recommended is Magee's *The Great Philosophers: An Introduction to Western* Philosophy;[31] this is a book to be read as a whole. There are to be sure many other introductory texts, but I should not recommend them. Of course these books merely offer an entry into philosophy; gluttons for punishment will want to read more. But for the purposes of understanding *The Concept of Law* what is needed is a grasp of some fairly simple ideas.

Criticizing the Masters

By the 1960s I had begun to have reservations over the argument presented by Hart in his inaugural lecture, and by now I had developed sufficient self-confidence and pushiness to risk publishing a criticism of Hart, the reigning jurisprudential guru. So it was that in 1964 the *Law Quarterly Review*

30. 1978. The more important dialogues for our purposes are 1 (Isaiah Berlin), 5 (Anthony Quinton), 6 (AJ Ayer), 7 (Bernard Williams), 10 (John Searle), and 13 (Ronald Dworkin).
31. 1987. Hereafter cited as Magee.

published an article of mine[32] which criticized both Hart's view, and views which had been published by Alf Ross[33] and Wesley Hohfeld.[34] My basic argument was that it was an error to suppose that the elucidation of the nature or meaning of legal concepts could be advanced by reference to the typical or regular function legal words or sentences served. This article was written in a somewhat irritating style, and would have been hugely improved if I had run a draft past a linguist, or lexicographer, which I did not do since I knew no linguists or lexicographers.[35] It has never provoked a response, and indeed has been more or less totally ignored. There is an odd practice in the academy of simply ignoring critical writings, sometimes perhaps because they are thought to be rubbish, but sometimes because those criticized can think of no reply. Hart himself was well able to crush opponents if he felt the need, his abilities being well illustrated in his demolition of Professor Bodenheimer in 1956–7.[36] But I escaped, albeit at the price of being ignored. The article was however discussed in the Hart group, Hart himself taking virtually no part in the discussion; I recall only that Tony Guest was unimpressed. Outside the group David Daube congratulated me. I continue to think that the arguments put forward were broadly correct.

Hart himself also came to the conclusion that the thesis he had advanced in his inaugural lecture was not quite correct, but he never suggested that my article played any part in this. The evidence is that it did not. For in the introduction to his *Essays in Jurisprudence and Philosophy* (1983) he wrote that his reservations over his lecture arose because it did not take on board JL Austin's distinction between the *meaning* and the *force* of statements. Austin had in his BBC talk, and much more fully in his *How to Do Things With Words*, distinguished between the meaning of an utterance such as 'I name this ship Peerless', and what he called in his ugly invented jargon its *illocutionary force*.[37] The distinction is basically quite simple: it is one thing

32. 'The Analysis of Legal Concepts' (1964) 80 LQR 531. Reprinted in my *Legal Theory and Legal History: Essays on the Common Law* (1987) at 335.
33. 'Tû-tû' (1957) 70 HLR 812.
34. *Fundamental Legal Conceptions* (1923) Chapter 1.
35. It was written when I was teaching in Dalhousie, and a draft was read by the late George Nicholls, who was a prominent Canadian academic lawyer.
36. 'Analytical Jurisprudence in Mid-twentieth Century: A Reply to Professor Bodenheimer' (1957) UPLR 105. See also the ferocious review of Dias and Hughes *Jurisprudence* in (1958) 4 JSPTL 143.
37. For discussion see KT Fann, *Symposium on J. L. Austin* (1969) at 26ff, 420ff, 445ff and Magee 10.

to say what the words 'I', 'name', 'this', 'ship', *'Peerless'* mean, and another to say what is going on when the statement is made, roughly affixing an identity to a vessel. It is not clear how Hart would have modified the text of his lecture to reflect this distinction, which can become problematic. He never did so.

Not very long after the discussion of my article I read to the Hart group a short paper on the unstructured and argumentative form of the common law judicial opinion—so utterly different from, for example, a French judicial opinion. Briefly, I suggested that originally judges in tricky cases, for example those determined on demurrer, or on special verdicts, argued openly with each other *before* the decision was taken. The hope was that in due course consensus would be achieved. Sometimes these arguments went on for years, voting not being viewed as a good way to resolve disagreement. *After* the decision was taken it was not the regular practice to provide any explanation as to why it had been reached. In the course of the sixteenth and seventeenth centuries such a practice did develop, but the post decision explanations retained their original discursive and argumentative form.[38] In the common law world this continues to be the case. Subject to some modifications in detail this is what did happen.[39] It was quite clear that Hart was not in the least interested in the form of the common law judicial opinion, and indeed did not even see that there was anything to be explained. Thus I came to realize that there were areas of legal scholarship which were of no interest to him at all. In time I came to realize how very extensive they were.

The Cox-Simpson Seminar of 1964–72

In 1964–1967 I collaborated with Harold Cox, who had been the philosophy tutor in Lincoln since 1929, in presenting each year a seminar on *The Concept of Law*, open both to undergraduates and graduates from the law faculty and to anyone else who wished to attend. It was advertised in the lecture lists for 'Greats',[40] and 'PPE'—Politics, Philosophy and Economics,

38. I still have a text of this paper.
39. See JH Baker, *The Legal Profession and the Common Law*, 167–9, 472–6; Baker is not however concerned with the form of the common law judicial opinion.
40. Classical literature and history, and philosophy. The school was also called *Litterae Humaniores*. If taken in full it involved a four year course, with two examinations, the first being known as Classical Honour Moderations, in both of which one could obtain a class.

also called 'Modern Greats'.[41] It was well attended both by graduates and undergraduates, and by some academics or future academics, such as JR Lucas,[42] and Joseph Raz, who attended in 1967. At the time Raz was I think a doctoral student. Back in 1951 Cox had collaborated with Tony Woozley in putting on a graduate class on the philosophy of ordinary language, and this may have encouraged in him an interest in applying linguistic analysis to legal questions. Cox was at this time the Sub-Rector, that is deputy head, of Lincoln College. There he was a dominating figure, renowned for his selfishness, cynicism, and often vicious and cruel wit. Indeed shortly before I came to Lincoln, the political scientist Kenneth Wheare had turned down an offer to be considered for the headship of the college because he did not want to spend the rest of his life having points scored off him by Cox.[43] During the war Cox had worked as a civil servant, becoming private secretary to Sholto Douglas,[44] who was an alumnus of Lincoln College, and who was Air Officer Commanding Fighter Command from 1940–2, and later of Coastal Command from 1942. Otherwise he spent his whole working life in Lincoln College.[45] In spite of the unattractive side of his character I came to get along well with him, and valued discussions with him on intellectual matters. Harold was gay, but any reference to this was wholly taboo.

His analytical skills may be illustrated by the following anecdote. The college had a scholarship to award, funded by alumni of the college. The trust required attention to be paid to the candidate's participation in 'manly sports'. The ablest candidate having been identified, Cox pointed out that his file lacked evidence of manly sports. Someone drew attention to the fact that he had once bravely rescued a boy scout, who had become stuck up a cliff. Cox pointed out that unless he had put the boy scout there this could not count as a manly sport. The candidate was recalled and asked if he had indeed done so. Plainly thinking he was in a lunatic asylum he assured us no. Further questioning revealed that he had, as he put it, 'felt good about it', and this enabled the scholarship to be awarded. But Cox dissented. Feeling

41. Introduced in the 1920s; a three year programme.
42. It is mentioned with approval in his *The Principles of Politics* (1966) and in his essay for Hart's 1977 *festchrift* at 85.
43. There is some account of Harold Cox in John Dancy, *Walter Oakeshott: A Diversity of Gifts* (1988).
44. (1893–1969). Later Lord Douglas of Kirtleside.
45. Previously RG Collingwood, of Pembroke, taught philosophy for the college.

good was not any kind of sport, much less a manly one. Cox, like other Oxford dons, was free to develop eccentricities of behaviour, and did so. One was that he only opened letters if he guessed that he would like what he would find in them; when he left his college rooms there were sackfuls of unopened letters left behind, some dating back twenty or more years. He was persistently rude to college servants, one of whom I once overheard smashing his teacups whilst chanting 'Cox, Cox, Cox'. But he was never rude to Mr Gray, the college chef.

I was delighted when he agreed to collaborate in the seminar, taking it in turns to open the discussion with a paper. Cox, rather like Hart, was deeply insecure, though he concealed this, and was terrified lest he should in his paper say anything which was incorrect; by midday on the day of the seminar he would tell me that he was unable to deliver his paper, and it was only with great difficulty that I was able to persuade him to utter at all. He was no publisher, and in his entire academic career he never published a single word; he burnt a book he had written on Kant.[46] He once told me that there were two jokes in that work; I regret never having noted them down. He also claimed that Kant corresponded with a Scottish sea captain; I have no idea if this is something only he knew. Eventually, after retirement, Harold contracted cancer, and having destroyed all his remaining papers, committed suicide, as he had always said he would.

So it was not surprising that this seminar, which we ran until 1972, did not lead directly to any joint publications, though my essay 'The Common Law and Legal Theory', published in 1973, ultimately derives from discussion in the seminar.[47] I have long since lost most of my notes, but the topics we discussed concentrated on central elements in *The Concept of Law*, such as social rules, the internal and external attitude to rules, the distinction between primary and secondary rules, and the like. In 1967 I think we discussed Dworkin's attack on Hart, taking the view that his distinction between rules and principles was muddled. Rightly or wrongly Cox and I did think that we had identified some serious difficulties in *The Concept of Law*, notwithstanding its merits. The rationale for the seminar was that it was an important and distinguished book.

46. Cox lectured on Kant's *Critique of Pure Reason* on numerous occasions, for example in Michaelmas Term 1956.

47. Published in *Oxford Essays in Jurisprudence* (Second Series) 1973.

Hart never attended, and indeed never showed the least interest or curiosity in what was going on in the seminar. I suspect that by this time he had come to be mired in the anxieties which prevented him from ever completing his reply to his critics, and just did not want to know, and in 1968 he had taken the extraordinary step of resigning his chair on the ground that he had nothing further to contribute to the subject. If adopted as a general policy this would surely convert the groves of academia into howling wildernesses.

This brief autobiographical account may explain how I came to adopt a more critical attitude to Hart's *The Concept of Law* and to his scholarship generally, but there was no sense in which I did not continue to think of it as having made a major contribution, given its purpose—the elucidation of the concept of law and the concept of a legal system in a book designed primarily for law teachers and law students, but also for political scientists, philosophers, and 'the general reader'. It appeared as the third volume of The Clarendon Law Series, edited by Hart, and as such was intended to be both readable and introductory in character. It was Hart who had persuaded the Oxford Press to promote this series.

From Explanation to Justification

But I need also to *justify* inflicting on the public yet another publication, ultimately parasitic on *The Concept of Law*. My justification is that I propose to discuss matters arising out of the text, and the context in which it was written back in the 1950s and 1960s which have, since then, either not been discussed or even mentioned at all, or discussed in an inadequate way.

But before we get into these matters we need to know a little about how it came about that Hart was elected to the Oxford Chair of Jurisprudence, a position which had begun life back in the nineteenth century in order to provide Sir Henry Maine with a platform in Oxford, and a little more about what was thought to constitute 'jurisprudence' in Oxford when Hart joined the law faculty in 1952.

2

The Corpus Chair and Oxford Jurisprudence as Evolved by 1952

An Auspicious April Fool's Day in 1952

Hart, at the time a fellow of New College, and philosophy tutor there, was elected to the Oxford Chair of Jurisprudence on 9 February 1952.[1] He was to take office on April Fool's day. The chair was vacant through the resignation of Arthur Goodhart, who had been elected in 1951 as Master of University College. It was duly advertised in the *University Gazette*. The duties attached to the chair were not, in a formal sense, onerous—not a thirty six hour week, but a thirty six hour year, for this was the number of lectures to be delivered. The job description was that of the Victorian Corpus Chair of General Jurisprudence:

> The Professor of Jurisprudence shall lecture and give instruction on the history of Laws and the comparative Jurisprudence of different nations; in addition he may, if he thinks fit, treat of the principles of laws in general, and of any other matters relevant to the subjects of his chair which he thinks advisable.[2]

The Board of the Faculty of Law had been asked if it had any views on the election, which could have included a recommendation that the statute governing the chair be amended, but, whether from indolence, or commitment, had none.[3]

1. The Oxford University Archives UR 6/JUR/1, file 1 contains surviving papers. See Lacey 148–151.
2. *Oxford University Gazette* 1951–2 at 240.
3. The minutes are in FA 4/6/2/6–7.

The Origin of the Corpus Chair[4]

The Chair of Jurisprudence began life back in the 1860s as a product of the reform movement which both broadened the range of subjects which could be studied at Oxford and which sought to establish there a distinguished professorate. For some the model was the German professorate. Since 1850 there had existed a School of Law and Modern History. To obtain a degree of Bachelor of Arts it was first necessary to take *Literae Humaniores*, or Greats.[5] Then you had to study and be examined in either Mathematics and Physics, or Natural Science, or Law and Modern History. This could be done either at the level of what was called a common degree (which came to be called a pass degree), or for honours. In the latter eventuality Law and Modern History included 'Jurisprudence, and especially the Laws of England'.[6] Under this scheme Law and Modern History was essentially a graduate school, but bore no relationship to modern graduate schools, for the academic standard involved was extremely modest.[7] At around the same time attempts were made to strengthen the professorate. The Vinerian Professor, JR Kenyon, did not bother to lecture, nor did the Regius Professor of Civil Law, J Phillimore.[8] But in 1855 Phillimore was succeeded by Travers Twiss. Twiss, who held the chair from 1855 to 1870, and had previously held chairs of Political Economy and of International Law, adopted the exciting new practice of actually delivering some lectures. Sadly his legal career came to an unfortunate end in 1872. He had married a lady reputed to be the orphaned daughter of a Polish officer; imputations were made against her chastity, and he sued for criminal libel. The case collapsed under cross examination, leaving his reputation in ruins.[9] Thereafter he betook himself to pure historical scholarship, at which he did not excel. His successor was the distinguished scholar and political figure James Bryce, who though non-resident continued to deliver lectures in Oxford

4. I am greatly indebted to Ray Cocks and Nick O'Brien who have investigated the Corpus Archives with a view to establishing how the chair came to be established.
5. Greats was examined in two stages, known as Honour Moderations and the Final Honour School.
6. For an account see FH Lawson, *The Oxford Law School 1850–1965* (1968) at 20 and ff.
7. Lawson 29. From 1860 separate papers were set for those seeking honours.
8. Kenyon held the chair until his death in 1880; Phillimore until 1855.
9. See my BDCL. 514, ODNB, and M Taggart, 'Alexander Chaffers and the Genesis of the Vexatious Actions Act 1896' (2004) 63 CLJ 656.

until 1893.[10] In 1859 All Souls College established the Chichele Chair of International Law and Diplomacy, the first holder being again a serious scholar, Mountague Bernard.[11]

In 1866 the system changed, and it became possible to obtain a Bachelor of Arts degree simply by taking one Final School. The Master of Arts degree was, after a decent interval, automatically conferred on payment of a modest sum, as it still is.[12] The content of the papers was determined by the examiners, appointed by the Vice-Chancellor and the two Proctors, who changed annually under a system of rotation around the colleges. There was no Board of Studies until 1872, and no Faculty Board until 1882. Hardly any individuals who were later to achieve eminence as lawyers took Law and Modern History, either before or after 1866.[13] Intending barristers did not normally study law at university, a tradition that lasted until after the second war. As for solicitors they did not count in the eminence stakes at all, and hardly any Oxford graduates would have considered joining the profession. You became a solicitor through apprenticeship.

In 1877 Law and Modern History died, and a Final Honour School of Jurisprudence was established under the supervision of a Board of Studies. The syllabus for this was always to include 'General Jurisprudence'. Somewhat grudgingly it could include some English law.[14] Even when I studied law in Oxford in the 1950s one third of the first examination was in Roman Law, and only four of the eight papers in my final examination were on current English Law. One of them, that on Real Property, was only remotely connected to the real world of property transactions. To a lesser extent this is true in American law schools; I have often had to explain to my Michigan first year property class that we are not engaged in studying any system of property law which actually exists in the USA. Our minds are fixed on higher things.

Underlying all this was the notion that a university law school was just not in the business of replacing the system of apprenticeship whereby barristers and solicitors were trained. It was not entirely clear what business it was involved in, but the basic idea was that it was the function of a

10. 1838–1922, became Viscount Bryce, Ambassador to the USA 1907–1913; he gave up the chair on becoming President of the Board of Trade.
11. 1826–1882, see the ODNB entry by M Lobban.
12. The basic rule is twenty one terms after joining the university (matriculation).
13. The most notable were James Bryce, later Regius Professor Civil Law, and WGF Phillimore, later a House of Lords judge. The abler individuals had normally obtained degrees in Greats.
14. See Lawson 36 and ff.

university legal education to provide what may loosely be called a theoretical foundation for legal study. I have explored the thinking on this elsewhere, but by way of illustration let me instance Sir William Markby's *Elements of Law Considered with reference to the Principles of General Jurisprudence* (1871). Markby saw his book as providing an essential and necessary intellectual contribution to legal study, which justified its being treated as a fit object for study in universities. Law could and ought to be studied as an organized body of knowledge, and not simply picked up as you went along in the manner in which children learn games:

> ... the only preparation and grounding which a University is either able, or, I suppose, would be desirous to give, is in law considered as a science; or at least, if that is not yet possible, in law considered as a collection of principles capable of being systematically arranged and resting, not on bare authority, but on sound logical deduction ... In other words, law must be studied in a University, not merely as it has resulted from the exigencies of society, but in its general relations to the several parts of the same system, and to other systems.[15]

I have explored all this more fully in a lecture delivered to the Salmond Symposium in 2006.[16]

There had to be some teachers, and there were a number of college tutors who performed this function. What they actually did by way of teaching is largely unknown, and none of them were legal scholars of any kind.[17] In the view of the reformers what was needed was the appointment of distinguished professors, whose appointment would raise the intellectual tone of the law school—much as was the idea when Hart was elected in 1952. One obvious candidate was Sir Henry Maine, whose *Ancient Law* had established him as the leading legal intellectual of the period. So the plan which emerged in the 1860s was to bring him to Oxford.

In 1865 the proposal was made in the governing body of Corpus Christi College that a professorship of jurisprudence be established. The proposal came from Dr JM Wilson, later to become White's Professor of Moral Philosophy, and President of Corpus. There is no direct evidence of any external pressure on the college. In 1867 the college decided that the professorship should be called The Corpus Professorship of General Jurisprudence, and should require residence for no more than three months.

15. Introduction at xiii.
16. (2007) 38 *Victoria Univ Wellington L Rev* 669.
17. See Lawson at 50.

This requirement was subsequently relaxed. The professor was to be paid £600 each year, roughly equivalent to £48,000 today. The initiative now came from Kenelm E Digby, who was to be from 1868 to 1874 the Vinerian Reader, attached to All Souls College, with the obligation to teach both English Law and Civil Law.[18] The Civil Law, leading to the BCL and DCL degrees, had been studied in Oxford since the early middle ages, but in the early nineteenth century the subject was moribund.[19] In 1851 the first steps were taken to introduce an elementary examination for the BCL.[20] Eventually it was to become the normal graduate law degree as it is today.

The Corpus Chair was thus created *ad hominem*.[21] Maine had been the Legal Member of the Viceroy's Council in British India from 1862, and this position came to an end in 1869. In 1867 Maine visited England, and it is clear from the Corpus archives that he was actively involved in discussions over details of the appointment, including the membership of the electoral board, and the residence requirement.[22] His appointment was published in *The Times* on December 8 1869. The statute governing the chair had been drafted for Maine. In its original form it read:

> *Professoris Sartremunus esto legum historiam tractare; leges diversarum gentium inter se comparare; principia iuris exponere; alia in materie sua docere quae usibus academiae expedire putaverit.*[23]

In 1882 a new statute was approved by the Queen in Council under the *Oxford and Cambridge Act* of 1877. This was drafted as a close English translation of the original statute:

> The Corpus Christi Professor of Jurisprudence shall lecture and give instruction on the history of laws and the comparative Jurisprudence of different nations; in addition to which he may, if he thinks fit, treat of the principles of laws in general, and of any other matters relevant to the subjects of his chair that he may judge advisable.[24]

Residence for twenty eight nights each year was now required. This was called pernoctation.

18. Later a County Court Judge (1892–4), then Permanent Under Secretary at the Home Office (1895–1903). Involved in public service until his death in 1916.
19. The study of Canon Law had been abandoned at the reformation.
20. Lawson 23.
21. Maine had been given an Honorary LLD in 1865.
22. In the event Maine appears to have spent around two days a week in Oxford during full term.
23. Text from *Statuta Universitatis Oxoniensie* 1874 at 59.
24. *Statuta Universitatis Oxoniensie* 1896 at 45.

The statute thus embodied the conception of the nature of jurisprudence which was associated with Maine. This came to be called historical jurisprudence, and might involve the comparative study of legal evolution. But also lurking in the job description was the notion of *general* jurisprudence, explained back in 1828 by John Austin in his *The Uses of the Study of Jurisprudence*:[25]

> Though every system of law has its specific and characteristic differences, there are principles, notion and distinctions common to various systems . . . Many of these common principles are common to all systems;—to the scanty and crude systems of rude societies, and the ampler and maturer systems of refined communities.[26]

The study of them in maturer societies Austin called general jurisprudence, or comparative law. Their study continued to form a large part of what counted as jurisprudence in Oxford and elsewhere in the 1950s and beyond. In his *The Early History of Institutions* (1875) Maine somewhat surprisingly accepted Austin's theory of sovereignty, that every political society had an uncommanded commander.[27] Why he did this is puzzling, and it certainly did not mean that he had changed his views on the historical evolution of law.

Lawson in his history of the Oxford Law School published some early examination papers, for example those from 1875, which give an impression of what undergraduates then studied as 'jurisprudence'.[28] Out of ten questions only four can, with a bit of stretching, be viewed as relevant to historical jurisprudence, and one gets the impression that comparing the history of English and Roman law was much emphasized. It is obscure what students were then expected to read.[29]

Maine's Lectures[30]

From 1870 Oxford published an official *Gazette*; the early issues simply contained professorial announcements of lectures. Later the *Gazette* published

25. Not in print until 1863. 26. 366. 27. 349. 28. At 198–9.
29. The two papers set in 1872 (see at 192–194), General Jurisprudence I and II, contained twenty questions in all, of which four or five fitted the subject; no less than five questions required knowledge of Bentham's writings.
30. Paul Vinogradoff's Inaugural Lecture of 1904 'The Teaching of Sir Henry Maine' (in vol 2 of Vinogradoff's *Collected Papers*) has interesting things to say about Maine at a high theoretical

termly lecture lists as approved by Faculty Boards.[31] Lawson did not make use of this source of information; a study of it would be a major undertaking. It is not at all clear who actually attended Maine's lectures, or who was expected to be interested. In 1870 he lectured on 'Ancient Systems of Law Surviving in the East' and in 1872 on 'The Attempts made in Indian Legislation to simplify certain parts of the English Law of Real Property'.[32] In 1872 his announced subject was Warkonig's *Institutes of Roman Private Law*; he only proposed to cover the Introduction and First Book.[33] Who, one wonders, would attend 'The So Called Codes of the Hindoos and the Primitive Relationship of the Lawyer to the Priest' (1876)? Or an 1877 offering, 'The House Communities of the South Slovenians, considered as illustrating portions of the Early History of Institutions'? Many of his lectures relate to interests which produced his *Early History of Institutions*, published in 1875, for example 'Some Problems in the Ancient Constitution of Hellenic or Latin Society and the light thrown on these by recent researches' (1877). Others do not, for example 'Theories of Judicial Evidence', and 'Sovereignty' both in 1872. It is implausible to suppose that the dimmer law students attended, and one cannot but wonder who else, if anyone, did. Maine himself became concerned and tried to descend from the heights; in 1871 he announced a proposal to form a twice weekly class for the discussion of the text of Austin. Again whether anyone attended is obscure. In 1872 there is a further entry in the *Gazette*:

> The Professor proposes to form a class for elementary instruction in Jurisprudence.

In 1875 he complained that the only lectures which attracted much of an audience had to be on 'elementary Austinianism', since this was relevant to the examinations. There was little interest in comparative jurisprudence.[34] Maine resigned the chair in 1878 in order to take up a position as Master of Trinity Hall Cambridge, but gave a final Oxford lecture in 1879 on 'Village

level, but does not discuss in any detail at all what teaching Maine actually provided in Oxford.

31. In what follows I shall not give detailed footnote references, since it is perfectly simple to locate entries. However for anyone working in Oxford one needs to know that the *Gazette* is shelved in the Radcliffe Science Library, Level 7, which is the same as Level 2.

32. Lawson at 48–9.

33. Leopold August Warnkonig (1794–1866). His *Institutiones juris Romani privati* was published in 1834. I am indebted to Tony Weir for identifying this author, of whom I had never heard.

34. Lawson at 49.

and other land communities in relation to recent researches'. Who would have attended? There was no school of anthropology in Oxford at this time, but perhaps there were medievalists interested. Or perhaps it was just Maine's friends. One has no idea, and I wonder if he gave formal lectures or conducted something in the nature of a discussion group.

The Amendment of 1968

The concept of historical jurisprudence as the subject of the chair persisted in a formal sense up to Hart's election. What was specified for the chair was not some version of analytical positivism associated with the writings of John Austin, but an ill-defined conception of historical jurisprudence, which had originated with one of his critics, married to the Austinian conception of general jurisprudence. Lurking somewhere was also the Austinian conception of positive law. Views on the merits of Maine's theories have fluctuated over time, and there is a school of thought which regards his conception of how early law evolved as simply rubbish. This view is for example maintained, not entirely convincingly, in AS Diamond's *Primitive Law Past and Present* (1971).[35] We shall have an account of his style of scholarship in Chapter 5 below, but here I shall not say more.

It was not until 1968, the year in which Hart resigned, that the statute was changed, and the attempt to define the scope of the subject was abandoned. It was brightly if unhelpfully provided that:

> The Professor of Jurisprudence shall lecture and give instruction in Jurisprudence.[36]

The revision was probably the consequence of a decision to publish all the University statutes in English; the moving spirit here was the distinguished natural scientist Rex Richards. So gems like *De Habitu et Vestitu Scholarum* vanished in the name of progress, and the opportunity was taken to do some tidying up. The consequence was that Ronald Dworkin was the first professor of jurisprudence in Oxford who was required to teach jurisprudence, and whatever he thought was jurisprudence would serve. This is somewhat odd since Dworkin has at times expressed the view that as an

35. vii, 45, 47, 61, 104, 124, 378. For discussion see below Chapter 6 at pp 171–6.
36. See page 7 of the revised statutes of that year.

independent branch of scholarship the subject simply does not exist at all. One is reminded of Thomas Erskine Holland, who held the Chichele Chair of International Law from 1874–1911. He did not think his subject existed, 'law' being a mere courtesy title. Unsurprisingly he, unlike Dworkin, did not make any notable contributions to the subject.

Maine's Successors

After Maine's resignation the chair remained vacant until he was succeeded by Sir Frederick Pollock in 1883.[37] He held the chair until 1903.[38] Why the chair remained unfilled I have no idea; Maine indeed wanted Pollock to succeed him.[39] Pollock gave lectures on a wide variety of subjects—some basically historical, as on early land tenure,[40] whilst others dealt with wider issues, such as 'The Theory of the State as in the English Publicists'.[41] His farewell lecture was on 'History of Comparative Jurisprudence'.[42] He had a reputation as being an intimidating person and a boring lecturer. But back in those days lectures were normally read out from texts, and were all somewhat boring. Nearer my time Sir William Holdsworth used to repeat everything three times through his walrus moustaches to ensure it was copied down correctly:

> The law of England. The law of England. I say the law of England.

So everyone knew what the subject was.

Pollock was succeeded by Paul Vinogradoff, who held the chair until his death in 1925. Vinogradoff was followed by Walter Ashburner. Ashburner's appointment was somewhat bizarre. He was an American who had been educated in England, and he had obtained a double first in Classical Honour Moderations and Greats. He became a fellow of Merton in 1887, and was called to the bar in 1892. Between 1898 and 1903 he acted as Assistant Reader in Equity for the Council of Legal Education. In that year he went to live in Florence, where he died in 1936. He was a classical scholar of considerable ability, and was privately wealthy, with no need to earn a living. He was nevertheless author of books on mortgages, equity, and the Rhodian

37. See generally Duxbury esp at 29 and ff.
38. Pollock continued to be one of the electors to the chair until his death in 1938.
39. Duxbury at 46–7. 40. As in 1898. 41. 1900. 42. 1903.

maritime laws; his two practical legal books may have been written in the hope that they would help his career at the bar. According to his obituarist:

> His lectures, thinly attended ('too good for the schools' they were called) exhibited an immense range of learning, and were diversified by most unexpected illustrations, narrated with verve, and punctuated by quaint, even mordant, comments upon mankind.[43]

Only the titles for his lectures survive. In 1927, for example, he provided 'Principles of Jurisprudence' and in 1928 'Elements of Jurisprudence'. In Trinity Term of that year he was loose on 'Criminal Jurisprudence' and 'Introduction to the Study of the Canon Law'. Whatever precisely it was he expounded, now undiscoverable, he made absolutely no impact on historical or any other kind of jurisprudence, and he resigned the chair when he found travel between Florence and Oxford too exhausting. It was with his appointment that the chair was transferred to University College. Possibly it was to offer lectures which the law students could understand that John Walter Jones of Queen's College offered a rival course on 'General Jurisprudence'.

Ashburner's successor was Carleton Kemp Allen,[44] who had acted as secretary to Vinogradoff, and was apparently groomed to succeed him. In October 1928 he had been appointed to a Lectureship in 'Theoretical Jurisprudence'; he was to lecture twice a week for two terms and 'make a special study of modern theoretical jurisprudence'.[45] He gave a series of courses on 'General Jurisprudence'. He was appointed to succeed Vinogradoff in 1929, but he resigned in 1931 on his appointment as a Warden of Rhodes House. His only major jurisprudential publication was *Law in the Making*.

In 1931 Arthur Goodhart was elected on a split vote of three to two. The electors were the then Master of University College, Sir Frederick Pollock, F de Zulueta, WS Holdsworth, and JL Brierly. There is no record of the voting, nor mention of other candidates. Goodhart was at the time a fellow of Corpus Christi College, Cambridge, and had edited the *Law Quarterly Review* since 1926. The votes against Goodhart could have come from those who thought that some attention should be paid to the statute governing the

43. See Lawson at 126–7. Obituary in *The Times* 24 February 1936.
44. 1887–1966.
45. Presumably this became the theoretical section of his book, *Law in the Making*.

chair, and thus may well have included Zulueta, Brierly, and Holdsworth.[46] Zulueta was a roman lawyer, whose life's work was supposed to have been burnt by Duff Cooper in a drunken orgy in New College; in my time the belief in the faculty was that this work was a myth.

Of those who had held the chair Pollock could, with some stretching, be thought to have had appropriate scholarly interests, and he certainly had little time for Austin. Allen's very successful *Law in the Making*, which was a product of the Empire, derived from the Tagore Lectures delivered in Calcutta in 1926. It went into seven editions, the last in 1965, and could certainly be viewed as a work of historical jurisprudence of a kind, though it could equally well have been categorized as legal history.[47] Goodhart regularly provided lectures which gave a potted history of legal theory, rather in the manner of Bertrand Russell's *A History of Western Philosophy*. For example in Hilary Term 1950 he gave lectures on 'Jurisprudence' on three days each week. These provided a guided tour starting, I think, for I never attended his lectures, with Plato, and in due course he moved into the middle ages with Aquinas. Then it was Grotius and Pufendorf, followed by Jeremy Bentham, John Austin and Henry Maine, the lectures ending up with contemporaries, such as Hans Kelsen. It was the practice in Oxford in my time to mock these lectures, texts of which were in circulation. I now think rather better of such introductions. But the reality was that Goodhart had not the slightest interest in the official subject matter of his chair. Indeed in the period between 1869 and 1952 the only professor who ideally fitted the job description was Vinogradoff. After his appointment he at first published and taught what could only be categorized as legal history, but his plan was to publish a multi-volume work under the title *Outlines of a Historical Jurisprudence*, developing an evolutionary theory of law. He envisaged six stages in legal evolution, the first three being universal: totemistic, with no technical law at all; then tribal, law discovered and declared by a chief;[48] then civic law, the law of city states. Two volumes appeared in 1922 and 1924, but he did not survive to complete the project.[49] They are largely and deservedly forgotten.

46. See OU archives cited above n1. Pollock had supported Goodhart's appointment as editor of the *Law Quarterly Review*.

47. I was indeed approached by the OUP to produce a revised edition, but took the view that the book had reached the end of its life.

48. The concept involved is that of the Homeric 'themistes'.

49. For an account see the life by P Stein in ODNB. His *Collected Papers* appeared in 1928.

By 1952 it had come to be accepted that the lectures, and subjects associated with the chair, should not be 'historical jurisprudence', however defined, but just be 'jurisprudence', whatever that was. There was no criticism of the fact that Hart, once appointed, paid not the least attention to the subject he was officially required to profess.

Hart's Legal Education

As Nicola Lacey points out in her biography, at the time of his election Hart had previously had little contact with the law faculty, and many of its twenty nine members had probably never even heard of him.[50] When filling in a questionnaire before he was interviewed in 1988 Hart stated, without any qualification, that he had never had a legal education. In a loose sense this was true, and no doubt the process of cramming whereby intending barristers like Hart prepared for the bar exams could not be counted as education in any serious sense. But Hart was for some uncertain but not inconsiderable time taught law by an academic lawyer, Charles AW Manning (1894–1978), who was the New College law fellow from 1924 to 1930.[51]

Hart obtained his first in Greats in 1929 and then set about the task of taking the final honour school of jurisprudence in one year, with the intention of obtaining a second first class degree.[52] This was a perfectly possible plan; Harry Lawson had obtained a first in Modern History in 1920, and one in Jurisprudence in 1921. If you set to work in July, you had eleven months for the task, not much less time than was available to those who followed the more normal route, and devoted two years, less vacations and parties, to hard study. Hart was taught by Manning, and the time was mainly devoted to the study of cases. The syllabus also involved subjects, such as Roman Law, for which familiarity with case law was irrelevant, but given his Greats background it is unlikely that Hart would have needed any help there. After something like six months—this would be around Xmas of 1929—Hart decided to give up the attempt and simply take the bar examinations. As Lacey explains he was at this time also working to prepare for his examination for an All Souls fellowship; he also apparently spent some

50. Lacey 148 and ff.
51. Appointed 1923; college fellowships were normally seven year appointments, renewable.
52. Lacey 40 and ff.

time on vacation. To have persisted in the plan and end up merely with a second was a risk not worth taking.

Who then was Charles Manning? He was a scholar of considerable distinction. There is a most informative life by Alan James in the *New Oxford Dictionary of National Biography*, on which what follows is largely based. He was a South African Rhodes Scholar who was admitted to Brasenose College in 1914. He served as a commissioned officer in the war, and then returned to Oxford to complete his studies. He was a pupil of 'Sonners' that is of Stallybrass, later Principal of Basenose Colllege.[53] He obtained the equivalent of a first in Greats in 1920, followed by a first in Jurisprudence (1921) and one in the BCL in 1922. In 1923 he was elected to a law fellowship in New College, which he took up in 1924. In 1930 he left New College to take up a chair at the London School of Economics in the newly invented subject of international relations, in relation to which he was the leading pioneer. He retired from the LSE in 1962.

It is on record that Hart got along well with Manning, though he noted by way of criticism that Manning 'believed in apartheid'. This was recorded many years later, and the chronology is of some importance. As a formal system of social organization, apartheid in South Africa only dates from 1948–1994, though long before this, back in the 1930s, the National Party had popularized the term amongst its supporters. It is, however, in the highest degree unlikely that it would have been a topic of conversation in Oxford back in 1930. After he retired from the LSE in 1962 Manning grew distressed at the criticisms levelled against the South African government, and became its vocal and prominent supporter. It was surely during this period that he became known as a supporter of apartheid.

Manning whilst at New College had shown interest in jurisprudential issues, and he must have taught the subject. He edited the eighth edition of *Salmond on Jurisprudence* (1930), though only making minor changes of which he thought Salmond himself would have approved. He contributed a notable chapter, 'Austin Today or The Province of Jurisprudence Re-examined', to a collection, *Modern Theories of Law*, edited by WI Jennings (1930). This had previously been delivered as a lecture at the London School of Economics in 1932; Hart could have attended but there is no evidence that he did. This was far and away the best critical analysis of Austin's theory of its time, and it let drop, though in an extremely elusive manner, ideas

53. See my BDCL.

which were later to be developed by Hart, for example the internal point of view (though not under this name),[54] power conferring rules,[55] continuity of law,[56] and the notion of a necessary hypothesis which is not empirically based.[57] I have no recollection of this article ever being mentioned in my time in Oxford, and have no recollection that I ever read it then.[58] It is nowhere cited by Hart, and I am not of course suggesting that he was in any way devious in this. If he read it back then, or discussed it with Manning, he may well have forgotten this, and there is no direct evidence that he did read it. But if Hart was planning to acquire a law degree in one year one of the subjects he needed to cover would have been jurisprudence, and he would have needed some instruction. So it seems to me to be inconceivable that at some point in their relationship Hart did not discuss jurisprudential issues with Manning, and it is possible that Hart's later work developed interests first encountered with Manning.[59]

The Election of Hart

Professorships were in the hands of an electoral board, chaired by the Vice-Chancellor, at this time the flamboyant and extremely opinionated Maurice Bowra, Warden of Wadham. The other members were the Master of University College,[60] the Regius Professor of Civil Law, HF Jolowich, the Professor of International Law, CHM Waldock, the Professor of Comparative Law, FH Lawson, the Vinerian (or as we called him the Venereal) Professor of English Law, Harold G Hanbury, the Warden of Rhodes House, Carleton Kemp Allen, and a Fellow of University College, AF Wells.[61] There were only two applicants for the chair, Hart and Norman S Marsh. Hart's referees were Sir Charles Harman, by now a judge, and former head of his chambers, and Wilfred M Hunt, Hart's pupil master at the bar. The third was Gilbert Ryle, the Waynflete Professor

54. 188, but only a hint. 55. 190. 56. 198. 57. 202, 208.
58. It is criticized by J Stone in his *The Province and Function of Law* 62 note 62.
59. Manning later published articles in the *Cambrian Law Journal* in 1970 and 1972 'Those South West African Cases: A Second Look' (CLJ 1970 at 29) and 'Political Justice at the Hague' (1972 at 64).
60. This would be the outgoing Master, not Goodhart.
61. The list in Lacey at 150 seems mistaken in including WD Ross and omitting the Master of University College and Wells.

of Metaphysical Philosophy,[62] and editor of *Mind*. Their letters of support survive. The choice of two referees from Hart's time in practice suggests a desire to emphasize the fact that he was a lawyer, and not just a philosopher.

His rival, Norman Marsh,[63] was a member of the Law Faculty, being the Stowell Fellow of Civil Law, and Bursar at University College. He had obtained second class honours in the Honour School of Jurisprudence in 1935, and a first in the BCL in 1936. Between 1937 and 1941 he practised at the bar; he had been a pupil of Gerald Gardiner, later Lord Chancellor. He served in military intelligence during the war,[64] and then on the Control Commission in Germany—he was a fluent German speaker. He became a fellow of University College in 1946.[65] His referees were Professor RW Lee, Professor of Roman-Dutch Law, Theo H Tylor, the Balliol law tutor, and EJ Cohn of Lincoln's Inn, presumably the head of his chambers. Their letters of recommendation are not in the archives. By 1952 Marsh had published two jurisprudential articles, 'The German Legal System under National Socialism'[66] and 'Principle and Discretion in the Judicial Process',[67] and two in comparative law, 'The Liability of the Gratuitous Transferor: A Comparative Study'[68] and 'Deduction and Induction in the Law of Torts: a Comparative Approach'.[69] He had also published two articles on English contract law.[70] His article on the judicial process was given a favourable mention in an article Hart published in the following year.[71] Marsh was a serious scholar whom I misjudged at the time. I attended some of his lectures on Roman Law and thought they were purely derivative of a French author, Monier, whose elementary work on Roman Law I happened to possess. This was a mistake.

62. Attached to Magdalen College.
63. 1913–2004.
64. He was not, like Hart, in either domestic intelligence (MI5), or in the Secret Intelligence Service.
65. He left Oxford in 1956 to become, on a two year appointment, Secretary General of the International Commission of Jurists. He was involved in the establishment of the British Institute of International and Comparative Law, becoming its first director (1960–65), leaving to become one of the Law Commissioners, a position he held until 1978. He became a QC in 1967 and was awarded the CBE in 1977.
66. (1946) 62 LQR 366.
67. (1952) 68 LQR 226.
68. (1950) 66 LQR 39.
69. 33 JCLIL, 3rd ser. 59.
70. 'The Severance of Illegality in Contract' (1948) 64 LQR 230, 347.
71. At 363. 'Philosophy of Law and Jurisprudence in Britain (1945–1952)'.

Julius Stone, Challis Professor of International Law and Jurisprudence at Sydney, who had a distinguished history of publication, and was an Oxford graduate, was an obvious possible outside candidate, but did not apply.[72] The electors were not, however, bound to confine their attention to those who had formally applied, and the archival records indicate that Jolowich suggested that AP D'Entreves should be considered, a suggestion which does not appear to have secured any support.[73] There is no indication in the records that anyone else was formally considered, and no way of telling whether other names were discussed informally by the electors, though no doubt they would have been. Apparently there was a division of opinion on the board, and Hart was elected by a majority, the opposition coming, so it is said, from Hanbury and Allen; the archives do not record the voting. Bowra, who played an extremely active role in appointments, would have strongly favoured Hart, for he viewed members of the law faculty with considerable disdain.

Hart's two legal referees, Harman and Hunt, say nothing of Hart's abilities except as a barrister. Gilbert Ryle's letter does speak warmly of his abilities as a philosopher and teacher, and of his interest in issues connected with the law. Ryle then went on:

> There is a general point on which I must explain my opinion. The philosophy of law is, in this country, in the doldrums. With one or two exceptions hardly anything of interest to philosophers has been produced here for a very long time. The subject has advanced in Germany, Scandinavia and the United States—not very much, but noticeably.[74] We are not helping it to advance. My chief concern is for the subject of philosophy itself.

This clearly states the thinking which was accepted by a majority of the electors, and which led to Hart's appointment. This point of view would have been put to members of the board informally in the process of

72. (1907–1985), he read law at Exeter College, Oxford, at the same time as Hart and suffered from anti–semitism there.
73. (1902–1985). Count Alessandro Passerin D'Entreves was Serena Professor of Italian Studies in Oxford from 1945–1956 and a fellow of Magdalen College. He had been Professor of International Law in Turin and became Professor of Political Theory 1958–72. It was said in Oxford that he actually lived for most of the year in idleness in the south of France. Jolowich had reviewed his *Natural Law* (1951) sympathetically in *Philosophy* 27:86 (1952). D'Entreves wrote an introduction to a translation by JG Dawson of *Select Political Writings of Thomas Aquinas* (1954), which translation John Finnis tells me contains mistakes. His *The Notion of the State: An Introduction to Political Theory* was published in Oxford in 1967, and he also published *Scritti Politici di San Tommaso d'Aquino* (1946).
74. The reference to Germany is puzzling—perhaps Ryle thought of Kelsen as being German.

lobbying and intriguing which regularly accompanied appointments in Oxford in my time, and no doubt still does. It is therefore not surprising that the appointment was warmly welcomed by philosophers, some of whom went rather over the top in their delight at the possibility of now putting the lawyers to rights. Amongst letters quoted in Nicola Lacey's biography Ryle wrote that he:

> . . . was glad for the sake of the students who want to think.

And Hart's friend George Paul, the philosophy don in University College, who had encouraged Hart's interest in the chair, wrote that:

> It is splendid to see the empire of philosophy annex another province in this way—not to mention the good you are going to do them.[75]

Thus did the Oxford philosophers look down their noses at the members of the Law Faculty. Since then the appointment has been presented as positively inspired, as by Hart's collaborator, Tony Honoré, writing in the *Oxford Dictionary of National Biography*:

> During his tenure of the chair (1952–1968) Hart rescued English jurisprudence from its century long decline and restored it to a central position in moral and political philosophy.[76]

At least one member of the Law Faculty, Robert Heuston, agreed with the philosophers, writing of the 'intellectual slum of English Jurisprudence'.

Lacey, in the chapter she entitled 'Selling Philosophy to the Lawyers: the Chair of Jurisprudence', gives a fascinating account of the negative view which Hart himself had of the state of the subject of which he was now to be the professor, and the low opinion which he also had for his new colleagues, including those who had never purported to be scholars of jurisprudence, much less philosophers of law.[77] In his 1953 article he did make kindly remarks about three of them: Marsh, Goodhart (both of University College which was now his academic home), and Lawson, his supporter in the election, for contributions to jurisprudence.[78] One wonders to what extent he was merely trying to be tactful; he had to live with them now. In my

75. Lacey 149.
76. ODNB vol 25 at 575.
77. See also Lacey at 148–9.
78. 'Philosophy of Law and Jurisprudence in Britain (1945–1952)' (1953) 3 AJCL 355. The mention of Goodhart is in a footnote.

recollection he was not infrequently dismissive of Goodhart's abilities, though I never recall his being dismissive of Marsh or Lawson. When interviewed by David Sugarman in 1988 he explained that he thought that in the 1940s and 1950s jurisprudence at Oxford:

> ... was in a very bad way. It had no broad principles, no broad faith; it confronted no large questions. Typical of the period.

And to be sure it cannot be said that any member of the faculty had published a book with much life in it except for CK Allen, and this adopted some strange theoretical views. But again Goodhart got a pat on the back:

> I owed a lot to Goodhart in many ways and I do not wish to decry him.

Philosophy and Jurisprudence in 1952

Leaving on one side for the time being quite what it was that philosophy could contribute to jurisprudence, the basis for thinking that Hart was the man for the job was, in 1952, slim. Hart's publications comprised three articles, and three book reviews, only one of each having any obvious connection with law.[79] His only substantial publication which was directly relevant was 'The Ascription of Responsibility and Rights'. When Goodhart had become a candidate for the chair back in 1931 he, or perhaps, those electors to the chair who favoured his appointment, felt he had to have published a book on jurisprudence to become professor of the subject, surely not an unreasonable view. So he cobbled together a number of periodical articles, most of which could hardly be labelled jurisprudential, into a book, *Essays in Jurisprudence and the Common Law*.[80] Hart made no such gesture, and indeed could not have done so. Being an Oxford philosopher he was above such things.

It is a sign of how much the English academic world has changed that Hart was even considered for a major appointment on so exiguous a record of publication, which today would not have the least hope of getting a

79. See Appendix I. He had also published a preface to HWB Joseph's *Knowledge and the Good in Plato's Republic* (1948). For a full bibliography see PMS Hacker and J Raz (eds) *Law, Morality and Society: Essays in Honour of H.L.A.Hart* (1977) at 309.
80. Published in 1931; it contained some nineteen pieces. See RE Megarry's memoir in *Proceedings of the British Academy* 94: 475 at 479–480.

candidate onto the short list for a senior lectureship. But there have been changes in the perception of the importance of publication in establishing one's status as an academic. Amongst the Oxford philosophers of this period publication, though valued, was not viewed as essential; my Lincoln colleague Harold Cox never published a single word in his whole career. When JL Austin was appointed to the chair of Moral Philosophy in 1952 he had published a translation of Gottlob Frege's *Foundations of Arithmetic*,[81] and a handful of papers: 'Are there A Priori Concepts' (1939), 'The Meaning of a Word' (1940), 'Other Minds' (1946), and 'Truth' (1950).[82] He had also published a number of book reviews, but no book of his own.

Anthony Flew, writing in 1950, explained the lack of interest in publication amongst the philosophers of Oxford, Cambridge, and London, and the consequential ignorance of their work:

> . . . those of them who have been in touch with the new developments have been so engrossed in the exciting work of following up their fresh insights that they have for the most part written little or even nothing at all . . .[83]

So it was enthusiasm, rather than idleness. I think the explanation different—the only people who really mattered in the world of Oxford philosophy were those who were already members of the club, to whom publication had already taken place. I am confirmed in this view by an account given by Isaiah Berlin:

> We were extremely self-centered. The only persons we wished to convince were our own admired colleagues. There was no pressure on us to publish . . . We felt no need to publish our ideas, for the only audience which was worth satisfying was the handful of our contemporaries who lived near us, and whom we met with agreeable regularity.[84]

This, it is true, refers to meetings of Oxford philosophers, attended by Austin and AJ (Freddie) Ayer, back in the 1930s, but I think it true also of the post war period.

More remarkable still was the extremely weak basis for the belief that philosophy, and Oxford philosophy in particular, had something special to contribute to jurisprudence. In the course of the twentieth century nobody

81. Published by Blackwells in 1950 and in revised form in 1953.

82. All reprinted in JL Austin, *Philosophical Papers*, 3rd edn reprinted 2007.

83. Introduction to AGN Flew, *Logic and Language. First Series* at 1.

84. I Berlin, *Personal Impressions* (1980) at 115. The same passage is in I Berlin et al, *Essays on J. L. Austin* (1973) at 16.

who held an academic position in Britain as a philosopher, or who would have been primarily identified as a philosopher, had published a book, or for that matter an article, with any central and explicit relevance to the concept of law or of a legal system. There was, to be sure, writing related to the philosophers of the ancient world, in particular Plato and Aristotle, and writings related, for example, to Locke. Leaving such writings aside the most recent book which addressed what might be thought to be a jurisprudential issue—the proper limits of the coercive control of the law—by a British writer had been JS Mill's *On Liberty* of 1859. Broadly speaking the philosophers had not the least interest in contemporary law; the same is largely true today.

If English jurisprudence was in the doldrums at the time of Hart's appointment it is perhaps worth noting that in the prewar period English philosophy was somewhat in the doldrums too. Insofar as there was a geographical centre for philosophy, albeit of a weird kind, for it was the home of logical positivism, it was Vienna, not Oxford or Cambridge. The great Cambridge days of GE Moore and Bertrand Russell were over, and the Oxford philosophers, with the possible exception of RG Collingwood, were hardly giants in the field. But in the 1930s ideas associated with the Vienna Circle began to migrate northwards, most dramatically through Ayer's *Language, Truth, and Logic* (1936), which was hugely influential in spreading the gospel of logical positivism in the English speaking world.[85] But all this was to change with the rise of Wittgensteinian linguistic analysis in Cambridge, and a distinct form of linguistic analysis which was developed in Oxford, where it was particularly associated with Ryle and Austin. It came to be thought in some circles that Oxford was the place where the most interesting ideas were being developed; Ryle encouraged graduate students to work in Oxford and this was influential.

Wittgenstein returned to Cambridge in 1929 and gave small classes and lectures from 1930 onwards until the outbreak of the war in 1939; after the war he taught there as professor for only two years. It took some considerable time for his philosophical ideas to become widely influential, and the enthusiasm of some of his acolytes for excluding outsiders from the club cannot have helped. His *Tractatus* was, as we have seen, published in his lifetime, and widely studied, but *Philosophical Investigations* (1953), the basis for the post war developments, was posthumous. *The Blue and Brown Books*

85. For a brief account see Magee, *Talking Philosophy* (dialogue with AJ Ayer), 95–102.

did have some circulation in typescript, but did not appear in print until 1958.

Some Minor and One Major Exception

There had however been some writers on the theory of law who had knowledge of philosophical literature, and who had been associated with the Oxford Law Faculty, a fact which seems to have been somewhat forgotten. Indeed, it was quite common for intending barristers to study some philosophy through reading Greats at Oxford. Sir Erskine Holland, author of the very successful *The Elements of Jurisprudence* (1880), had taught philosophy at Exeter College for some years from 1859, probably on a part time basis to supplement his income as a barrister. This would have been on philosophers of the ancient world. After some years in practice he became an academic in Oxford from 1874, holding the Chichele Chair of International Law at All Souls from 1874–1911.[86] But he was thought of as a lawyer, not a philosopher, and he published only on law, making no use of his philosophical expertise in his writings. He was of an inflexible disposition and in revisions of his book took little note of criticisms. Sir Frederick Pollock, holder of the chair of jurisprudence from 1883 to 1903, and surely to be classed primarily as a lawyer, was also a competent exponent of philosophical ideas. Neil Duxbury, in his *Frederick Pollock and the English Juristic Tradition*, discusses the fact that he did make limited attempts to apply philosophical ideas to juristic issues; the conclusion he reaches is that Pollock was in general fairly unenthusiastic in this enterprise.[87] Pollock did publish a monograph on Spinoza, though Duxbury discusses the very limited degree to which he related his study of Spinoza to his juristic work.[88] As for periodical articles, Glanville Williams had published a series of articles under the title 'Language and the Law' in the *Law Quarterly Review* in 1945 and 1946; these articles did not present a philosophical theory and were not related to the methodology associated with linguistic analysis.[89] He had also published 'International Law and the Controversy Concerning

86. (1835–1926), educated Balliol, first in Greats.
87. See Duxbury 85–6.
88. *Spinoza, His Life and Philosophy* (2nd edn 1899); see Duxbury at 91–7.
89. 61 LQR 71, 179, 293, 384 and 62 *LQR* 387.

the word "Law"', and this article did develop a nominalist philosophical theory, whereby the controversy was presented as being devoid of significance.[90] So whether you called international law 'law' or decided not to call it law, who cared?

A story which circulated in my time in Oxford was that Williams had been imprisoned as a conscientious objector during the war, and had acted as librarian in Wormwood Scrubs Prison, whiling away the time there by studying philosophy. There is, unfortunately, no truth in this.[91] He was indeed a conscientious objector, which did him no good in stuffy Cambridge after the war, but merely had to undertake some public service work. I do not recall who first told me the story, which was elaborated with the claim that the job of librarian was later filled by Alan Nunn May, the atom spy and my colleague in Ghana. Williams was categorized as a lawyer, not a philosopher, and he was never associated with Wittgenstein's Cambridge acolytes. Indeed so far as I know he had no contact with the Cambridge philosophers.

Outside the world of the law school, and outside the Oxford faculty, the political scientist Michael Oakeshott had, back in 1938, published, 'The Concept of a Philosophical Jurisprudence'. It was written in his typical pontifical style, appropriate to a cat who is happy to walk by himself. Oakeshott made no effort to present his views lucidly. The essay argued both that jurisprudence, in the sense of theory of the nature or law, was in a state of chaos. I guess you could say it still is, but does that matter? Oakeshott thought it did, and what was needed was a philosophical jurisprudence. His article will be discussed later in this book in Chapter 3.[92] But the article had not galvanized the philosophers into action, and its very existence seems to have been forgotten until it was recently disinterred by Neil Duxbury.[93] It is nowhere mentioned in Hart's own writings, and in all the time I knew Hart I never recall his mentioning Oakeshott's name. This is puzzling, but one explanation is that Oakeshott was thought of as an apologist for conservatism, and that may have excluded him, for Hart was susceptible to political prejudices. Another, which is more probable, is that such of his

90. (1945) 22 BYIL 146.

91. I am indebted to Peter Glazebrook for this.

92. See pp 68–71.

93. This was first published in (1938) *Politica* 3 at 203 and 345; reprinted in L. O'Sullivan (ed) *Essays and Reviews 1926–1951* (2007).

writings as addressed legal issues date from 1970 and later, in particular his *On Human Conduct* (1975) and his essay *The Rule of Law* (1983).[94]

Hart, in his 1953 article, mentioned one book by a philosopher, WD Lamont's *The Principles of Moral Judgement* (1946), as having special relevance for lawyers for its:

> . . . most original and valuable analysis of the concept of Justice and of the related concepts of Right, Duty, Interest and Responsibility.[95]

He also concluded his article by arguing that the 'auspices are very favourable for a rapprochement between jurisprudence and philosophy', but the rapprochement was to be in the future. He listed a number of topics and ideas which had attracted the attention of philosophers, and which were of interest to lawyers. I discuss this shopping list later in this book.[96]

All in all it is fair to say that there had developed no academic tradition of publication in which the insights of philosophers were related to the nature of law or to legal matters, though the potential for the development of such a tradition existed. One has to be careful here, since the evolution of a conception of philosophers, typically holding academic teaching posts, as belonging to a profession with a distinctive identity, like engineers, surgeons, or aroma therapists, is a development originating in the late nineteenth century. The first philosophical journal was *Mind*, which dates from 1876. The Aristotelian Society was founded in 1880. The first World Congress of Philosophy apparently took place in 1900, but I suspect that it was only well after the Second World War, when impediments to travel passed away, that any Oxbridge philosophers attended such events, which in my experience could be of a hideous character. I recall one in the University of Lancaster from which I fled for a day's fly fishing on the River Lune, where I met another refugee from the conference, similarly engaged.[97] As a profession philosophy only developed very slowly in the first half of the twentieth century. Many scholars we would now think of as philosophers did not conceive of themselves thus, rather, for example, as classical scholars, or political economists.

94. Reprinted in a Liberty Fund edition in 1999.
95. See 357. In CL this book is not mentioned, but there is reference at 254 to another book by Lamont, *The Value Judgement* (1955).
96. See below Chapter 4.
97. There is a considerable amount of information on philosophy conferences in AJ Ayer's *More of My Life* (1985), eg at 157.

Interdisciplinary Teaching Initiatives

As for teaching which mingled legal and philosophical ideas, or techniques, there had been some developments. The pioneer was the philosopher Tony (Anthony D.) Woozley, a Fellow of Queen's College since 1937.[98] He had, according to his *Times* obituary:

> Early in his teaching career ... [been] struck by the idea that there was a fundamental similarity between the way lawyers and philosophers went about their arguments ... He took this up with the Law Fellow at Queen's, who had no interest whatever in pursuing the matter.[99]

This was John Walter Jones, who, as I can say from personal experience, had considerable skill in getting rid of people whom he thought would waste his time. His time was valuable to him, for he was a compulsive devotee of western movies. He was Provost of Queen's when I was an undergraduate, where one was welcomed, over a diminutive glass of dry sherry, by him, his sister, and their cat, with the following ritual:

> What's your name?
> What are you going to read?
> [Looking at watch]. Well it's time to start now.

At the end of three years it went:

> What's your name?
> What have you been reading?
> [Looking at watch] Well it's time to go now.

The obituarist continued:

> But fortunately for the study of law and philosophy the Law Fellow became Provost of Queen's in 1948, and a new law fellow, Tony Honoré, was appointed ... When ... Woozley broached the idea of their doing a joint graduate class in law and philosophy, Honoré leapt at the idea. The class they organized in 1951 was the first class in law and philosophy at Oxford, and probably the first such class in the U.K.[100]

98. (1912–2008). In 1954 he became Professor of Moral Philosophy at St Andrews, and he moved to the University of Virginia in 1967.
99. Author of *Historical Introduction to the Theory of Law* (1940) and *Law and Legal Theory of the Greeks* (1956).
100. *The Times*, 7 May 2008. See Lacey at 149. In 1952 Honoré spent time on sick leave, and in 1953 Woozley became Senior Proctor, which would have caused him to cut back on teaching.

This was first given in Michaelmas Term 1951, being advertised in the Law Faculty list as intended for BCL students, and in the lecture list which catered for those reading PPE, Philosophy, Politics and Economics, or 'Modern Greats'. But it was a graduate class to which no mere undergraduates reading PPE would be admitted. It was repeated in 1952, and was then included in the lecture list for 'Greats'. Hart attended this class, probably in 1952, and gave a paper on the concept of intention.[101] A reading list for this class survives; the topics covered were Acts, Negligence, Cause, Promises, Meaning and Intention, Identity and Attributes, and Personality. The surviving reading list is typed, with hand-written additions. It appears that Woozley led the discussion on Acts, and Honoré on Cause, and that students were signed up to make presentations on some topics.[102]

The Woozley-Honoré class was not in fact the earliest interdisciplinary initiative, though it was certainly the first which crossed faculty boundaries. A little earlier, in Michaelmas Term 1950, Hart and Austin offered a graduate class in the Greats list under the title 'Legal and Moral Responsibility'. One legal case discussed was *R v Finnis*. This was a manslaughter case arising from an incident in which a lunatic had been scalded to death by an attendant.[103] Quite why this case was selected out of the many which have raised problems over the conception of responsibility I do not know, but it was a case which we had to read for criminal law in my time. It is probable that Hart had the task of providing the 'legal' material. One session, Hart explained when interviewed, was devoted to 'excuses', and as we shall see Austin's 'A Plea for Excuses' emerged from this. Little seems to be known about this class. Austin's account suggests it ran for more than one year, but the evidence is that it was only offered once, in Michaelmas Term 1950. Apparently it soon lost its audience. The story, which Nicola Lacey got from me, and I got from Hart, was that Austin nevertheless insisted on continuing to conduct the seminar without an audience.[104] In Trinity Term 1951 Hart lectured on 'Moral and Legal Reasoning'; I take it that this was by way of a replacement for the joint class with Austin, which Austin presumably was not prepared to offer again. Or perhaps it was Hart who was unwilling.

101. See the memoir 'Herbert Lionel Adolphus Hart' by Honoré in PBA 84:295 (1994) at 301.
102. The reading list is available through <http://www2.law.ox.ac.uk/jurisprudence/history.htm> accessed 31 April 2011.
103. (1874) 12 *Cox CC* 625.
104. Lacey 142.

Austin, whom I never met, was a strange person, with a reputation for exaggerated cleverness, pedantry, bullying, and negativity. There are numerous accounts of his behaviour and eccentricities in print. Thus in PJ Conradi, *Iris Murdoch: A Life* (2001) it is said that he was 'as terrifying as possible, with a taste for self-congratulatory complicity'.[105] He sounds quite awful. Yet he nevertheless inspired affection in some, and respect from other philosophers, and he did not always bully his students. It is not unusual in academia to meet persons who are abrasive with colleagues, whom they fear, but cuddly with students, whom they can dominate. He certainly dominated his colleagues in the group, though how much it is impossible to say.[106] Austin's appearance was odd; Noel Annan described him as looking like an inscrutable crane.[107] I have no idea whether all cranes are supposed to look inscrutable or only some; none I have seen fits the description. At the time of writing they are being reintroduced in England so before long we can check up.

Isaiah Berlin, who somewhat curiously viewed him with great affection, gave an extraordinary account of Austin's pre-war teaching technique:

> He put questions to the class. If, petrified by terror, everyone remained silent, he would extend a long, thin, finger, and after oscillating it slowly to and fro for a minute, like the muzzle of a pistol, would suddenly shoot it forward, pointing to one man, chosen at random, and say in a loud, nervous voice 'You answer!'. The victim would, at times, be too terrified to utter.[108]

Nevertheless this did not drive the pre-war audience away. Perhaps the post war generation of students were less tolerant. Austin was educated at Shrewsbury School, parodied in the movie 'If'. Warnock's biographical sketch says that:

> As a House Monitor his authority, *which he did not hesitate to exercise*, was unquestioned, as was also the strict sense of justice by which it was directed. . . .

105. 203.
106. See Lacey 141, 133–6; *Essays on J. L. Austin* (1973) esp 'Austin and the Early Beginnings of Oxford Philosophy' by Isaiah Berlin, 'Austin: a personal memoir' by George Pitcher, 'Saturday Mornings' by GJ Warnock; KT Fann (ed), *Symposium on J. L. Austin* (1969) esp the Biographical Sketch by GJ Warnock; J. L. Austin, 1911–1960 by S Hampshire; and generally PMS Hacker, *Wittgenstein's Place in Twentieth Century Analytic Philosophy* 151, 172; N. MacCormick, *H. L. A. Hart* 5–6, 24–27; PJ Conradi, *Iris Murdoch. A Life* (2001) at 301–5.
107. Quoted M Ignatieff, *Isaiah Berlin* (1998) at 83 from N Annan, *Our Age*, 303.
108. *Essays on J. L. Austin* at 8.

This is code for saying that he administered corporal punishment to his juniors, as was then normal in such schools. So he perhaps brought to classes in philosophy disciplinary habits acquired elsewhere.

We may guess that the reason for the failure of the Austin-Hart class was Austin's manner, rather than any defect in Hart as a teacher.

So such interdisciplinary teaching initiatives as there had been were on a very modest scale.[109] It might be imagined that in PPE there would be interdisciplinary teaching, but this was certainly not at all usual; in my time the philosophers, political scientists and economists inhabited their separate worlds.

The 'Hacks' or College Tutors

In Oxford at this time, and indeed today, the tutorial was the basic educational exercise in the humanities, conducted by a single tutor, and some college tutors could teach for some twenty or more hours a week. At his interview Hart noted the term hack as describing the work horses of the system. The term 'college tutor' could mean merely any academic associated with an undergraduate's college who provided tutorial teaching. It could be applied to an academic holding a fellowship and tutorship in a college, or to an academic who held a college lectureship, a position normally held only for a limited period and without membership of the college's governing body, or to a person hired on a part time basis to provide teaching. Some law teaching was provided by 'weekenders'—barristers who provided tutorials on a Friday evening or Saturday morning in order to finance their career at the bar. They too could be called 'tutors'. Hart had done some weekending in the 1930s. Austin's group was principally directed towards educating college tutors who held fellowships in a college.

At this time the principal function of Oxford was still conceived to be the teaching of undergraduates reading in the various Honour Schools. The tutorial in its ideal form involved a single undergraduate meeting with his college tutor once or twice a week, and presenting written work in the form of an essay. This was read out for criticism and discussion; it was not the practice for the essay to be submitted to the tutor in advance, or returned

109. There were of course also more orthodox lectures and classes on, for example, Aristotle's *Ethics*. Thus in Trinity Term 1950 Hart, Austin, Grice and Hare ran a class on the *Ethics*, and in Hilary Term 1952 Hart lectured on 'Legal and Political Theories in Plato'.

with written comments. The tutorial encouraged spontaneous negative criticism of written work, orally presented.

In various ways real tutorials might depart from the ideal; there might for example be more than one pupil, and the customary hour might be extended, and might be devoted to other activities of one kind or another. I recall one tutorial when my pupil persuaded me to devote the allocated time to trying out a high performance car on the Oxford ring road; it was the first occasion on which I drove a car at 100mph. My own tutorials with Derek Hall were sometimes devoted to trips to inspect manuscripts in the Bodleian Library. One could give other less reputable examples. Sarah Cockburn, best known as a detective story writer under the name Sarah Caudwell, weekended for Merton College and conducted tutorials in the bar of the Randolph Hotel, with predictable results on sobriety.

Professors only rarely taught undergraduates in tutorials. Indeed there was a rule whereby if professors got out of line and did so, they could not be paid extra for this work. A college to which the undergraduate belonged might find it convenient to hire a professor to fill a gap in the teaching arrangements. Perhaps the idea was to prevent their dangerous ideas infecting the young; more plausibly the idea was that professors had other functions: to deliver formal lectures, to write books, and to supervise graduate students. The teaching of undergraduates by professors took place either through the delivery of formal lectures, or through what were called seminars or classes, which could be attended either by anyone who cared to turn up, or sometimes only by graduate students reading for higher degrees. In the Law Faculty for example such classes became common for candidates for the BCL where the teaching might be shared between a professor and a tutorial fellow.

Austin's Saturday Morning Group

It was not an unusual practice in the world of the philosophers to set up discussion groups with regular meetings.[110] An element of patronage was involved, since membership was by invitation and people could be excluded

110. On the pre-war group known as 'the brethren', which comprised Ayer, Berlin, Hampshire, Austin, MacNabb, Woozley and the wildly eccentric Mackinnon see M Ignatieff at 84–5. For the group established by AJ Ayer after he became Wykeham Professor of Logic in Oxford in 1959 see *More of My Life* at 183. For The Metaphysicals, Eric Mascall, Austin Farrer, Basil Mitchell, and Dennis Nineham, see Conradi 305.

if their views or personalities were not thought to be correct. A private group organized and led by Austin's met in one or other of the colleges on Saturday mornings to discuss philosophical issues. This was intended to provide an intellectual forum for the hacks, on whom fell the main task of instructing undergraduates in philosophy, with Honoré, who was a law tutor, as the exception. Another idea was that the philosophical insights developed in it would be fed into the teaching graduates too, of whom there were a growing number. Ryle had been influential in establishing the Bachelor of Philosophy degree in 1946, which attracted many overseas graduates to Oxford—by 1956 there were some twenty six such students. In part it was through participation in this group that Hart generated support from Ryle and others as a candidate for the chair, though Ryle did not attend the group himself.

Those who attended in addition to Hart were George Paul, Jim Urmson, Tony Woozley, Richard Hare, Peter Strawson, Geoffrey and Mary Warnock, Philippa Foot, Tony Honoré and Friedrich Waismann. There were some notable absentees—Isaiah Berlin by choice, he having given up the attempt to participate in Oxford philosophy. Arguably Austin's greatest contribution to the intellectual world was to scare Isaiah Berlin away from continuing to be a member of the Oxford philosophy circle associated with Austin, (which led eventually to his appointment as Chichele Professor of Social and Political Theory and to the remarkable body of literature he left behind him). Iris Murdoch and Elizabeth Anscombe were not there perforce, since they were not invited. In retrospect the exclusion of Iris Murdoch seems notably bizarre, for as things have turned out she was one of the most distinguished Oxford philosophers of her time, though the vehicle for her work was mainly to become the novel. She never went along with the crowd, and her monograph on Sartre, *Sartre: Romantic Rationalist* (1953), separated her from Austin's world; it had also criticized Ryle's *Concept of Mind*. Only a handful of philosophy students today read the works of JL Austin, or for that matter Wittgenstein; Murdoch is, of course, far more widely read. The exclusion of Anscombe was also curious, and based on prejudice because of her Catholic views. She was a devout Catholic convert, married to one Peter Geach, another convert. Both were eccentric.

Honoré alone of the members of this group was not a teacher of philosophy; he was the law tutor at Queen's and was qualified as a barrister, as of course was Hart. Woozley, though as we have seen interested in law, had no formal training as a lawyer. Those who attended formed a self-defined elite. Thus in 1952 there were around twenty college philosophy tutors, most of whose names have long been forgotten; they too were mainly excluded, or excluded themselves.

Waismann, because of his background, was a particularly significant member of the group, though it is not known how actively he participated in discussions.[111] After a short period in Cambridge he became Reader in the Philosophy of Mathematics in Oxford in 1950, and Reader in the Philosophy of Science in 1955. He was a refugee from Vienna, driven out by the Nazis at the time of the Anchluss. He had been an assistant to Moritz Schlick, the leader of the Vienna Circle, and he had become a collaborator with Wittgenstein on a work to be entitled *Logik, Sprache, Philosophie*. In the summer of 1930 Wittgenstein dictated to Waismann a list of 'theses' as preparation for this joint book; at this time Wittgenstein had adopted a verification principle in the form 'The sense of a proposition is the way it is verified'. Between 1927 and 1933 or so he collaborated on the proposed book, an early version of which was apparently completed by 1931. The relationship between Waismann and Wittgenstein, who was sometimes very nasty indeed, turned sour, and collaboration ended. A rewritten version of the proposed book (if indeed it is a version) eventually appeared as *The Principles of Linguistic Philosophy* in 1965.[112] It is a largely forgotten book, which had been overtaken by events. Waismann's life was mired in tragedy and ended in loneliness. His original mentor Moritz Schlick, the leading figure of the Vienna Circle, was murdered by a deranged student before a lecture in June 1936; in England both his wife and son committed suicide. In Oxford he was apparently an isolated figure; his command of English idiom remained poor, and he apparently detested English food as served in his academic home, University College. Later in this book I shall say something about an article of his, 'How I See Philosophy', which I am

111. (1896–1959). On Waismann see PMS Hacker, *Wittgenstein's Place in Twentieth Century Analytic Philosophy* at 153 and 281–2, R Monk, *The Duty of Genius*, esp 296–7, 283–4, 357–8, B McGuiness, *Friedrich Waismann. Philosophical Papers* (1977) (with introduction by Anthony Quinton). A number of papers found after Waismann's death were published as *Ludwig Wittgenstein and Friedrich Waismann. The Voices of Wittgenstein: the Vienna Circle* (ed G Baker) in 2003.

112. Edited by R Harré, who gives no clear account except to say that the original had been extensively revised. A version, now lost, existed in proof until 1939.

pretty sure was originally published in 1950.[113] This was republished on a number of occasions in a collection *Contemporary British Philosophy*.[114] Waismann was responsible for disseminating some of Wittgenstein's ideas in Oxford, and as we shall see he influenced Hart's ideas on the nature of language.

I can well recall the day of Waismann's funeral. Hart, who had a considerable respect for him, attended, and arrived late at the Hart group, wrapped in his gown, which was soaked by heavy rain. Waismann was a Jew, but apparently non practising, so there had been no religious ceremony, and the philosophers, after silently consigning Waismann to his grave, were about to leave, when Ryle leapt onto a nearby tabular grave stone and delivered an extempore Periclean oration. The proceedings, attended only by philosophers, all in soggy flapping academic dress, resembled a gathering of immense crows clustered around carrion, and excited the bewildered attention of some passing locals. But this was Oxford, and the burial took place in the graveyard close to the site of Osney Abbey, near the railway station, where the trains in those days always paused as a token of respect as they entered the city of dreaming spires, and where strange things were known to go on. So was buried the Oxford philosopher who had enjoyed or perhaps suffered the longest connection with Wittgenstein.

An Excursus on Wittgenstein

Since there will be numerous mentions of Wittgenstein in this book it may be convenient here to mention a small selection of highly readable books which can be used to gain, or at least try to gain, some sort of impression of what this brilliant, or perhaps phoney, and certainly very strange person, was like, and how he thought philosophical enquiry should proceed. I have therefore done so in this excursus. Start with Brian Magee, *Talking Philosophy*, the conversations with Anthony Quinton,[115] Bernard

113. On this see G Baker, Friedrich Waismann. 'A Vision of Philosophy' *Philosophy* (2003) 78: 163.
114. The Third Series of this collection, edited by HD Lewis, appeared in 1956. A different collection which included other writings by Waismann appeared under the title *How I See Philosophy*, edited by R Harré, in 1968.
115. 'The Two Philosophies of Wittgenstein'.

Williams,[116] and John Searle.[117] Then try Anthony Kenny, *Wittgenstein* (2006). This makes a start on the great man's ideas. Then go to Alexander Waugh, *The House of Wittgenstein: A Family at War* (2008) which tells of his bizarre and tragic family. Next stop is David Edmonds and John Eidinow's highly entertaining *Wittgenstein's Poker: The story of a ten-minute argument between two great philosophers*. The other philosopher was Karl Popper. Then for a full life read Ray Monk, *Ludwig Wittgenstein: The Duty of Genius* (1990); do not be put off by the alarming photograph of the author with staring eyes, which reminds me of a well-known photograph of Sir Oswald Mosley. If you then want to learn of his influence you start with PMS Hacker, *Wittgenstein's Place in Twentieth Century Analytic Philosophy* (1996). Beyond that lies the vast corpus of literature produced by the Wittgenstein industry, which is not for the faint hearted.[118]

Be warned however that no clear picture will emerge at the end of the day. One view is simply that he was a charlatan, which was the view of Kelsen. I incline to agree but with no great conviction. It is compatible with the view that he was also very clever, but used his strange antics to conceal his inability to sort out his philosophical ideas into any form of order. Although much of the derivative literature is miles above my head, and so far as I am concerned can stay there, he has long fascinated me, more perhaps as a person than as a philosopher. He was by any standards an arrogant, vain person, but in his lifetime there were many who admired him and even loved him. In Cambridge he encouraged the formation of a ludicrous band of devoted acolytes, who imitated his behaviour and dress code, whilst lapping up every word which fell from the master's lips. And although there is endless disagreement over what his philosophical ideas were it is, rather oddly, idle for anyone to dispute his importance, whatever that means, without having to run for cover.

One general point can however be made about his legacy. There are numerous theoreticians who have, one way or another, had a profound effect on the way in which educated people generally think about the world; we could all offer our own list, which might include, for example,

116. 'The Spell of Linguistic Philosophy'.
117. 'The Philosophy of Language'.
118. Much of Wittgenstein's correspondence has been published, and the latest addition to the corpus is B McGuinness (ed), *Wittgenstein in Cambridge. Letters and Documents 1911–1951* (2009). McGuinness has written a biography of the early part of Wittgenstein's life, which I have not read.

Darwin, Marx, Freud, Keynes... Such a list would not be confined to the particular intellectual world of the compiler. Wittgenstein would not I think feature in any such list which was not compiled by a philosopher or student of philosophy. His only legacy is the Wittgenstein industry, and if he had never existed, our understanding of the human condition would, we can be quite sure, remain the same.

What Went on in Austin's Group?

Accounts of what actually went on at meetings of Austin's group, which came to be viewed as the home of Oxford linguistic philosophical analysis, do not provide a clear picture. It is known that the group discussed Aristotle, Chomsky, Frege, and Merlau-Ponty.[119] Members of the group did not produce a cult samizdat literature, unpublished but circulated in typescript or manuscript, recording the thoughts of Austin, as happened with Wittgenstein's classes in Cambridge. Nor did they, mercifully, imitate his dress and mannerisms. It is difficult to assess the significance of these meetings for Ryle's decision to support Hart for the chair; after all Ryle did not attend, and could have thought that any philosopher was better than any mere lawyer for the chair. Ryle was certainly committed to a kind of cultural imperialism. Oxford philosophy, as he understood it, was to become internationally dominant, with the B Phil students to serve as the missionaries, and any chance of acquiring a new colony was to be taken. As initially established Austin's group excluded professors; the point was presumably to exclude the domineering Ryle, described as being like a Prussian sergeant major—a description I can confirm, who threatened Austin's position as leader of the pack. When Austin became a professor in 1952 he did not resign from the group, nor did Hart; the objection was not to professors, but to Ryle.

As for the significance of Hart's participation in Austin's group for his later work, and in particular for *The Concept of Law*, it seems very probable that it was discussions within the group which led to Hart's fascination with the concept of a rule, which dominates his analysis of the concept of law and

119. Lacey 134. Merleau-Ponty (1908–1961) was a phenomenological French philosopher influenced by Marx. I confess to have never heard of him before the mention by Lacey.

of a legal system.[120] There is no doubt that Austin was interested in 'the diversity of rules and standards of conduct and analysis of various concepts connected with it'.[121] Hart in the 1988 interview said that:

> We devoted term after term to studying rules and the concept of a rule in the Saturday morning meetings. We used to look at every kind of rule—rules of games, moral rules, legal rules. I thought that a lot of muddle, say, about the notion of a corporation, whether it was a real or fictitious entity, was not seen; and that what was at stake was the specific use of language in the application of rules of various sorts.[122]

Hart himself was appointed to become expert on the rules of baseball. Why? In 1956–7 Hart visited the USA and presumably attended a game of baseball, and my guess is that this explains why he was chosen. If this is correct then it means that the discussion of the rules of games was underway in 1957–8, the time when Hart was at work on *The Concept of Law*. It would I suppose have been possible for members of the group to have published interesting work on the rules of games, about which a great deal could be said. They never did.

Discussion in the group also furthered the ideas both that some issues traditionally conceived of as jurisprudential could be illuminated by Austin's ordinary language philosophy, whatever that amounted to, and that the expertise of lawyers might even have something to contribute to the work of philosophers. This idea was most effectively developed by Hart and Honoré in *Causation and the Law*, but also seems to have been entertained by Woozley.

It also seems likely that discussions may have contributed to Hart's interest in criminal responsibility. Austin's presidential address to the Aristotelian Society in 1956, 'A Plea for Excuses'[123] seems clearly to have been a product of this interdisciplinary cooperation, as was Hart's own 'The Ascription of Responsibility and Rights'.[124] Who influenced whom, and to what extent, is inevitably uncertain. And although Austin was certainly domineering, Hart was a person normally well capable to standing up to this; he had enjoyed a good relationship with his philosophy tutor at New College, the bullying and destructive HWB Joseph. Maurice Bowra, who

120. Honoré's memoir at 300. 121. Hart Interview at 274. 122. At 277.
123. JL Austin, *Philosophical Papers*, Chapter 6. See N Maccormick 218 note 18.
124. Hart later disowned this piece; see his *Punishment and Responsibility* (1968) at v.

fought in the first world war, used to say that he would have preferred to spend time back in the trenches than again suffer a tutorial from Joseph.[125] There were however those who took a more kindly view of Joseph; they included John Sparrow, for many years Warden of All Souls, and earlier, like Hart, a chancery barrister of promise. Sparrow became one of those sad Oxford figures who never lived up to their potential; in the end he became a professional reactionary and a parody of himself. He also became a notorious drunk.[126] I used to dine with him in the Chicago Quadrangle Club in 1978, where he would consume, after martinis, a bottle or so of wine. He was there preparing to deliver some lectures. One evening he explained to me that he had absolutely nothing to say.[127] He was right. I urged him not to let this stand in his way—many professors in Chicago were in the same situation, though he had the advantage of being aware of the problem. I was not successful; his lectures were an embarrassment.

It is noticeable that Hart did not acknowledge any debt to Austin for commenting on *The Concept of Law*, though a draft must have existed well before Austin's death in 1960.[128] Those who read and commented on the text were Rupert Cross, Peter Strawson, and Tony Honoré; George Paul read the proofs. The reason for not running the text before Austin must surely have been nervousness over the certainty he would tear it apart, as he certainly would have done. It is also striking that Hart never contributed to the extensive secondary literature on Austin, though he must have been invited to do so.[129] Nor, after his appointment to the chair, did he collaborate with Austin over any seminars, even that on 'Excuses', which had legal aspects, which Austin gave again in 1958. Perhaps there was a cooling of the relationship, though Hart after Austin's death was apparently supportive of Austin's widow and may have been reluctant to have distressed her by

125. Lacey 26–9, L Mitchell, *Maurice: A Life* (2009), 51–54.
126. See J Lowe, *The Warden. A Portrait of John Sparrow* (1998) esp 40ff on Joseph. Edward Levi appears in this book as Devi.
127. He had earlier delivered some lectures in Chicago, and the invitation was engineered by one Philip Kurland of the law school, who was profoundly hostile to rioting students, as was Sparrow. The law school had admitted one who had been involved in riots in Berkeley, and Kurland, outraged, sulked over this throughout my time there.
128. In Michaelmas and Hilary Terms 1958 Hart gave a series of twenty four lectures under the title 'The Concept of Law', and these were repeated in 1959.
129. For example *Essays on J. L. Austin* by I Berlin *et al* (1973) and KT Fann, *Symposium on J. L. Austin* (1969). This contains a bibliography of writings on Austin at 470.

criticisms of her late husband. A friend of mine who was taught by her said she would burst into tears at any criticism. He did write a friendly DNB entry on him for the Oxford Press:

> He was often reserved in manner, and on occasions formidable. But he had great natural courtesy, gaiety and charm, and much manifest benevolence, especially to his pupils.[130]

Hart also wrote an obituary in the *Oxford Magazine* in 1960.

The Scope of Oxford Jurisprudence in 1952

What was understood as Oxford 'jurisprudence' when Hart became its professor? 'Jurisprudence' was the name then given in Oxford to the academic study of law generally. Hence undergraduates pursuing degree programmes in which it was possible to obtain honours,[131] in contrast with pass degrees—firsts, seconds, thirds or fourths—were examined and classified in what was called the Honour School of Jurisprudence. By the 1950s undergraduates were no longer admitted to read for pass degrees; they were taken only by those who had for one reason or another not been able to cope with an honours degree, and could not even make it into the fourth class. At the end of two terms law students took an examination known as Law Moderations in which no classes were awarded, but it was possible to get a distinction. Under a reform of 1950 undergraduates had to take a final examination in eight subjects,[132] one of which was called 'General Jurisprudence'. So 'Jurisprudence' was the name of this subdivision of legal study. The 1950 reform also removed from the examination a paper in which the candidates had to write a single general essay; in Oxford scholarship examinations at this time candidates were confronted in one paper with a single word, such as 'Death', or 'The Zeitgeist', or 'Decomposition', on which they were expected to write an elegant essay. The jurisprudence essay topics, from which they had to choose one, did not all take this form,

130. The entry on Austin in the ODNB is by PMS Hacker.
131. Also called a class.
132. The subjects included for example a branch of Roman Law, the Law of Land (or Roman Dutch Law), Contract, Torts and two of a list of subjects which included for example International Law and Legal History. Lawson at 151 and ff.

and covered some of the same ground as the questions which were set in the general jurisprudence paper.[133]

In his 1953 article, 'Philosophy and Jurisprudence in Britain (1945–1952)'[134] Hart explained that the expression 'philosophy of law' had 'never become domesticated in England', adding that:

> . . . what is taught and discussed in English universities as jurisprudence is, and always has been, a loosely related family of questions about law.[135]

One might have expected him to have provided an official syllabus, but nothing of the sort existed. It was however the practice for the Faculty Board to approve and publish in the annual *Examination Statutes* a list of books 'suggested for study'; no great attention was directed to keeping this up to date, and Hart's own *The Concept of Law* first made it in 1965.[136] Hart reproduced the 1952 list, but added to it Cardozo's *The Nature of the Judicial Process*, Holmes' *The Common Law*, Gray's *The Nature and Sources of Law* and Hohfeld's *Fundamental Legal Conceptions*; Cardozo, Gray, Hohfeld and Holmes first appeared in the officially suggested books in 1954, perhaps in response to Hart's article. He described his list as 'a typical list of the books the student is recommended to read'; perhaps he got it from one of the college tutors. It comprised twenty items, of which the most recently published were CK Allen's *Law in the Making*, the then current edition dating from 1939, W Friedman's *Legal Theory* (1944), and GW Paton's *A Text-book of Jurisprudence* (editions in 1946 and 1951). One notable omission

133. In the essay paper set in 1951 candidates had to write on one out of seven topics. They were (1) Law and Justice; (2) Codification; (3) 'A country gets the constitution it deserves'; (4) 'Next to the Bible, no book has left a deeper mark on the history of mankind than the *Corpus Iuris Civilis*'; (5) 'How far does the law still recognize private ownership in land?'; (6) 'English law neither knows nor needs a doctrine of Restitution'; and (7) Law and Fact. Apart from (4) and (6) these vaguely specified essay topics echoed the more precise questions which featured in the jurisprudence examination. Thus in the jurisprudence paper for 1953 question 9 reads 'Discuss the meaning and importance of the distinction between Law and Fact'. The essay paper was last set in 1953, the topics being (1) The Rights of Man; (2) The Judge and the Statute; (3) Restitution as a Legal Concept; (4) The Merits of Codification; (5) The Machinery of Law Reform; and (6) The Value of the Study of Roman Law.

134. (1953) 2 AJCL 356.

135. At 358. In his 1988 article he claimed that 'It focused on technical, legal problems' which is simply wrong.

136. That published in 1952 listed 16 authors and 19 works; only in one instance is an edition specified. The authors were Allen, Bryce, Friedman, Goodhart, Holland, Jethro Brown, Jones, Maine, Maitland, Jennings, Paton, Pollock, Pollock and Wright, Pound, Salmond, and Vinogradoff.

was Kelsen's *General Theory of Law and the State.*[137] Another striking omission was any of the writings of the jurist John Austin.[138]

He also provided a specimen set of 'the questions [the student] is expected to answer in his written final examination'. The topics addressed by the questions were legal fictions and the fiction theory of corporate personality; the theory of statutory interpretation; the concept of ownership; the distinction between law and equity; notable jurists, giving an opportunity to compare and contrast the theories of Cardozo and Frank, or of Savigny and Maine; abuse of rights; the definition of negligence; intention and motive as legal concepts; the theory of sovereignty; natural law; and sources of law (with particular reference to custom, the law of nature and the concept of a *grundnorm*). No source is given, and the questions do not come from an examination paper which was ever actually set. It was at this time common for the more conscientious college tutors to make their pupils take mock examinations, called 'collections',[139] usually at the beginning of the term following that in which they had received tutorials in a subject. Hart must have got hold of a paper, perhaps one set by Butterworth, the New College law tutor. Butterworth, who was my tutor for the study of real property, was an able and charming man, but an appalling teacher. I went to him with one Frank Logan, an American Rhodes Scholar, for property law. Butterworth expected us to read out by way of an essay a chunk of Cheshire's treatise on property law; any hint of individuality was met by reproof:

> You are departing from the words of the master.

Meanwhile Butterworth would be on the phone organizing his social or professional life, or writing letters. On occasions I nearly had to restrain Frank Logan from physical assault. Oddly enough all serious students taught this subject by Butterworth did reasonably well in the final examinations; they had to repair the situation by hard private study. I do not know if he

137. Kelsen's *General Theory of Law and the State* (1945) was written in the 1940s at the Harvard Law School. It was published in English translated, from a draft in German, by Anders Wedberg. This was reprinted in 1949 and Hart gives references to this. It was republished in the American *Twentieth Century Philosophy Series* in 1961 in an edition which also has an Appendix with a translation by WH Kraus of Kelsen's *Natural Law Doctrine and Legal Positivism*. This edition has a list of Kelsen's publications and a bibliography. In 1941 the HLR had published Kelsen's 'The Pure Theory of Law and Analytical Jurisprudence'; see 55 HLR at 44.

138. The 1954 list did include Hart's edition of *The Province of Jurisprudence Determined*.

139. The term was also used for sessions at which reports on the industry of students were read out and considered.

taught jurisprudence. He was known as 'Honest Jack' because of a reputation for deviousness; he took a prominent part in managing the finances of the University. He went on to become a controversial Vice-Chancellor of the University of Warwick.

Establishing the Boundaries of Oxford Jurisprudence

Hart did not explain how, in Oxford of the 1950s, the boundaries of 'jurisprudence' were established, maintained, and changed. Teaching was, as I have explained, provided in part by the Professor of Jurisprudence (and any other member of the faculty who chose to lecture on the subject), and in part by those college tutors who taught it.[140] This amorphous group never met. Nor were the boundaries decided by the Faculty Board, whose list of suggested books was largely reactive, nor by meetings of the whole faculty, which never discussed the scope of the subjects taught and examined. There was a strong convention (enforced by the University Proctors, who ultimately controlled the examination system) whereby the examiners could not be directed or controlled either by resolutions passed by the Board of the Faculty, or by the whole Faculty. The final examination was set by a Board of Examiners, which in 1952, the year of Hart's appointment, comprised Alan Brown, Jack Butterworth and Norman Marsh, from Worcester, New and University Colleges. Marsh would have produced the draft jurisprudence questions, but the whole board was collectively responsible, and other members might, and in my experience did, propose amendments.

What was within the subject, and what outside it, depended on informal convention, based on past practice (as enshrined in examination papers), and on informal modes of communication.

140. Students could be sent to other colleges under swapping arrangements. I used to send pupils to RFV Heuston for international law; in exchange I taught his students legal history. Heuston thought there were only five 'discussable issues' in international law, so they only went to him for five of the eight weeks in the Oxford term. I was never happy with this, and made other arrangements. Lawson at 171 records a rumour that before 1939 'some tutors left jurisprudence, and others Roman law, largely to take care of themselves.' Expecting students to master subjects with no instruction was not unusual in my time; thus students of English Literature were expected to learn Anglo-Saxon, but no instruction whatever was provided.

This system was very different from that obtaining in American law schools, where the individual teacher has considerable freedom to define the scope of a subject, for he has virtually total control over what his students read, and over the setting and grading of the examination. He operates as an individual and not as a member of a team. He chooses the case book, most emanating from one of the more prestigious law schools. Their compilers ultimately define the scope of a subject. This is how, for example, simplified versions of economic theory have come to feature prominently in the teaching of subjects such as Property, Contracts and Torts. A teacher may supplement the case book with personally selected additional reading, and require or recommend students to use commercially published collections of additional material. The influence of the compilers of case books and other collections is limited by market forces, by the extent to which these works sell, and one thing which encourages sales is a good *Teacher's Manual*, which provides what the compiler of the case book conceives to be the correct understanding of the material. These manuals serve much the same function as comfort blankets for babies. Successful case books are frequently revised so as to destroy the value of second hand copies.

Oxford Boards of Examiners did not enjoy similar power. Unless they were to provoke outrage from their colleagues, they had to respect the informal consensus. It was not unusual for the examiners to make enquiries as to what topics had been covered in lectures which students might have attended. The need to respect the consensus functioned as a strong conservative force, softened to some extent by the practice of setting a considerable number of questions, but requiring the candidates only to answer four or five. Thus the jurisprudence papers set in 1951 and 1953 provided eleven questions, and those of 1955 fifteen, out of which either four or five had to be answered. Given this choice it was possible to set questions which departed from the conventions, and modestly shifted the boundaries of the subject.

Readers may wonder how the scripts could be graded, when candidates could answer four or five questions. Under the Oxford theology of examinations marking was conceived as an attempt to identify the inherent ability of the candidate, merely evidenced by the written answers, and if need be by an oral examination; it was not viewed as an exercise in adding up points scored. The results were expressed in a scale running from $\alpha+$ down to $\delta-$, which could be refined creatively to meet the individual case. In Oxford, examining was treated as something in the nature of a religious exercise, on which much energy and time was spent. By the end of the process it could be that quarrels had emerged, and I recall one occasion when the chairman refused to speak at all, so outraged was he over the classification of one candidate. She was a young woman who had been given a second; he suspected charm had done it. But the proceedings always ended happily with a sumptuous dinner.

In 1954 Hart for the first time became an examiner, with Harold Hanbury, the Vinerian Professor, Barry Nicholas (Brasenose), and Robert Heuston (Pembroke). Hart would have produced the first draft of the jurisprudence questions. In 1955 he was again an examiner, with Hanbury, Christopher Davidge (Keble), Nicholas, Heuston and Derek Hall (Exeter). It might be imagined that the examination papers set in 1954 and 1955 would on their face reveal the presence of a new broom. Nothing of the sort is the case. The 1954 and 1955 papers could just as well have been set in 1950, for most of the topics to which the questions related were permanent features of the Oxford jurisprudential firmament. Thus one such topic was 'the definition of law' which might be treated as more or less the same as 'the Austinian theory of law and its critics'. So in the 1951 paper Question 1 read 'How do you define law?' and in the 1953 paper Question 3 read '"Austin's definition of law has met with constant criticism, but no one has yet been able to devise a better". Discuss'. In the 1954 paper there was no question which directly addressed this topic, but there was, in Question 13, a 'great jurists' question:

> Assess the principal contribution to Jurisprudence of any one of the following: Hobbes; Locke; Bentham; Maine; Holmes; Kelsen.

A student, by choosing to write either on Bentham, Holmes, or Kelsen could make use of reading which would have been as usable in the 1951 or 1953 paper. In 1955, when Hart was an examiner, a number of quotations from Austin were provided and the candidate had to comment on three. One, for example, was 'All judge-made law is the creation of the sovereign'. In 1964 Question 1 asked, 'Is it ever desirable to define law?' This could have been answered using a knowledge of the discussion in *The Concept of Law*.

Another much favoured topic was some aspect of 'the doctrine of precedent'. In 1951 Question 6 read: '"All attempts to analyse the nature of the judicial process must fail, since all are based on the false assumption that law is a science." Consider this criticism.'

In 1953 Question 4 asked: 'How do you determine the *ratio decidendi* of a case?' and Question 1 had asked: 'Is law a science or an art?' In 1954 Question 12 read:

> 'The Court creates a principle when it determines which are the material and which are the immaterial facts on which it bases its decision' (GOODHART).
>
> 'The judge in the present case may find irrelevant the existence or absence of facts which previous judges thought important' (LEVI).
>
> Which of these two views best represent the English doctrine of precedent?

In 1955 Question 14 asked: 'Can a judicial decision be authority (a) only for the rule of law the judge has in mind in deciding the case, (b) for more than one rule of law?'

In 1958 Question 9 asked: 'How would you determine the effect of (a) a case in which different judges came to the same conclusion but for different reasons; (b) a line of cases which are not inconsistent with each other?'

In 1962 Question 2 asked: 'Why is it so hard to determine the *ratio decidendi* of a case?'

Other topics, some of uncertain scope, to which I here attach my own labels, included 'theories of possession';[141] 'theories of statutory interpretation';[142] 'the concept of ownership';[143] 'marxist theories of law';[144] 'the concept of human rights';[145] 'legal fictions';[146] 'the concept of rights';[147] sanctions;[148] 'theories of punishment';[149] 'change and stability in law';[150] 'the merits of codification';[151] 'Kelsen';[152] and 'the status of custom'.[153]

So 'jurisprudence' was something of a ragbag of topics, what was included being determined by tradition, rather than by any general theory of the matter. Insofar as it is possible to impose some order it comprised first of all of what were viewed as competing general theories of law—Austinian positivism, Kelsen's pure theory, historical jurisprudence associated with Maine, Vinogradoff, and to some extent Pound, sociological jurisprudence associated with Pound, American realism, mainly associated with Jerome

141. 1953 Q. 7, 1954 Q. 7, 1955 Q. 3, 1962 Q. 8.
142. 1951 Q. 11, 1954 Q. 11, 1955 Q. 15.
143. 1954 Q. 8, 1955 Q. 4, 1958 Q. 7.
144. 1954 Q. 1, 1953 Q. 11.
145. 1951 Q. 2. See below p 178.
146. 1951 Q. 6, 1954 Q. 13 (general opportunity to write about Maine), 1958 Q. 12 (on general theories of legal development).
147. 1954 Q. 5 and 6, 1955 Q. 5, 1958 Q. 10.
148. 1954 Q. 3, 1958 Q. 2.
149. 1954 Q. 15 (on capital punishment), 1955 Q. 10 and 11.
150. 1953 Q. 6.
151. 1954 Q. 14.
152. 1955 Q. 2.
153. 1951 Q. 8.

Frank, and Marxist theories, and, very superficially, theories of natural law. Secondly it comprised the study of what were called sources of law, which included theorizing about the working of the doctrine of precedent, the concept of the *ratio decidendi*, and the interpretation of legislation. Thirdly it comprised the analysis of what were thought to be fundamental legal conceptions, such as rights, ownership, possession, intention, negligence, and equity. Fourthly it comprised a varying number of questions dealing with issues of general legal policy—the merits of codification, or of capital punishment, or of the desirability of having a doctrine of abuse of rights.

The lecture courses certainly helped to define the scope of the subject. Goodhart's extensive course on 'Jurisprudence', extended over two terms, and tutors and examiners would have a general idea of what was covered.[154] The other member of the faculty who regularly offered a course of lectures was SN Grant-Bailey of Christ Church, who offered a course called 'Discussion'.[155] He contributed nothing, for he was a fraud and, so far as I know never actually delivered this regularly advertised course. I once told Honoré that I planned to attend Grant-Bailey's lectures, 'Let me know if he attends too' was his response. Grant-Bailey was, indeed, eventually sacked in 1954; technically his fellowship at Christ Church (called a studentship), which would have been held for a term of seven years, was not renewed. During the war he had pretended to be engaged in highly secret war work; in fact he ran a restaurant. He moved to the University of Southampton, which also soon sacked him. Very occasionally other faculty members gave jurisprudence lecture courses, such as HJF Jones of Merton, who gave a course on 'The Law of Nature' in 1949–50 and 1950–1951. He was primarily a Wordsworth scholar, appointed to teach law until a suitable fellowship could be found for him, and he transferred to the English Faculty in 1956. I never knew of anyone who went to his lectures.

Reading and Private Study

The Oxford system depended primarily on reading and private study, guided by one's tutor, and not at attendance at formal instruction, which was wholly optional. What is difficult to determine is what the more serious

154. Goodhart also regularly ran a course on 'Recent Cases'; as editor of the *Law Quarterly Review* he devoted most of his energies to writing comments on recent cases for the review.
155. See eg the *Oxford University Gazette* for 1949–50.

undergraduates actually read. The better college tutors produced elaborate reading lists with recommended books and articles. My primary tutor was Tony Honoré, but he was on sick leave in the term when I studied jurisprudence, though I am sure I based my work on his comprehensive reading list. I supplied copies of his reading lists to friends in colleges with low quality law tutors, such as Keble and St. John's. I went to some tutorials with a weekender, one Tony Walton, who filled in for Honoré, but took a low view of his abilities, and rudely absented myself from a number. Thereafter I went to tutorials with Derek Davies, an able and conscientious teacher. Authors I read included, as I recollect, for I did not keep a list, CK Allen, John Austin, Lord Bryce, WW Buckland, Benjamin Cardozo, G Del Vecchio, L Duguit, Jerome Frank, Wolfgang Friedman, Arthur Goodhart, Wesley Newcomb Hohfeld, Thomas Erskine Holland, Oliver Wendell Holmes, Hans Kelsen,[156] Albert Kocourek, Henry Maine, Bronislaw Malinowski, William Markby, Frederick Pollock, Roscoe Pound, John Salmond, Julius Stone, Glanville Williams, and Paul Vinogradoff. The list was long. I suppose I was a bit of a glutton for punishment. Many students who were not as ambitious as I was simply read one or other of the going 'textbooks' written for law students, such as that by GW Paton or Sir John Salmond, whose treatise was by this time antique and extensively edited by Glanville Williams. I myself certainly also read these works.

How Bad were the Bad Old Days?

By wide reading it was possible, in the supposedly bad old days before Hart's appointment, for an Oxford undergraduate to obtain an excellent education in jurisprudence, even if most of what he read had not been produced by members of the Oxford Law Faculty, if that was thought to matter. The quality of the instruction he received in tutorials differed widely; able students set about remedying this by private initiatives. I have taught for many years in American law schools, and have often been struck by the fact that any reasonably hard working and intelligent Oxford law student of my time there left with a much greater knowledge and understanding of theoretical writings on the nature and history of law than does the average

156. I suspect that I may as an undergraduate have only read second hand accounts of Kelsen, or perhaps the article in the (1941) 55 HLR 44.

American law student; one has to except economic theories, which are peddled *ad nauseam* and uncritically in numerous courses as embodying received truth. I have devoted much time in courses on such subjects as property and contract to smuggling in teaching on issues which would have been covered for all students in Oxford jurisprudence. The problem does not arise for those who have elected a course in legal philosophy, and in some schools some form of general theoretical course for all students has survived, such as the *Elements of Law* course in the Chicago Law School, originally taught by Edward Levi. In my time there students grumbled endlessly about this course, but many came around in the end to value what they had learned in it. By way of contrast, American law students leave the law school, if they select suitable courses, with much more knowledge of hard law than did Oxford students in my time, who learnt hardly any at all.

It was these bad old days which Hart's supporters, and in particular the Oxford philosophers, hoped would now be over. In some not very obvious sense Oxford jurisprudence, and through it perhaps jurisprudence in general, was to be *philosophized*. What this was supposed to mean is the subject of the next chapter.

3

The Gladsome Light of Philosophical Jurisprudence

Reasons for Optimism

One reason for optimism over the appointment of a person viewed as a philosopher, rather than a lawyer, needs to be briefly stated. At this time the law faculty did not have a high reputation in Oxford. Hence bringing in new blood from outside was thought the right thing to do. Indeed quite a number of academics thought that the study of law, unlike that of mathematics, or history, or economics, did not belong in a university at all. In this spirit some Oxford colleges long refused to teach the subject, or admit undergraduates to study it. A striking example was Corpus Christi College, the original home of the Corpus Chair of Jurisprudence, though back in Maine's time it apparently did employ a law lecturer. Law and legal institutions formed a respectable subject matter for university study by scholars from other disciplines, such as mediaeval historians, or thinkers who it was impossible to label, such as Maine himself. But English law as a practical going concern was like plumbing, and belonged in a trade school, with skills to be assimilated through apprenticeship. The notion that the common law encapsulated a body of intellectually fascinating ideas or even, perish the thought, wisdom, developed by able individuals in the conduct of adjudication over the centuries, was not widely entertained. Hart himself reflected this negative point of view in his interview with David Sugarman when he said that although he practised law for many years, and with success, and that legal practice:

> ... provided me with a vast range of examples about which to philosophize. It stimulated me as a philosopher, because I saw that in the law there were

> questions which arose, and answers given, which could be explored philosophically.

he went on to add the bizarre qualification that:

> But when I got very busy I soon began to discover that I had no real interest in law as such.

Another reason for disdain of academic lawyers was that those who practised, especially at the bar, viewed those who taught law in universities as self-defined failures, unable to make it in practice. Some might have excuses; thus Rupert Cross was totally blind, and Theo Tylor of Balliol almost totally. There were also special exceptions; thus Goodhart enjoyed a high reputation amongst the judiciary and members of the bar, and in any event he was an American. Yet another reason for disdain was that some of those in the Oxford law faculty were indeed of scant attainment as legal scholars, however judged, with little dedication to their legal work. There was the disreputable Grant-Bailey, and John Jones, a Wordsworth scholar, excellent at his subject, but it was not law.[1] Other examples are Edwin Slade of St. John's, appointed to fill the law tutor's slot until a philosophy position became vacant; before it was realized that Slade had no promise there either, so he soldiered on as the law tutor until retirement. In St. John's jurisprudence was taught by the able philosopher John Mabbott, and not by Slade, who taught the common law subjects such as tort law. Then there was Vere Davidge of Keble, a person of considerable but unrealized ability as a lawyer, who served the college as bursar for many years. One of his pupils was Robert Stevens who went on to a distinguished academic career; he was a schoolfriend of mine, and I used to supply him with Honoré's reading lists. Davidge was most widely known for his alcoholic performances on guest nights; I once was there when he persuaded a Benedictine monk, whom he had contrived to intoxicate by constant filling of his glass, to propose a toast to the damnation of the Jesuits. He was the inventor of Davidge's Law: *The Poorer the College the Better the Food*. Both he and his son were rowing men and members of the prestigious Henley-based rowing club, Leander; the pink colour of the Leander tie conveniently matched his ravaged complexion. Coming from a relatively modest social background, Davidge turned himself into an enthusiastic fox hunter, his hunting pink adding yet another item to the palette. By the time he retired, his colleagues had endured him too

1. See above Chapter 2 at p 59.

long to wish to pay for his portrait, so he paid for it himself; it was of spectacular ugliness.

Quite a number of college law tutors had never taken law degrees at all; law was a subject which any intelligent person, especially one with a good degree in Greats, could get up in the long vacation. An example is Phillip Landon of Trinity College, who had obtained a first in Greats and practised at the bar for some years, but had no law degree. He was an appalling snob, and was noted for his attempts to drive away any women who attended his criminal law lectures by detailed discussions of the more squalid cases. On his retirement in 1956 he was succeeded by Patrick Fitzgerald, who had also obtained a first in Greats and taken the bar exams, but again had no law degree. William Stallybrass, always known as Sonners—his original name was Sonnenschein which he changed in the First World War—became Principal of Brasenose in 1936, and was for a long time the editor of Salmon's treatise on tort law. He was in like case. His career ended when, as Vice-Chancellor, he fell or was pushed off the train from Paddington in 1948; his demise was celebrated annually by one Stanley Cohen, his former colleague, until he too succumbed to alcoholic excess.[2]

The Dumping Ground

The law school was at this time used by some colleges as the dumping ground for undergraduates whose abilities, or enthusiasms, were too low for them to have any chance of success in more serious schools. It was common when I first taught in Oxford for schoolteachers writing on behalf of candidates to say that Snooks lacked imagination, and did not possess the ability to cope with Greats or History, but had a good memory, and would therefore be ideally suited to study law. Competition for admission was nothing like as strong as it has become, and colleges, for financial reasons, were anxious to recruit undergraduates. In many colleges the head of the college could, on his own, admit commoners—those without scholarships or exhibitions. Some of the intellectually under endowed law students were 'founder's' or 'old member's' kin, or kin to potential benefactors. Some

2. Oxford and Cambridge colleges served as schools for potential alcoholics. Cohen, towards the end, was much troubled by the pheasants he saw wandering around his rooms in Brasenose, but a stiff glass of whisky would drive them back to their coverts. For information see BDCL.

were athletes. Under Davidge's reign those members of the Eton rowing eight who could not get in elsewhere arrived in Keble *en masse*; it was said that they simply rowed their boat up the river to Oxford, disembarking at Folly Bridge. Davidge would arrange an annual champagne party where they met the examiners in the first year examination, Law Moderations, in the hope that their charm, which Old Etonians possessed in abundance, would influence their marks. I once, as examiner, attended one of these functions, at which one was treated rather like the local vicar on a landed estate, with superior solicitude. I and my fellow examiners, Young Turks dedicated to raising standards, failed them all without exception, but felt a little guilty. Some few came to Oxford because of representations from the Foreign Office (Sebastian here on the Middle East desk) to the effect that it would be helpful to British interests if the son of the Sheikh of Wherever was able to read law in Oxford, Greats or History being rather too much for him. A significant number of those who read law ended up with fourth class honours degrees, for which little more than ability to write something entertaining was required; a certain cachet was attached to this bizarre qualification, which was not finally abolished until 1968.[3]

In the first years of Hart's membership of the law faculty it continued to be a dumping ground, but in 1956 and 1957 the Board of Examiners decided to take drastic action, the moving spirit being Peter Carter of Wadham. In 1956, though 20 fourths were given, 45 candidates were simply failed completely.[4] One was Plantagenet Somerset-Fry, who elaborated and hyphenated his name at Oxford, and later became a distinguished writer of children's stories. I was shown one of Plantagenet's exam scripts by Derek Hall, a strong supporter of Carter's initiative. He had written stories about his aunt, explaining that although he knew no law he had interesting things to say about her which he hoped the examiners would enjoy. He had indeed, but they had no connection with the study of law.

The message from the examiners took time to affect admissions. Law Moderations was taken in March of the first year, and could be retaken in June. Even as late as 1961 21 per cent of the 184 candidates were failed at their first attempt, and 51 per cent of the 37 who retook in June failed again. Indeed some undergraduates who later went on to distinguished careers did not perform well. The point of the Roman Law course was obscure, that on

3. See Lawson, Appendix VIII at 258–9.
4. 11 obtained firsts, 97 seconds, 72 thirds, and 20 fourths.

the English Legal System was profoundly boring.[5] But in the end another dumping ground had to be found. English and Geography were candidates, but they soon refused to take dim law rejects.

Raising the Intellectual Tone

Against this background it is easy to understand the idea that the appointment of an established philosopher to the faculty would raise the intellectual tone. For whatever could be said for or against the activities of the Oxford philosophers, it was impossible to deny that they were true intellectuals, and clever with it. They were, as Americans in law schools say, 'smart', a term which would never be used in England without derogatory overtones. This was not something that either they or anyone else in Oxford at this time ever doubted. Scholars such as Ayer, Ryle, and Austin, and those associated with them, further believed that they were participants in a philosophical revolution of international significance, in part at least now centred in Oxford.[6]

The only problem was the existence of the University of Cambridge, home to Moore and Russell, both now past their sell-by dates, but inhabited by the ghost of Wittgenstein, who was certainly not past his. He had only set foot in Oxford on one fraught occasion in May 1947, when he attended a meeting of the undergraduate-run Jowett Society. One Oscar Wood, himself then an undergraduate, delivered a paper. Wittgenstein simply ignored it, and then became embattled with a long-retired moral philosopher, Harold A Pritchard, whom he described as 'a very silly old man'. According to one story it was all too much for Pritchard who died a week later; in fact it was seven months later that he died, on 29 December.[7] Later Wittgenstein was invited to deliver the Locke lectures in Oxford in 1950,

5. I was an examiner and still have my notes, peppered with comments such as 'incredible gaps and howlers' 'vast ignorance' 'not the faintest idea of relevance' and the like. In 1962 18 per cent (30) failed at their first attempt, and of the 32 who retook the examination in June 40 per cent failed.
6. In 1960 a series of talks originally delivered on the BBC Third Programme were published as *The Revolution in Philosophy*; there was an introduction by Gilbert Ryle, and contributions by AJ Ayer, WC Kneale, GA Paul, DF Pears, PF Strawson, GJ Warnock and RA Wollheim. The revolution described in these talks was however thought to have extended over the whole of the first half of the 20th century.
7. Lacey 139–141 and 407. He had been White's Professor of Moral Philosophy from 1928–1937. Monk at 496–7 is confused about this and names the person as Joseph Pritchard, conflating Pritchard with Horace Joseph, Hart's tutor, who had died in 1943.

but declined.[8] His ideas were fed into Oxford philosophy in part by former pupils, such as George Paul, or Elizabeth Anscombe, or former collaborators, such as Friedrich Waismann, and in part through *The Brown and Blue Books*, notes dictated to pupils which date from 1934–5. For over twenty years these circulated only in typed or handwritten copies, with a trade in them developing. They first appeared in print in 1958 with a preface by Russ Rhees, an American friend and literary executor of Wittgenstein. The *Brown Book* may originally have been a draft of a possible book. Paul gave Hart a copy of *The Blue Book*. Probably he also gave him a copy of *The Brown Book*, but Hart does not mention this in the interview. Then, in 1953, and after Wittgenstein's death in April 1951, *Philosophical Investigations* was published.[9] In time Oxford became the centre of Wittgensteinian linguistic analysis, but at the time with which we are concerned this development lay largely in the future.

Michael Oakeshott on Philosophical Jurisprudence

Back in 1938 Michael Oakeshott had, as we have seen, argued the need for the development of philosophical jurisprudence.[10] His article, it has to be admitted, is not at all easy to follow; like much of his other work it is driven by vanity. It is written in an arrogant style typical of his writings, with no serious attempt to make his views easy to follow. It is mercifully not necessary for present purposes for me to attempt to set out, much less attempt to evaluate, all his arguments, if indeed I was able to do so. What is important is that he put forward dogmatically an elaborate and highly abstract theory of the form a philosophical enquiry into the nature of law ought to take if it was to count as being philosophical. This starts from the idea that:

> Jurisprudence is the name given to the unresolved variety of explanations of the nature of law;[11] and an unresolved variety is chaos.[12]

8. Monk 564.
9. Edited by GH von Wright, R Rhees and GEM Anscombe. There is now a 3rd edition of 2001 with the German text and a revised English translation by Anscombe. Part I was complete by 1945 and Part II was written between 1947 and 1949.
10. 'The Concept of a Philosophical Jurisprudence' *Politica* 3: 203 and 345 (1938).
11. Other expressions he used included 'a theory', 'an interpretation of the nature of law', 'an explanation of the nature of law'.
12. 162.

He provided a description and analysis of what he thought to be the going theories or explanations; these were the analytical, the historical, the psychological (which remained undeveloped), the economic, and the sociological. In addition there existed explanations which purported to be philosophical, philosophical being variously defined. So Oakeshott provided an elaborate map of the going philosophical explanations or theories, all of which he found wanting. His claim that jurisprudence was in a state of chaos was based on the fact that these various forms of explanation simply competed with each other and:

> ... until a relationship, or a series of relationships, have been established between these different types of interpretation the confusion will remain.[13]

The way to resolve the chaos was through a truly philosophical enquiry. This, he thought, would be concerned with definition, but definition:

> ... not of words, but of concepts. And definition is the making clearer of something which is already to some extent apprehended and to some extent clear.[14]

The first step had to be the identification of the subject of the enquiry:

> If we are to examine the meaning of the concept 'law', we must first know how to apply the word 'law'. And this is to be learnt only by a critical examination of the way in which the word is ordinarily used.[15]

But this was merely the starting point. Oakeshott presented the ordinary meaning of law as analogous to a text with its context,[16] and such a text can only be understood through:

> ... knowing its relationship to other things, knowing it in a world of related things, knowing it in its context.[17]

So this must be the aim to be pursued, which will (or at least ideally ought to be) pursued until no further enquiry is thought possible. The reason is that:[18]

> ... a philosophical explanation [of a concept] is one which, in principle, is the relationship of its subject to what I have called the totality of experience because this alone is a self complete context, a context which criticism cannot turn into a text itself requiring a context.

13. 162. 14. 171. 15. 175.
16. He does not explain what he means by the context of a text.
17. 175. 18. 175.

Accordingly, so Oakeshott argued, a philosophical jurisprudence, if successful, would occupy a place of primacy over other theories of law, being:

> . . . at once the most complete kind of explanation of the nature of law (for *ex hypothesis* the context to which it relates law is complete) and the criterion by means of which the relative incompleteness of other explanations can be determined and established.[19]

Elsewhere he argued that a philosophical concept must be 'categorical' in the sense that:

> . . . definition in philosophical enquiry aims at comprehending the whole character of its subject as a single whole.[20]

He claimed that his notion of a philosophical jurisprudence of law, having as its aim the most complete possible explanation of the nature of law, was no speculative pipe dream. Without developing the point he argued that it was the conception underlying the work of Aquinas, Hobbes, and Hegel.

Oakeshott's argument is elaborately adorned with views about the nature of philosophical enquiry, and presented in a wholly abstract form; at times it becomes extremely difficult to gain any vision of what a philosophical jurisprudence would look like. And he himself never made an attempt to develop one; one suspects an element of the fraudster and the charlatan, in that he really had not the least idea. He confined himself to meta-theory; a theory as to what a jurisprudential theory which was truly philosophical would be like rather than what it would be. I suspect that the fact that Oakeshott's article seems to have had no influence on either Hart or anyone else is that its arguments are obscure and at the same time absurd. And it must be said that to write an article which lays down a blueprint for a philosophical theory of law, and then fail to attempt to provide such a theory, has all the air of chickening out.

All this is strikingly unlike the approach followed by Hart. I do not know of any evidence that Hart knew of Oakeshott's article, though he could have done; he would surely have mentioned it if he had thought it important. The only jurisprudential text of the period in which it is cited, unenthusiastically except in one instance, is J Stone's *Province and Function of Law*.[21] But Hart, unlike Oakeshott, actually developed and published a theory of law. Although he published a 'Prolegomenon to the Principles of

19. 176. 20. 173. 21. At 11, 15, 16, 27, 43, and 48.

Punishment',[22] he never published a 'Prolegomenon to the Principles of General Jurisprudence', or offered in some other form a general account of how the knowledge, insights, and experience which he or other philosophers possessed could be harnessed to the task of revitalizing the study of jurisprudence. Hence we have to try to construct his ideas from scattered hints and indications to be found either in *The Concept of Law*, or in his other writings, particularly those which appeared early in his tenure of the chair. The nearest he came to a prolegomenon was his 'Analytical Jurisprudence in Mid-Twentieth Century: A Reply to Professor Bodenheimer'.[23]

The Publication of *The Concept of Law*

The Concept of Law was published in The Clarendon Law Series in 1961. Between his appointment to the chair in 1952 and around 1958 Hart must have been working on his edition of Austin's *The Province of Jurisprudence Determined* (1954), though this would not have detained him long, since he merely wrote a preface. Then he would be busy with his collaborative work with Honoré, *Causation and the Law* (1959), arguably the only major achievement of the Oxford school of ordinary language philosophy which has stood the test of time, but that is another story. Back in 1953 he and Honoré had offered a seminar on the subject, which I recall attending. Work on this must have reached a fairly advanced stage before Hart spent his year at Harvard in 1956–7, and contacts there with Herbert Wechsler, and reading of the American literature, persuaded him that the text of the book required extensive revision.[24] This work, which involved the two authors in disagreements as to how to proceed, seems to have been begun in late 1957 and continued well into 1958;[25] it was published in 1959.

Then, amongst a number of other projects, Hart seems to have then turned his attention to producing the text of *The Concept of Law*. From early in his tenure of the chair he had offered teaching in issues with which it was concerned. Thus in Hilary Term 1953 he taught a seminar on 'The Nature of the Basic Norm', where presumably he developed his criticisms of Kelsen, and in Michaelmas Term 1954 he delivered two lectures each week on 'Definition of Law and Related Concepts', a course repeated in

22. PAS 60: 1 (1959–60). 23. (1953) 105 UPLR 104:953.
24. Lacey 188, 190. 25. Lacey 209–214.

Michaelmas 1957. In 1958 and again in 1959 he delivered over two terms, courses of twenty four lectures under the title 'The Concept of Law'. These would be formal lectures, and it was a common practice in the British academic world, then as today, for monographs to originate as lecture courses. By late 1959 or so what was to become the final text must have been in an advanced state.[26] Eventually published, the book has ten chapters, divided into thirty three sections; it prints out at 237 pages. That is roughly ten pages of text per lecture. As we have seen the text was read and commented on by Rupert Cross, Peter Strawson, and Tony Honoré, and this would have taken some time. There was also a disaster, or two disasters which delayed publication; for details of this I have to rely on uncertain memory. The type for the book was hand set in Oxford, where an apprentice dropped a tray of type. Fearing trouble he did his best to reset the gathering, thereby producing sixteen pages of gibberish. The actual printing of the book, or perhaps just the binding, had been farmed out to a firm in Aylesbury, where this accident was not noticed; fortunately Hart himself spotted it when he received an advance copy. Setting matters to rights inevitably delayed publication.[27]

The Preface was signed by Hart in February 1961, and the book was published later that year. So *The Concept of Law* was on the stocks from 1958 until 1961, with something like a final draft in existence from late 1959 or early 1960.[28]

Hart as Analytical Jurist and Elucidator

One thing on which there is general agreement is that Hart's *The Concept of Law*, whatever else it is, falls into the category 'analytical jurisprudence'. As he himself put it:

> The lawyer will regard this book as an essay in analytical jurisprudence, for it is concerned with the clarification of the general framework of legal thought, rather than with the criticism of law or legal policy.[29]

26. See below Chapter 7 at p 197.
27. The bad luck did not end there, a van containing revised copies was involved in an accident.
28. See also Nicola Lacey's account of the writing process on pp 222–3 of her biography.
29. CL vii.

Later in the chapter he has recourse to metaphor, and writes not of 'clarification', but of 'elucidation'.[30] This became for him a favourite term for what his work was about: analytical jurisprudence's function was to *elucidate*. Thus when, later in the book, he sets out his own theory of law as the union or primary and secondary rules he writes:

> We accord this union of elements a central place because of their explanatory power in *elucidating* the concepts that constitute the framework of legal thought.[31]

Though the conception of seeing the light, elucidation, was much used by philosophers around the time in which we are interested nobody seems to have explained even loosely what the sense to be conveyed by the metaphor was supposed to be.

A feature which runs through both Hart's writings and the writings of other linguistic analysis philosophers of the period, and which makes it difficult to pin down what their ideas actually were, was their extensive use of metaphors—we shall soon come across, for example, 'family resemblances', 'language games', 'open texture', and 'the core and the penumbra'. Here we meet elucidation. Use of such metaphors hints at what the author is trying to convey, but provides an excuse for not trying to spell out more precisely what it is. One can unflatteringly view this as involving intellectual indolence and sloppiness of thought. Much the same charge can be levelled against Wittgenstein on language games, and perhaps against other passages in *Philosophical Investigations*, but my remarks here are not based on other parts of the book which I have not read for many years. The discussion of language games is self-evidently banal, and from this one can come to varied conclusions. One is that he just had nothing of interest to say. Another is

30. Also used by Oakeshott in his 'The Concept of a Philosophical Jurisprudence' included in his collection edited by L O'Sullivan, *The Concept of a Philosophical Jurisprudence: Essays and Reviews 1926–1951* at 174. It can be traced back to Wittgenstein's *Tractatus* 4.112, 'A philosophical work consists essentially of elucidations', quoted PMS Hacker, *Wittgenstein's Place in Twentieth Century Analytic Philosophy* (1996) at 287. See also A Kenny, *Wittgenstein* xv quoting *Tractatus* 6.54 'My propositions are elucidatory in this way: he who understands me finally recognizes them as senseless'. cf R Monk, *Ludwig Wittgenstein: The Duty of Genius* at 296. As discussed above in Chapter 2, in the summer of 1930 Wittgenstein dictated to Waismann a list of 'theses' as preparation for a joint book; at this time Wittgenstein had adopted a verification principle in the form 'The sense of a proposition is the way it is verified' and he then 'elucidated' it, ie explained more fully what this meant.

31. CL 79 and ff. In Hart's inaugural lecture and in (1957) UPLR 105:953 the expression is used on numerous occasions.

that he might have had something to say, but lacked the determination to do so. Another is that he discovered from experience with his class of acolytes that he could get away with rambling remarks (so different from the delphic utterances of the *Tractatus*), and ill thought out ideas, and from a sort of indolence, or perhaps from vanity, since his followers liked it, but did not think it worthwhile to explain his ideas (if indeed he had any) clearly. There are other possible explanations. But readers need to be careful about a version of the Emperor's Clothes syndrome. Just because the great Ludwig wrote something banal there is no reason to suppose it is not really banal just because Ludwig wrote it.

One way of looking at the matter would be to start from the fact that the practice of philosophy involves brooding over some difficult idea, and once the idea has been elucidated the brooder feels comfortable of achieving a level of understanding which makes further brooding unnecessary. Philosophy according to this view is therapeutic, rather like chattering to an analyst, but much cheaper. Presumably in relation to philosophical puzzles or conundrums, elucidation would dispose of the puzzle completely. There is no need to worry about the nature of the good, or the problem of induction, or the frustrations of Achilles in pursuit of the tortoise any more. One can have a gin and tonic, or go fishing, or whatever. Waismann, Hart's colleague, gave the following account of the philosophical enterprise of elucidation as therapy, but did not actually use these words, when it achieved success:

> Whoever has pondered some time over some dark problem in philosophy will have noticed that the solution, when it comes, comes with a suddenness. It is not through working very hard towards it that it is found. What happens is rather that he suddenly sees things in a new light - as if a veil has been lifted that screened his view, or if the scales had fallen from his eyes, leaving him surprised at his own stupidity not to have seen what was there quite plain before him all the time. It is less like finding out something and more like maturing, outgrowing preconceived notions.[32]

This dates back to 1950,[33] and although there is no direct evidence Hart may well have been familiar with it. How do you know that elucidation has taken place? Presumably by intuition. The sort of philosophical engagement

32. F Waismann, *How I See Philosophy*, 37.
33. HD Lewis (ed), *Contemporary British Philosophy*, Third Series, London 1956 pp 447–490 reproducing an article originally written somewhat earlier. See above Chapter 2 at p 46.

described by Waismann is a solitary activity, rather like a three pipe problem confronting Sherlock Holmes, though with no empirical frame of reference. Hart himself never addresses the matter. I shall quote an attempt I made some time ago to make sense of the idea:

> If you visit an art gallery in the company of a communicative person who has a deep knowledge of the history and philosophy of art, you come away with the feeling that you now understand much more clearly what the artists were trying to do, why the paintings are as they are, where the artists have perhaps not achieved what was intended, what symbolism lurks in the compositions, and so forth and so on. But at the end of the day, no profound problems or puzzles may have been solved, and nothing concluded. Indeed the process of elucidation throws up new fields for enquiry.[34]

But this explanation differs from Waismann, for whom no further elucidation is needed. And is this the best that can be done? Or is some experience rather like that of St Paul on the road to Damascus involved?

Which Concepts Require Elucidation?

The concepts which in Hart's thinking required elucidation comprised the concept of law itself, and a collection of other concepts which were traditionally called legal concepts, and which were thought to be in some way 'fundamental' in the sense originally developed by John Austin. Hart here identifies them as those that 'constitute the framework of legal thought'. In his 1953 article he wrote of 'the fundamental notions involved in the structure of a legal system'[35] and of 'fundamental legal concepts and distinctions'.[36] Where or how the boundary line was to be drawn between fundamental and non-fundamental concepts remained somewhat uncertain. It is easy to think of legal concepts which under this test do not qualify, such as the concept of a contingent remainder, or of anticipatory breach of contract; legal thought, however understood, could go on without them. It is harder to come up with a definite list of those that do, or a principle for telling us how the list should be compiled. The subject was ventilated in a very inconclusive way in a 1955 symposium on Hart's inaugural lecture, the

34. (2006) 104 MichLR at 1458.
35. At 363.
36. At 364.

participants being Jonathan Cohen and Hart himself.[37] Cohen suggested that:

> ... requests for general juristic definitions arise when people are puzzled about, or interested in, concepts which seem to belong peculiarly and necessarily to all developed legal systems.[38] And it is this kind of request that men like Austin and Kelsen have (most of the time) thought themselves to be meeting...

He distinguished between what he called 'framework concepts' (eg right and duty) and 'material concepts' (such as possession or corporation); his idea was that framework concepts are logically necessary to any system of rules for human conduct, whereas there could be such a system of rules which said nothing about material concepts, meaning concepts related to the substance of the law.[39] Cohen in a note refers to Austin's distinction between 'general' and 'particular' jurisprudence, citing to the posthumous *Lectures on Jurisprudence*. Cohen's arguments simply elaborated Austin's conception of general jurisprudence.[40] In his response Hart disagreed with Cohen's suggestion that the philosophical problems of the kind he addressed in his lecture, for which he argued for a special technique of elucidation, were peculiar to framework concepts as defined by Cohen.[41] But in one passage he said that:

> ... it is certainly arguable that the concept of a legal right and a legal duty are logically necessary parts of the concept of a legal system.[42]

But neither in the symposium, nor in *The Concept of Law*, did he ever give a general explanation of what the difference was between fundamental and non-fundamental concepts, or say whether he thought there were concepts which either necessarily, or as a matter of empirical fact, belonged to all developed legal systems. What does 'logically' mean here—not surely formal logic, but some loose idea of making sense.

In the main Hart simply accepted the canon of general jurisprudence topics which had come to be established in Oxford jurisprudence. This is the explanation of the fact that the examination papers set in Oxford in his

37. 'Symposium: Definition and Theory in Jurisprudence', PAS, Supp, Vols (1955) 29 *Problems in Psychotherapy and Jurisprudence* 213–264.
38. Neither Cohen nor, as we shall see, Hart, had extensive knowledge of the world's legal systems.
39. At 218. 40. At 220. At 32–3 and 107. 41. At 241–7. 42. At 250.

time related to the topics long established by convention. His inaugural lecture particularly well illustrates this, addressing how such questions as 'What is law?',[43] 'What is a state?', 'What is a right?', 'What is possession?', and the concepts of duty, or of a corporation should be elucidated, old chestnuts in Oxford jurisprudence. The one concept which he did add to the canon was what he called a rule;[44] in Kelsen's theory a similar notion appears as a norm. The analysis of rules or norms had not played so central a role in earlier analytical jurisprudence, though the concept of a legal system as comprising rules had featured in Austinian jurisprudence, analysed in a different way.

Elucidating the Concept of Law Itself

Hart's title for his book, *The Concept of Law*, echoed Ryle's *The Concept of Mind*, and so a starting point must be the assumption that the *concept of law* is both what the book is about, and what makes it a philosophical enterprise. Ryle, in an article published in 1968,[45] pointed out that:

> Sometimes philosophers say that they are analyzing or clarifying the 'concepts' which are embodied in the 'judgements' of the plain man or of the scientist, historian, artist, or who-not [he could have added lawyer]. But this seems to be only a gaseous way of saying that they are trying to discover what is meant by the general terms contained in the sentences which they pronounce or write.

Ryle had begun his article by pointing out that philosophical arguments largely and perhaps always are about what it means to say this or that, attention being focused on 'more or less radical types or classes' of general expressions. He went on to discuss various problems as to the purpose, value and perils of this philosophical enterprise which need not concern us here;[46]

43. Though in this lecture he does not apply his ideas to this question.
44. The passage in which Hart argues that it is impossible 'to elucidate even the more elementary forms of law' without the idea or concept of a rule appears in CL at 78.
45. 'Systematically Misleading Expressions' in AGN Flew, *Logic and Language First Series* Chapter 2.
46. In particular his argument, as applied to 'the concept of law', is that insofar as the use of this expression is taken to refer to an entity, or to entail the existence of such an entity, it is systematically misleading. In *The Concept of Mind* (1949) Ryle argued against 'the ghost in the machine', the idea that the language with which we commonly describe and analyse human behaviour, which may often reflect a mind-body dualism, can be understood without the assumption that its use entails the idea that there exists in some mysterious sense an entity called the mind, which controls the body.

I quote him only because his account helps us to understand what Hart's title seems to say is the subject matter of his book. Hart, as I have said, never spells this out, or discusses what is meant by the analysis or elucidation of a concept. But his opening chapter does convey the idea that at least the starting point for the elucidation of the concept of law is an enquiry into meaning.[47] And his argument that trying to answer the question 'What is law?' by offering definitions *per genus et differentiam* is misguided, is consistent with Ryle's account of the philosophical enterprise. Its concern is with questions of meaning, here the meaning of the abstract word 'law'. Consistently with this, Hart wrote in his preface:

> The lawyer will regard this book as an essay in analytical jurisprudence, for it is concerned with the clarification of the general framework of legal thought, rather than with the criticism of law of legal policy. Moreover at many points I have raised questions which may well be said to be about the meanings of words.[48]

So that is what his philosophical work of analytical general jurisprudence was about.

Other passages in his preface to *The Concept of Law* seem at first sight at least quite at odds with this, for they say that the aim of the book is to provide, in addition to an analysis of the structure of a legal system, a better understanding not of the meaning of the abstract word 'law' (and other abstract terms discussed in the book, most importantly 'coercion', 'legal system', 'obligation') but rather of social phenomena:

> . . . its [ie The Concept of Law's] purpose is not to provide a definition of law, in the sense of a rule by reference to which the correctness of the use of the word can be tested; it is to advance legal theory by providing an improved analysis of the distinctive structure of a municipal legal system and a better understanding of the resemblances and differences between law, coercion, and morality, *as types of social phenomena*.[49]

He also wrote:

> Notwithstanding its concern with analysis the book may also be regarded as an essay in descriptive sociology; for the suggestion that inquiries into the meanings of words merely throws light on words is false.[50]

47. 17. 48. CL vii. 49. CL 17, emphasis added. 50. CL vii.

So the book was presented as an essay in social science. But he went on:

> Many important distinctions, which are not immediately obvious, between types of social situation or relationships may best be brought to light by an examination of the standard uses of the relevant expressions and of the way in which these depend on a social context. In this field of study it is particularly true that we may use, as Professor J. L. Austin said, 'a sharpened awareness of words to sharpen our perception of the phenomena'.

Does this mean that the book is intended to be about social phenomena, or rather about questions of meaning, meaning however being dependent upon social context?

Many years later Hart, with hindsight, gave in the *Postscript* a much clearer statement of what *The Concept of Law* was about:

> My aim in this book [ie *The Concept of Law*] was to provide a theory of what law is which is both general and descriptive. It is *general* in the sense that it is not tied to any particular legal system or legal culture,[51] but seeks to give an explanatory and clarifying account of law as a complex social and political institution with a rule-governed (and in that sense 'normative') aspect. This institution, in spite of many variations in different cultures and in different times, has taken the same general form and structure, though many misunderstandings and obscuring myths, calling for clarification, have clustered around it.[52]

In his 1988 interview he gave perhaps an even clearer explanation. David Sugarman asked him:

> So what did you mean by its being 'an essay in descriptive sociology?'

He replied:

> What I should have said is that it provides the tools for descriptive sociology, not that it is descriptive sociology. It meant that if you read that book you can see we need to discriminate various types of situations - say where people habitually follow somebody, where they accept him as their guide to conduct, and therefore his word is a reason for acting, therefore he is [sic] a guide to criticism of other people's conduct.

51. This expression does not occur in CL. 52. CL 239.

General Philosophical Ideas in *The Concept of Law*

Hart was supposed to bring new philosophical insights, analytical tools, and techniques to revitalize the moribund jurisprudence of the Oxford Law Faculty. I shall call these general philosophical ideas.[53] It is not difficult to identify some which are recurrently used in *The Concept of Law*, and which do not feature at all, or only in a very shadowy way, in earlier jurisprudential writing. In the next chapter I shall try to state in a simple and largely non-critical form what they are. I shall also say a little about their pedigree, which it is not always possible to establish.

First I shall say something about Hart's discussion of the strange question 'What is Law?', and his argument that no satisfactory answer could be provided by a definition *per genus et differentiam*. Instead one had to ask why such a question was asked. And the answer Hart gave to this was critically important in that it determined the structure of *The Concept of Law*.

Early in his book Hart raised the question why 'thoughtful men with a firm mastery and knowledge of the law'[54] and, it should be added, with an ability to use the word law and related terms correctly, should be puzzled when they tried to answer the question 'What is law?'. Why on earth do they ask the question at all?[55] It is as if some leading surgeon, half way through a transplant operation, suddenly turned to his registrar and said in tones of anguish: 'What is surgery? I just can't go on until someone tells me'. And when his registrar, nervous lest he is having a *crise nerveuse*, replies 'It's what you are doing', and the surgeon, in tones of desperation, replies 'I know that, but what am I doing?'. By now the patient is dead.

In my own long experience as a teacher and to some modest extent a practitioner of law I have never once been asked the question 'What is law?'.

53. PMS Hacker in Hacker and J Raz, (eds), in *Law, Morality and Society. Essays in Honour of H. L. A. Hart* (1977), a *festchrift* for Hart's 70th birthday, in 'Methodological Remarks' at 2-12 analyses the use made by Hart of techniques associated with English analytical philosophy, which, he argues, were both applied and ingeniously adapted so as to illuminate numerous outstanding issues and raise a number of new problems.

54. CL 6.

55. cf (1957) 105 UPLR 104 at 964 and ff where there is a full discussion.

Back to St Augustine of Hippo

Hart's initial explanation is to offer the classic statement of this puzzle by St Augustine:

> What then is time? If no one asks me I know: if I wish to explain it to one who asks I know not.

In his 1957 article he gave a fuller text:

> What then is time? If no one asks me, I know; if I wish to explain it to one who asketh, I know not; yet I say boldly, that I know, that if nothing passed away, time past were not; and if nothing were coming, a time to come were not; and if nothing were, time present were not.[56]

This serves to identify the question as being philosophical in character. Augustine's concern was in fact over how time could be measured: the past has gone, the future has not yet arrived, and the present has no extension. Hart's contention, of central importance for *The Concept of Law*, is methodological: such philosophical questions cannot usefully be addressed by the provision of a definition *per genus et differentiam*, here of the word 'law'.

Hart was surely right in this basic contention, but the way he developed his scepticism over the value of defining law *per genus et differentiam* seems problematic. The problem, he thought, is the same as that of someone who can recognize an elephant, but cannot define it. Why anyone should worry about this is beyond me, but it is I suppose all part of life's richly varied pattern. For Hart the function of a definition *per genus et differentiam* is to provide a form or words into which 'elephant' can be substituted whenever it occurs.[57] The idea that this is an achievable end is little short of weird. If it was true then simultaneous translators who, as one once explained to me, spend much of their time translating rubbish into rubbish in the UN or at other international institutions, would find their work hugely simplified. The weirdness is the more striking coming from a philosopher who, with Austin, sought support in the ordinary use of language.

I do not think this was St Augustine's problem at all, and dictionary definitions certainly do not have the function Hart here attributes to them.

56. CL 13. *Confessions of St Augustine* 11.14.7. 57. CL 14–15.

Hart provides a possible 'definition' of an elephant:

> . . . a quadruped distinguished from others by its possession of a thick skin, tusks and a trunk.

This is the sort of 'definition' one might indeed find in a dictionary. My *Shorter Oxford Dictionary* has a more elaborate definition:

> A huge quadruped of the Pachydermate order, having long curving ivory tusks and a prehensile proboscis. Only two species now exist, the Indian and the African; the former of which (the largest of extant land animals) is often used as a beast of burden.

Now some elephants do not possess tusks, and some have been poached and skinned. They are still plainly elephants, albeit in bad shape, and not aardvarks, or law professors. Baby elephants? Nothing huge about them. Yet someone well able to identify an elephant, dead or alive, mutilated or unmutilated, baby or adult, may still be puzzled as to how it is we can treat obviously different things as the same. Attempts to address this problem by producing more and more elaborate definitions simply do not work. Try it.

On all this there is a vast philosophical literature, with which Hart would be familiar. He does not address it in *The Concept of Law*, or indeed anywhere else. One long established response assumes that all elephants must have in common some fundamental or basic quality of elephant-ness. But we do not seem to be able to state clearly what this is, and it seems deeply implausible to suppose that when, on safari in Africa, one's friend calls out 'Look over there, there's an elephant just visible behind that baobab tree' they were able to identify what they can see as an elephant because it possesses the true quality of elephant-ness. In real life the nearby presence of an elephant may be known because of smell, or noise, or by identifying tracks or droppings. Our dictionary definitions mention none of these indicia. And any attempt to say what the 'true nature' of elephants is will probably end up with some absurdity like 'It's being an elephant'. Similar puzzles arise over the abstract concepts of social organization. We may agree that today Germany, France, South Africa, India and even the USA. are all democracies, but their systems of government are wildly different in many respects. So what is the 'true nature' of democracy? Was Stalin's Russia really a democracy? The Russians said it was. Was Franco really a fascist? Is Somalia really a state? What is the essence or true nature of fascism? Or of statehood?

In his reply to Bodenheimer, Hart handles the matter differently; he does not run together his views as to the function and nature of definitions *per genus et differentiam*, and his explanation of St Augustine's concern. He provides two other illustrations: someone who can find their way around a town, but cannot explain how it is he does so, or draw a map of the town,[58] and the ability to use mathematical notions without being able to give any account of the problems as to the nature and interrelationship between mathematical concepts. He seems to have found it extremely difficult to answer the general question he had posed. And for a philosopher this does seem to be a matter for concern, for they were supposed to be well aware of the problem. It is also noticeable that no mention is made of the fact that people differ very considerably in their ability to put their ideas into words. Some can hardly rise above profanity and grunting as I discovered in the early days of my military training.

One Rejected Response: The Silly Question Solution

One radical response to the elephant problem, which Hart might have adopted, though at the price of never writing *The Concept of Law*, would have been to say that anyone who has no problem over identifying elephants, and using the word elephant, but persists in asking 'What is an elephant?' is just asking a silly question. If he needs philosophy he needs it as therapy only. For he assumes that there is, out there somewhere, something he does not know about elephants, when the truth is that he already knows all there is to be known.

I am reminded of a story once told me by Derek Hall. One of his pupils, a Welshman, came to see him in a state of anguish about the concept of 'a fee simple absolute in possession'.[59] He knew how this property interest was created, how it could be transferred, how one established that one was possessed of such an interest. He explained that he knew how long it could last, what happened if someone in whom such an interest was vested died intestate, and what if any rights of enjoyment it entailed. He was

58. I think this comes from Ryle, but have mislaid the reference.

59. I once had an obsessive pupil who was on the edge of a breakdown over the alienability of contingent remainders.

distressed by the fact that in spite of all the work he had put in he remained fundamentally ignorant. His question to his tutor was this:

> What I want to know, Mr. Hall, is this: what is the essential nature and quality of the fee itself?

The context in which he told me this story was a discussion of Hart's inaugural lecture, which we had both attended.

Hart's response was not to treat the question 'What is law?' as silly, but to seek to identify what underlay the puzzlement which had prompted lawyers (a handful of them only, it has to be conceded) to ask the question 'What is law?'.

This was a critically important move, for it was the answer he gave to this question which provided him with the basic structure of *The Concept of Law*.

Context and Meaning

Hart's basic insight here can be explained quite simply. When we communicate with each other, whether by speech, or text, or significant signals, the action of communication will normally take place in what I shall loosely call a context. The context, which is not the same thing as the conventions governing the use of particular words and expressions, may, for example, clarify the meaning of the act of communication—pass the cat means one thing in a veterinary surgeon's office, and quite another on Captains Bligh's *The Bounty*. In face to face communication the context will include a wide range of significant gestures, tones of voice, and so forth, similar to those which animals use to communicate with each other. Again if on a square rigger you call to a friend 'Race you to the futtock shrouds' the wind direction, the manoeuvre in which the vessel is engaged, *etcetera*, will normally identify which futtock shrouds, for there are a number of pairs of them at the junction between masts, you mean. Sometimes it may be difficult or even impossible to establish what the context was—we shall come across this problem later on in connection with the mysterious remarks by the poet Archilochos on the abilities of the fox and the hedgehog.[60] It would not be possible to list everything that can be included in the loose

60. For a classic attempt to recreate the context largely from a text see Moses Finlay's *The World of Odysseus* (1954).

concept of context, but the context can include the reasons why the act of communication took place, including the purpose of the communicator.

So when a question is asked the questioner will usually, though not always, have some reason for asking the question—perhaps simply to irritate, or insult, or humiliate the person questioned, or enhance the status of the questioner, a phenomenon which can be witnessed in Prime Minister's Question Time in the House of Commons, or in the questioning of candidates for appointments in American Law Schools, where the merits of the candidate commonly get forgotten as members of the faculty compete with each other over asking really smart questions. So keen was the competition at Michigan that you had to put up your hand as if requesting permission to visit the loo in an infant school; a list was compiled and those on it called on in sequence. One faculty member's chief aim appeared to be to make it virtually impossible to understand what the question was, though the consensus was that it was probably a most important question, and the questioner a very smart person, which he indeed was. The candidate would at this point freeze with terror or just sound off at random. Silence for thought was taboo.

One of the ways in which puzzles were generated in post war Oxford philosophy was by discussing propositions either without specifying their context, or by covertly assuming a context without specifying what it is or was. By way of example one such proposition, which came to rank as an old chestnut, and was in fact first raised by Bertrand Russell back in 1905, was the proposition:

> The King of France is bald.

Well, one is supposed to note, since there is no King of France, it is not obvious that one can say the statement is true, or false. But at the same time the statement is not some logical tautology, true by definition, nor is it meaningless; it is quite clear what it means. Nor is it just nonsense, like:

> Twas brillig, and the slivy toves,
> Did gyre and gimble in the wabe...

At the time when I read law in Oxford I recall numerous occasions on which friends who were studying philosophy gave accounts of the knots they tied themselves up in during tutorials in which this proposition was discussed. But I do not recall them ever explaining the context in which the proposition was supposed to have been put forward, or why anyone would have advanced such a proposition, except to generate a puzzle for academic discussion. In fact for it to serve this function some sort of context had to be covertly assumed, for it had to be put forward at a time when there is no King of France. And even this was problematic, for although in the 1950s (and for that matter back in 1905) most people, including French constitutional lawyers, would have agreed that there was indeed no King of France, there were out there some monarchists who took the opposite view. A contemporary of mine in Oxford, David Urch, claimed to be the true King of England, descended from some Saxon monarch or other; I fear we did not take him very seriously. And when I was a fellow of St Edmund Hall, the college had a club which annually invited the Stuart Pretender to the English Crown to a dinner, and he would politely explain that he was unable to attend. The present Stuart is Francis, Duke of Bavaria, but he does not press a claim.

In fact it is easy to provide a context for 'The King of France is bald' in which its capacity to generate a puzzle vanishes. You take your children to see a historical drama about France; one asks 'Which one is the King of France?' and you answer 'The King of France is the one who is bald'. Question answered. Here what has been specified is why the statement was made; once clear the mystery goes away, and the proposition ceases to provide tutorial or seminar fodder. Numerous other examples of similar tutorial fodder could easily be provided.

I wonder if Hart's provision of a context to the asking of the question 'What is law?' reflected an awareness, based on his experience as an Oxford philosopher, that contextless questions, or questions with unspecified contexts, served only to create puzzles, and do not contribute to elucidating the concept under discussion, here the concept of law. But if so he never explicitly said so; hence any explanation along these lines must be speculative. And in his famous 1957 exchange with Lon Fuller over the vehicle in the park he doggedly maintained the view that in what he called the standard instance, or case falling within the core of meaning, the decision as to whether a particular thing was a vehicle should be decided without reference to context.[61] In particular any use of the supposed purpose of the legislation was not to be treated as relevant. All you needed was the word, and the normal conventions of ordinary language.

61. See at 607.

Identifying the Four Issues

Be all that as it may, it was Hart's contention that continued concentration on the single question 'What is law?' would not be a useful way of proceeding:

> Plainly the best course is to defer giving any answer to the query 'What is law?' until we have found out what it is about law which has in fact puzzled those who have asked or attempted to answer it.[62]

He went on to argue that the reason why the question was asked was puzzlement over three recurrent issues:

> How does law differ from and how is it related to orders backed by threats? How does legal obligation differ from and how is it related to moral obligation? What are rules and to what extent is law an affair of rules?[63]

Later he added a fourth issue: in what sense can laws constitute a system of law?[64] In terms of the conception of context, Hart's analysis is contextual in that it gives central importance to the reasons why the blanket question, 'What is law?' is asked in the first place. And his identification of the four issues or sources of puzzlement provided the structure of *The Concept of Law*, and, at the risk of some simplification, led him to write a book not so much on the concept of law, as on the concept of a legal system. A book on the concept of law, the term law being used in a wide variety of senses, would have been utterly different. So the title of the book is quite misleading.

Given the fundamental importance to Hart's analysis of why the question 'What is Law?' was asked, and his identification of the four issues, it is tempting to enquire whether a specific philosophical pedigree or source of this emphasis on context can be established. One problem here is that Hart, though he had much to say on the functioning of language, never explicitly spelled out the idea of linguistic context which I have loosely set out, notwithstanding the frequent emphasis in *The Concept of Law* on the social context in which claims and assertions are made. Indeed in his writings which relate to questions of interpretation of rules of law context hardly features at all; this it seems is a serious defect, most obviously in his

62. CL 5. 63. CL 13.

64. Developed in CL Chapters V and VI; a concise summary is provided on 116, bottom paragraph.

exchange with Fuller. At one level however there is nothing to explain, for in Oxford linguistic analysis of the period, particularly that associated with Austin, the attachment of importance to some impoverished version of what I have called context was common form. This is particularly so in his *How to Do Things With Words*.

But the idea that there was a philosophical pedigree for his analysis may simply be wrong. Just as life was possible before the invention and without the assistance of scotch tape, or electricity,[65] or the computer, or the psycho analysts, so it is possible without the philosophers. You surely do not need to have studied philosophy to take the view that it is easier to answer a question if you try to work out why the question has been asked. That is not a profound insight for which we have to thank the Oxford philosophers. Yet it is worth noting *en passant* that Hart seems to have been the first person who applied this commonsense idea to legal theory. And that itself is surely both curious and important.

65. I grew up from 1931 to 1937 in a house without electricity apart from that provided in rechargeable cells for the radio, acquired I think in about 1936. Everyone in the valley came in to listen to this amazing contraption.

4

The Elusive Sources of Hart's Ideas in *The Concept of Law*

Oxford Linguistic Analysis and Ordinary Language

In the immediate post war period a view was mooted, and perhaps by some accepted, which was neatly summed up by one PL Heath:

> Philosophical problems are generally, if not always, due to unnoticed or unadvertised departures from Standard English, and are to be solved, or cured, as the case may be, by pointing out the normal use of the words employed and the normal grammatical form of the sentences in which they appear. For ordinary language is correct language.[1]

Well before *The Concept of Law* was written the more extreme versions of this view had been subjected to radical criticism, as in Heath's article. Softened versions persisted, and Austin was particularly associated with such a version, which he, somewhat uncharacteristically, explained very clearly:

> In view of the prevalence of the slogan 'ordinary language' and of such names as 'linguistic' or 'analytic' philosophy or 'the analysis of language', one thing needs specially emphasizing to counter misunderstanding. When we examine what we should say when, what words we should use in what situations, we are looking again not *merely* at words (or 'meanings', whatever they may be) but also at the realities we use the words to talk about; we are using a sharpened awareness of words to sharpen our perception of, though not the final arbiter of, the phenomena. For this reason I think it might be

1. PL Heath, 'The Appeal to Ordinary Language' (1952) *Philosophical Quarterly* 2:1.

> better to use, for this way of doing philosophy, some less misleading name than those given above—for instance, 'linguistic phenomenology', only that is rather a mouthful.[2]

This passage occurs in Austin's paper 'A Plea for Excuses', itself ultimately a product of cooperation between Hart and Austin,[3] and it is not surprising that when Hart in the preface to *The Concept of Law* set out his own view he wrote as follows:

> ...the suggestion that inquiries into the meanings of words merely throw light on words is false. Many important distinctions, which are not immediately obvious, between different types of social situation or relationships may best be brought to light by an examination of the standard uses of the relevant expressions and of the way in which these depend on a social context, itself often left unstated. In this field of study it is particularly true that we may use, as Professor J. L. Austin said, 'a sharpened awareness of words to sharpen our perception of the phenomena'.[4]

There are many examples in *The Concept of Law* of Hart's use of the methodology which he states in this passage. It is impossible to say whether it was Austin or Hart, or both of them, who developed this view.

Precursors to *The Concept of Law*

Though Hart made his ideas clear on this methodological issue, he did not, as we have seen, publish a prolegomenon to *The Concept of Law*. So we have to do our best to tease out his ideas and their sources, if discoverable, from some of the more important of his publications which preceded the publication of *The Concept of Law*.

The earliest such publication which is at all relevant is his inaugural lecture of 1953. But although it opens by saying that it proposes to discuss the perplexities which have arisen over attempts to answer such questions as 'What is law? What is a state?', it is largely concerned with what it calls the elucidation of legal concepts such as right, corporation—the fundamental legal conceptions of general jurisprudence, rather than with the analysis of the overarching concept of law, or of a legal system. And it deals with the

2. Austin, *Philosophical Papers* 3rd edn 182.
3. See above Chapter 2 at p 50.
4. The passage omitted is that which claims that the book is an essay in descriptive sociology.

inappropriateness of attempting to resolve the puzzles to which they have given rise by the technique of definition *per genus et differentiam*. The source is Bentham's *A Fragment on Government*.[5] From time to time in this lecture Hart lets fall remarks which indicate that he was already developing ideas which were to be worked into *The Concept of Law*, he gives no indication of external sources for his ideas. Thus at one point he writes:

> That is, we must elucidate the expression 'the same legal system' by showing what are the conditions sufficient for the truth of statements of the form 'The same legal system is in force in England now as in 1900'. The fundamental question here is the elucidation of the expression 'the same rule'.[6]

Again at one point the concept of a *legal system* even makes a cameo appearance:

> . . . a special and very complicated setting, namely the existence of a legal system with all that implies by way of general obedience, the operation of the sanctions of the system, and the general likelihood that this will continue.[7]

The context is the argument that statements such as 'A has a legal right to X' assume, but do not state, that such a legal system exists. But that is all there is, apart from a considerable use of the analogy between the operation of the rules of games and the working of a system of law, which analogy we know was a concern of the Austin group's discussions, and which was to feature prominently in *The Concept of Law*.

In 'Philosophy of Law and Jurisprudence (1945–1952)'[8] Hart set out a list of topics and ideas which had attracted the attention of philosophers, and which were of interest to lawyers. It might be thought that this would shed some light on what general theory, if any, Hart espoused as to the relevance of philosophical thought to problems in jurisprudence, and who had influenced him. It is not in fact helpful or informative.

The first item in the list is the notion of a rule, and the logical features of expressions which invoke or apply rules. There is a citation to Austin's 1946 paper 'Other Minds'.[9] It is not at all clear what precisely Hart is referring to in this difficult article, which discusses epistemological problems involved in the action of communication. It contains no analysis of the concept of a rule, only using the word rule once,[10] and says nothing about the logical

5. Cited at page 2 n 2. 6. 20 n 1. 7. 9. 8. (1953) AJCL 2:355.
9. Austin, *Philosophical Papers* (3rd edn) at 76. 10. 115.

features of expressions which invoke or apply rules. It does contain an analysis of the significance of engaging in what Austin calls the ritual of promising, but this does not rely on the concept of following a rule.[11] It also contains a passage which anticipates Austin's later work on performatives, and conceivably this is what Hart had in mind.[12] There is also a citation to RM Hare's *The Language of Morals* (1952), which is not helpful.

The second item is the concept of an action (relevant to the elucidation of intention, will, motive) as an aspect of a re-description of notions of mind and body. There is inevitably a citation to Ryle's *The Concept of Mind*, and whatever Hart had in mind it has no relevance to *The Concept of Law*. The discussion seems relevant to Hart's later work on punishment and responsibility, although his *Punishment and Responsibility* (1968) nowhere so much as mentions Ryle.

The third comprises analyses of the function of names and descriptions which might be relevant to problems over identity and mistake in contract. There is no citation and this again has no relevance to *The Concept of Law*.

The fourth item is more intriguing: the discovery that one statement or rule could be *about* another statement or rule in various ways, which could provide the basis for an improved account of the structure and interrelation of legal systems and the relation between legal and moral rules. There is no citation, and in particular no citation to the writings of Sir John Salmond, the earliest source of this idea, which I discuss below. In *The Concept of Law* one of the distinctions between the two types of rule on which Hart's analysis relies is that power conferring rules are said to be 'parasitic or secondary' to duty imposing rules.[13] Later he says that secondary rules:

> ...are on a different level from the primary rules, for they are all *about* such rules; in the sense that while primary rules are concerned with the actions that individuals must or must not do, these secondary rules are all concerned with the primary rules themselves. They specify the ways in which the primary rules may be conclusively ascertained, introduced, eliminated, varied, and the fact of their violation conclusively determined.[14]

The text of the article provides no indication as to the provenance of this idea, which of course may have been original to Hart.

The fifth item mentions two quite distinct ideas. One is an interest in types of argument which may be rational but not conclusive. Hart himself

11. 99. 12. 101–3. 13. CL 81. 14. CL 94.

never developed this idea, which is critical to understanding, for example, legal reasoning and indeed all practical reasoning. The other is the way in which concepts which cannot be rigidly defined, but are open textured, could emancipate jurists from the belief that deductive proof exhausts the notion of reasoning.[15] The reference to the concept of 'open texture' is to the use of this metaphor by Waismann; it is an English version of an expression *Porosität der Begriffe*.[16] So Hart's shopping list perhaps gives some general indication of the philosophers who had influenced him: Austin, Ryle, Rees, King, Waismann, and Wisdom—all but King associated with Oxford linguistic analysis. Hart makes specific reference to the influence of J Wisdom's article 'Gods', which appeared in a collection edited by AGN Flew.[17] This does contain[18] a very brief discussion of the character of legal reasoning in disputed cases in which there is agreement on 'the facts' but not on the categorization of the facts for the purpose of determining the legal consequences; for example 'whether Mr. A who admittedly handed his long trusted clerk signed blank cheques did or did not exercise reasonable care'. Three points are made. One is that the process of judicial decision in such cases involves:

> . . . the weighing of the cumulative effect of one group of inconclusive items against the cumulative effect of another group of severally inconclusive items . . .

The second is that decisions in such cases, though not the product of deductive reasoning, are not arbitrary. The third is that a judicial decision in such a case evinces what Wisdom calls 'an attitude' and has not only a

15. With citations to WJ Rees, 'The Theory of Sovereignty Restated' (1950) *Mind* 59, 495 (an elaborate analysis of the various senses of the use of the concept of sovereignty and of the utility of the concept in political theory); BE King, 'Propositions About Law' (1951) *Camb LJ* 2 (1951) 31 (develops a distinction between propositions about law and propositions of law and offers a theory as to when law or a system of law can be said to exist; King was a member of the Cambridge Law Faculty, and not by profession a philosopher); F Waismann, 'Verifiability', Hart, 'The Ascription of Responsibility and Rights' and J Wisdom, 'Gods' in A Flew (ed), *Logic and Language First Series* (1951) at 117, 145, 187.
16. It is used in Waismann's 1945 article 'Verifiability' PAS Supp. Vol XIX 119 has been suggested (see PMS Hacker, *Wittgenstein's Place in Twentieth-Century-Philosophy* at 164–5) that it was invented by W Kneale in his *The Development of Logic*, but since this was first published in 1962 this cannot be right. See also GP Baker and MS Hacker, *Wittgenstein: Understanding and Meaning, Volume I of an Analytical Commentary on the Philosophical Investigations* PII paras 4–7 and Exegesis para 80.
17. *Logic and Language*. First Series (1951) at 187.
18. 195.

purpose but a 'logic', which he says is surprisingly like the 'logic' of 'futile', 'deplorable', 'graceful', 'grand', and 'divine'. What on earth he meant by this one can only speculate. I have not the least idea. I wonder if he did.

One of the cases he refers to in a note by way of illustration is the case, well known to common lawyers, of *Hannah v Peel* (1944)[19] which he appears to have spotted when reading his copy of *The Times*. Briefly the agreed facts were that in the course of his military duties a corporal was adjusting the blackout curtains in a house in which he was billeted. It had been commandeered under wartime legislation by the Crown. The house was owned by one Major Peel, but he had never gone into possession of it. In doing so the corporal came across an extremely valuable brooch. How it got there nobody was able to discover. The corporal handed the brooch in to his commanding officer, who handed it to the police. When, after an interval, nobody came forward to claim the brooch the police gave it to Major Peel. Plainly quite a number of possible claimants to the brooch existed—the 'original owner' if such a person could be identified, the person who put it up on the curtains (a thief perhaps?), the Crown (which made no claim). In the course of its life since original manufacture the brooch might well have had a series of legitimate owners, but the dispute was confined to Corporal Hannah and Major Peel. The former won the case.

In the course of my academic career I must have devoted many hours to *Hannah v Peel*, since it is a wonderful case on which to hang a discussion of the nature of legal reasoning in complex disputed cases. This was the more so because, under a body of elaborate legal doctrine, based on a number of earlier legal decisions, out of which it was extremely difficult to distil any clear body of principle, the outcome of the case was supposed, according to one view, to turn on whether Major Peel had 'prior possession' of the brooch, thereby trumping Corporal Hannah's claim. For according to this doctrine a prior possessor should normally win such a case in a dispute with a later possessor. The judge who decided the case, Norman Birkett, more or less gave up on the abstract doctrinal reasoning surrounding the concept of possession.[20] But his decision was, arguably, not arbitrary, in that he

19. [1945] 1 KB 509. He also refers to a case in which a cruiser was cut in two by a liner, in which the facts were in dispute. The reference is to the incident in 1942 in which the Cunard liner Queen Mary sank its escort, HMS Curacao. Litigation eventually reached the House of Lords, with the Curacao being held two thirds to blame.

20. Later Lord Justice and a judge at the Nuremberg Tribunal.

provided reasons for it, and made a case for saying that it was at least not inconsistent with prior decisions. But here, as elsewhere, Wisdom, the philosopher, did not devote any time to doing his homework on the case, with the consequence that he had nothing to say on the nature of legal reasoning which extended beyond the banal.

The Roasting of Bodenheimer[21] and *Legal and Moral Obligation*[22]

As I have said Hart's response to Bodenheimer is the closest he ever came to publishing a prolegomenon to his analysis of the concept of law, and of a legal system. It sets out in some detail ideas which were to feature prominently in *The Concept of Law*, for example the limitations on the usefulness of definition *per genus et differentiam,*[23] the analysis of the concept of legal obligation,[24] the importance in conceptual analysis of identifying the paradigm or standard case,[25] the distinction between ambiguity and structural complexity, and the Aristotelian insistence that the application of one word to different things does not entail the idea that they all share a common feature, but that the explanation might lie in 'varying relationships to a central notion, or by analogy'.[26]

Hart's article does not however provide much in the way of evidence as to the philosophical influences which underlay it. The importance of attending to the conventions of ordinary language is emphasized in a passage which criticizes Kelsen's argument that all legal rules can best be understood as being fundamentally of one kind, directions to officials to apply sanctions,[27] and in a passage which distinguishes between being obliged and being under an obligation.[28] There is a passage emphasizing the importance of identifying the varied ways in which legal rules function in a legal system

21. 'Analytical Jurisprudence in Mid-Twentieth Century: A Reply to Professor Bodenheimer' (1957) 105 UPLR 1080.
22. AI Melden, *Essays in Moral Philosophy* (1958).
23. 960.
24. 966.
25. 968.
26. 269.
27. 959. Here this is called the 'reductionist drive' whereas in CL the favourite expression is 'recasting'.
28. 966. In CL at 82.

and the manner in which this is reflected in language.[29] But the only earlier writers whose work is discussed in any detail whatever are Hohfeld and Kelsen Both receive pats on the back[30] for their contributions to analytical jurisprudence, but Hart is at pains to differentiate his theory from that of Kelsen. Otherwise such references as there are to philosophical writings amount to little—there is for example a very brief and undeveloped citation to Gottlieb Frege's *The Foundations of Arithmetic*.[31] 'Open texture' pops up, but there is no reference to Waismann.

Hart's essay on legal and moral obligation appeared not long before a draft of *The Concept of Law* must have existed, and it too is disappointingly uninformative. The only earlier writer whose work is discussed in any detail is again Kelsen.[32] In the 1957 exchange with Fuller in which he sets out some of the ideas developed in *The Concept of Law* the citations make it clear that his principal philosophical mentor was Bentham, in particular the *A Fragment on Government* and *Principles of Morals and Legislation*, though numerous other of his writings are cited too from the Bowring edition of 1859. There are other citations to other writers, many of them lawyers, but they add little to understanding Hart's philosophical influences.[33]

Wittgenstein and Language Games

What more can be said about the influence of leading philosophers of the period? Let us begin with Wittgenstein. Hart once told me that he had been present at Wittgenstein's visit to Oxford, which is what one would expect. He was no uncritical admirer, and on a number of occasions expressed his strong disapproval of the rudeness and wanton obscurity of expression, as it seemed to Hart, which Wittgenstein affected in his role as guru.[34] He never contributed to the corpus of Wittgensteinian secondary literature. His contacts with Wittgenstein's ideas came in part through his friend

29. 958.
30. 957–8.
31. 961. JL Austin published a translation of this book in 1953.
32. 88, 91 Goodhart (89) and Hagerstrom (86) are mentioned for their mistakes; RM Hare (102) receives praise but mild criticism for his 'illuminating' book, *The Language of Morals*.
33. They are to Amos (*The Science of Law* 1881), Markby, Holland, Holmes, Gray, Kelsen, Pound, and Stone. There is also reference to Hagerstrom.
34. cf Lacey at 357 noting Hart's negative view of Wittgenstein as a person, expressed in 1988 to Bob Summers.

George Paul,[35] who had been Wittgenstein's student, and his colleague Friedrich Waismann, and in part through typescript copies of *The Blue* and *Brown Books*.[36] Conceivably Hart derived knowledge of Wittgenstein's ideas from other philosophers who had attended his seminars, in particular Elizabeth Anscombe and Peter Geach, but I know of no evidence of this. Geach had a post in Birmingham but lived in Oxford; he had married Anscombe in 1941. They used their staircase in a house in St John's Street, Oxford as a filing system and they ate their way round a table, only washing up when spaces lacking dirty dishes ran out. One of my Lincoln pupils had an alarming experience at a social event at the Catholic Chaplaincy attended by Anscombe. Standing next to her he became edgy and found he was holding a thread of wool in his hand, which he tugged, until he realized it was attached to her knitted skirt. He was indeed unravelling Anscombe, and fled in terror.

In 1953 the posthumous publication of *Philosophical Investigations* provided scholars such as Hart, who had never attended the great man's Cambridge seminars, an entrée to his later philosophy.[37] His belief in the importance of this book and his fascination with it is on record from the interview. It is a reasonable hypothesis that some of the philosophical insights and ideas which Hart brought to his analysis of the concept of law might have been derived from or influenced by Wittgenstein. In the notes to *The Concept of Law* Wittgenstein's *Philosophical Investigations* is indeed cited twice,[38] though the text does not contain any discussion.

Philosophical Investigations is a strange book, but one charitable way to understand the style adopted is to view it as an account of Wittgenstein holding a conversation with himself. I have met this phenomenon elsewhere in the academy. The last time I attended a seminar at the Chicago Law School I was surprised to find the local academics in the school quietly listening to a paper delivered by a visitor. What, I wondered, had become of

35. Paul, much to Hart's distress, died in a boating accident in 1962. He published little, but contributed a piece on 'G. E. Moore: Analysis, Common Usage and Common Sense' to AJ Ayer, *The Revolution in Philosophy*, and contributed to Flew's *Logic and Language* (First Series). He lectured in 1956 on 'The So Called Revolution in Philosophy'. See also Hart's *Punishment and Responsibility* at 238 for Paul on Locke.

36. This would be long before their publication in 1958. cf the Hart interview only mentioning the *Blue Book*.

37. Wittgenstein's *Tractatus Logico–Philosophicus*, which had been published in German in 1921, and in an English translation by CK Ogden in 1922, is not here relevant, though Hart would of course have been familiar with it.

38. CL 280, 297.

the school? For back in my time there a speaker was lucky to be listened to for more than five minutes; one indeed simply got up and left, and nobody noticed. But after a few more minutes a loud voice could be heard as my one time pupil Richard Epstein entered the room, loudly discussing the paper, not with his colleagues, but with himself, and making some good points as he did so. Earlier when I was at Chicago I was able to establish a new measure of frigidity, the RE Windchill Index—the level of wind chill which would silence my colleague when in full cry, once experienced crossing the Chicago Midway en route to lunch in the Faculty Club.

In the conversations in which we are interested, Wittgenstein gives the impression that he is fascinated by the concept of a game; indeed the passages which are most obviously relevant for our purposes all concern games.[39] This is a little strange, since the idea of Wittgenstein playing cricket or darts is quite incongruous, but I have on credible hearsay an account of a game he did indeed play in Cambridge. In Trinity College there was an eccentric don known as 'Snipper Simpson'. It was his habit to walk around colleges armed with a pair of secateurs, with which he would snip plants, telephone cables, or whatever. Often he would pass Wittgenstein in the Great Court, and instead of speaking to him he would whistle a phrase of Bach, and when he fell silent, returned to snipping. Wittgenstein would complete the phrase. This can I think be viewed as some kind of game.[40]

One Wittgensteinian use of the concept of a game, which has generated a huge literature, involves the concept of what he called by the silly name 'language game'.[41] This expression would in everyday English be applied to such games as Scrabble, or Chinese Whispers, but Wittgenstein's notion of a language game was not so confined. His own explanation is, typically, elusive, and readers who wish to go into the philosophical complexities must look elsewhere. But the basic idea of a language game is neither mysterious, nor for that matter some original discovery of Wittgenstein's. I shall try to explain it in a simple way by giving some examples.

39. For some reason or other philosophers seem wholly uninterested in bull fighting, on which there is a substantial theoretical literature, or in very dangerous sports such as mountaineering. Are these games?

40. I think there is another example in N Malcolm, *Ludwig Wittgenstein: A Memoir* (1984) when Wittgenstein and his companions imitated the movements of the planets whilst walking in Cambridge, but I have mislaid my copy.

41. In *Philosophical Investigations* the idea first surfaces in 1–7 and is developed in 7–53 and elsewhere.

Had you been in Eastbourne in 1944 you might have seen Regimental Sergeant Major Copp of the Coldstream Guards, standing on the sea front and clutching his pace-stick, bellowing 'Muark Toime' whilst facing a group of officer cadets who were, in neat ranks, standing up to their thighs in the sea. And you would have seen the officer cadets dutifully marking time. Some sort of action of communication was underway, but what on earth was going on? Mr Copp perhaps was for some reason displeased with the standard of drill exhibited by the cadets and was *punishing* them. Or he just thought it good for them to be subjected to a bit of ill treatment, *teaching* them that if they, as officers, ill-used their soldiers the soldiers would deeply resent this. Or he was *conditioning* them to obey orders, however stupid the order seemed to be. Only by understanding the context in which he bellowed 'Muark Toime' can sense be made of the act of communication and the response to it. And once the language game that was being played is understood it will in a sense control the range of critical ideas which can be sensibly applied to Mr Copp's actions—was he for example, entitled to punish the cadets in this way? It would make no sense to ask whether Mr Copp's bellowing 'Muark Toime' was a good way of encouraging the cadets to reflect on their mortality.

Each language game has what is sometimes called its own 'logic', or 'informal logic', which means that what makes sense for one game will be different from what makes sense for another—whatever sense 'makes sense' makes. And each language game derives its identity from the rules, conventions, call them what you like, which underlie the actions of communication involved, and the context in the loose sense I have explained earlier.

Wittgenstein himself gives a list of possible language games, including 'Giving orders and obeying them', 'Making up a story and reading it', 'Singing catches', 'Guessing riddles', and 'Requesting, thanking, cursing, greeting, praying'.[42] The list is not of course meant to be exhaustive. In the case of some of these games the conventions and understandings and presuppositions which underlie them will be of a very informal nature. But some language games are quite specifically governed by formal and quite explicit rules; you can for example buy books setting out what they are. Thus when I took flying lessons in Ann Arbor I had to learn and use the language game which is played between pilots and the air traffic controllers, the function of which is to avoid accidents and collisions. Initially this is

42. *Philosophical Investigations* I 23.

quite unintelligible, but after a while you pick it up, and start saying things like 'Negative. Holding short. Traffic on short finals',[43] or 'I have the figures',[44] or 'Looking',[45] or 'Turns for spacing',[46] or if you are in serious trouble 'Mayday'. And you soon come to understand what the air traffic controllers, who always speak too fast, are saying. Within the world of air traffic control it all makes sense, and works.

There is no explicit reference in *The Concept of Law*, or indeed elsewhere in Hart's writings, to Wittgenstein's conception of a language game.[47] This is I think surprising, since it seems obvious that in the world of the law, language games abound. Indeed, though nobody seems to have made the point, no better example of a language game could be thought of than the one which counsel and the judges play in appellate cases. Possibly Hart was unimpressed by Wittgenstein's use of the idea, or perhaps he may have thought it unwise to introduce any discussion of its applicability to jurisprudential questions in what was intended to be a book primarily directed at those who had no background in philosophy. However, a case can be made for the view that it may have influenced his analysis. Hart argued that a legal system comprised a body of rules identifiable as valid by what he called a rule of recognition, whose existence could be shown by the fact that it was used by officials to identify the subordinate rules. In his 1966 interview he coined an expression, 'the master concept of a rule', which captures the centrality of the idea of a rule in his legal theory. He was asked:

> What were your major aims in writing *The Concept of Law*, in addition to attacking sloppy views on the relationships between law and morality?

His response was:

> The truth as I saw it about the relationship between what law was and how the master concept of a rule—which I had studied so closely under J. L. Austin—could be used to throw light on it.

We simply do not know to what extent Austin was influenced by Wittgenstein's idea of language games, and he too never uses the expression. Austin

43. Although you have cleared me for take off I am not going to taxi onto the runway because there is an aircraft just about to land on it whose presence you have (idiotically) missed.
44. I already have the wind speed and direction, and the barometric pressure.
45. I have not yet spotted the aircraft cleared to land before me.
46. I am too close to the aircraft in front and am going to do some turns to increase the separation distance.
47. There is a fleeting reference in the 1988 interview at 274, making the point that Austin's notions on the variety of the uses of language were different from those of Wittgenstein.

may indeed for reasons of vanity have been at pains to conceal any derivation of his ideas on language from Wittgenstein. In his *Philosophical Papers* and *How to Do Things With Words* Wittgenstein is never once mentioned.[48]

In Hart's analysis much emphasis is placed on a distinction between the attitude or point of view of an external observer who does not in any sense accept the rules of the system, which he calls the external point of view, and the attitude or point of view of someone who does in some sense accept the system. This he calls the internal point of view:

> The use of unstated rules of recognition, by courts and others, in identifying particular rules of the system is characteristic of the internal point of view. Those who use them in this way thereby manifest their own acceptance of them as guiding rules and with this attitude there goes a characteristic vocabulary different from the natural expressions of the external point of view.[49]

Is the 'characteristic vocabulary' another name for a language game? It is conceivable. In the notes to *The Concept of Law* Hart cites *Philosophical Investigations*,[50] and states that Wittgenstein makes 'many important observations concerning the notions of teaching and following rules'.[51] One suspects that these may well have been discussed in Austin's group, but Hart does not tell us what they were.

Wittgenstein and Family Resemblances

Wittgenstein also used games in connection with the supposed problem of universals—how do we call different things by the same name? He argued that it was a mistake to suppose that all games must share some common feature:

> Don't say: 'There *must* be something common, or they would not be called "games"—but *look and see* whether there is anything common to all'.

This typically uses his technique of advancing philosophy by exhortation. He goes on to suggest that the explanation for the use of the same word is the existence of a 'family resemblance' between them. Wittgenstein makes little effort to explain clearly what he means by a 'family resemblance'

48. There is a reference in *Sense and Sensibilia*. 49. CL 102.
50. I paras 208–238. 51. CL 297, note to CL 125.

though it is clear that he has in mind personal characteristics, for example hair colour, not kinship relationships. Metaphor enables him to avoid explaining himself clearly. Nor is there any evidence that Wittgenstein took the time to look, for example, at the *Oxford Dictionaries* to see if the relationship between the various senses of words which are there distinguished are indeed linked by 'family resemblances'. In general they are not. It seems clear that the idea that games (all games?) resemble each other in the same sort of way as family members who have, for example, similar coloured hair, and big ears, is neither self-explanatory nor plausible. It is ridiculous. In *The Concept of Law* Hart explicitly refers to the relevant passages in *Philosophical Investigations*.[52] He does not himself use the expression 'family resemblance', but makes what is essentially the same point, adding that sometimes the various instances where a term may be used may be 'different constituents of some complex activity'. He also suggests that perhaps here we have 'a principle similar to that which unifies the different types of rule which make up a legal system'.[53]

In his earlier 1957 riposte to Bodenheimer, Hart makes the point that the various instances of the use of the same word may not share a common feature, but the citation is to Aristotle, not Wittgenstein.[54] And since the point being made is perfectly obvious to anyone who has, for example, devoted five minutes to looking at an *Oxford Dictionary*, and was made a fair time ago by Aristotle, it is not very obvious that Wittgenstein's discussion was of much significance for *The Concept of Law*. Indeed it is much more likely that Hart was here influenced by Austin's 1940 paper, 'The Meaning of a Word', parts of which are echoed in *The Concept of Law*.[55]

Wittgenstein's Constitutive Rules and Parley Castle

It is a familiar fact that games have rules. All games? Well perhaps, with the possible exception of a Free For All, which used to go on in the Officer's Mess in my time, though in reality there were no doubt limits—no use of

52. CL 280 I, paras 66–76.
53. CL 15–16. This passage I am fairly sure echoes a passage in the lectures of Isaiah Berlin on feet which my friend Dyson Heydon used to parody.
54. *Nichomachean Ethics* 1.6.
55. *Philosophical Papers* 3rd edn 55 esp at 71ff.

hand grenades for example—though this was not something one had in mind in joining the game.[56]

Back in my childhood in a Yorkshire vicarage, life could be pretty boring, and my elder brother and I developed a curious game, associated with the world of chivalry, known as Parley Castle, which served to while away the time. One of us would retire behind the wood pile and sit on a log, donning an old dustbin which had lost its base, and which functioned as a suit of armour. One's head would be protected by an ancient rusty bucket. The other would retire to an agreed distance, and then hurl lumps of clay; the score was the number of hits on the dustbin or helmet. Rocks were not to be thrown. The inadequacy of the protection meant that minor injuries could still be caused, and when the passive participant could stand it no longer he called out 'Parley', and the game either came to an end, or the participants exchanged roles. I do not recall that there was any great significance attached to winning; playing Parley Castle was an end in itself. There are various intellectual questions which can be raised about the game of Parley Castle—for example how did it come into existence in the first place as a game, in contrast simply to random sibling violence? There is a chicken and egg problem; do you need to have a game first before you can regulate it? Or do you have to have rules first before you can have a game?[57] Plainly what was essential to the transition from random violence was the establishment of at least some of the rules of Parley Castle. Is that right? What is to happen if a tennis ball is used instead of a lump of clay? Does that score? If so have we a new rule, or did the old rule permit other missiles so long as they were no more dangerous than lumps of clay? Is this supposed to be the purpose of the rule? Is there some correct way of formulating a text of what the rules are? These are tricky questions, but without some conventional rules the game of Parley Castle could not exist. Other strange games of my childhood included competitions to make each other become unconscious for the longest period, achieved by over breathing, and compression of the diaphragm, and waking sleeping children by lighting newspaper under their beds, with betting on whether the unfortunate victim would, on waking, run as far as the fire escape door before realizing that it was all a game. It was not at all clear what game rules, as distinct from ordinary moral

56. cf Wittgenstein, *Philosophical Investigations*, footnote on 28.

57. This issue is briefly discussed in P Winch, *The Idea of a Social Science and its Relation to Philosophy* at 34–5 but in relation to the establishment of a language.

rules (must not actually set the child on fire), governed these practices. Part of the Public School culture, they hardened us up in preparation for running the Empire or leading our men into battle.

The claim that you cannot have games without rules is sometimes made by saying that the rules are *constitutive* of the game, though neither Wittgenstein (nor for that matter Hart) use this expression.[58] The expression is unfortunate, since it can be taken to convey the idea that the whole activity involved in a particular game is a product of the rules of the game, which is not the case. For there are numerous problems over the conception of constitutive rules—if for example you only look at the official and formalized rules of some well established game such as cricket, or soccer, you would obtain a miserably inadequate understanding of these games, and of their place in contemporary society. Commonly the rules of games give no indication of what the point of the game is supposed to be, which will usually but not always involve trying to win, but may be much more complicated than that, as the Olympic Games reminds us. Again it is perfectly possible to play a game whilst having virtually no knowledge of what the rules of the game are, and in the case of games which have some kind of textual set of official rules, copies of which one can purchase, many players will never have seen a copy, and their understanding of the rules will be picked up in the course of playing the game. You can play a lot of philosophical games with games.

In *Philosophical Investigations*, and earlier in the *Blue* and *Brown Books*, Wittgenstein engages in elusive discussion of the relationship between games and rules, and between playing games, and following or observing rules. One game much used by way of illustration is chess. I suppose chess is chosen because of the idea that everything that counts as chess is rule defined (which is not I think the case) and because any action which might affect the result of a match is comprehensively covered by the rules (thought this too is not correct). Examples of Wittgenstein's throw away remarks are:

> But isn't chess defined by its rules?[59]
>
> There is no doubt that I want to play chess, but chess is the game it is by virtue of all its rules (and so on).[60]

58. It is however used by the editors in the index to *Philosophical Papers*.

59. I 205. 60. I 197.

> But after all, the game is supposed to be defined by its rules! So if a rule of the game prescribes that the kings are to be used for drawing lots before a game of chess, then that is an essential part of the game.[61]

One purpose in all this was to use the rule governed character of the game of chess, or of other games, as a model for understanding the rule governed nature of language, a point most clearly made in *The Brown Book:*

> Words can in many ways be compared to chess men.[62]

It seems that this was indeed the principal purpose. The comparison, not spelled out of course, is to my mind pretty limited.

In the notes to *The Concept of Law* Hart, as we have seen, says that:

> Wittgenstein . . . makes many important observations concerning the notions of teaching and following rules.[63]

This is a note to a passage in which Hart discusses the teaching of standards of conduct by example, which he treats as a model for understanding the use of precedent in establishing what the law is. But as I have said, Hart does not here spell out what if any insights have been derived from Wittgenstein.[64]

Elsewhere Hart makes extensive use of analogies between the legal world and the world of games,[65] and chess features in a number of them;[66] though there are no explicit references to Wittgenstein.

Peter Winch's Prolegomenon to a Philosophy of the Social Sciences

Winch's elusive and difficult book, *The Idea of a Social Science and its Relation to Philosophy*[67] was published when the draft of *The Concept of Law* was probably in a moderately advanced state; his surviving working notebook

61. I 567. 62. *The Blue and the Brown Books* at 83 v–4.
63. CL 297, *Philosophical Investigations* I 208–38 and reference to the discussion in P Winch, *The Idea of a Social Science* 24–33 and 91–3.
64. CL 124 and ff.
65. See in particular 9, 34 (the rules of games are of two types), 59, 63 (rules explain continuity in games), 102 (similarity between scoring rule of games and rule of recognition), 56–7, 102 (internal aspect of rules), 140 (notion of compliance with rules), 142–3 (analogy between adjudication and umpiring in games).
66. eg 31, 140.
67. 1958. In the 1990 edition Winch modified some of his views; for present purposes these modifications are not relevant.

shows he was reading it in 1959. Hart explicitly refers to its discussion of the internal aspect of rules, and the distinction between rules and habits,[68] and to its discussion of Wittgenstein's observations on the teaching and following of rules.[69] So we know he read it. Winch was never a student of Wittgenstein, but he was influenced by him through his teacher Russ Rhees.[70] It would be surprising if the book was not discussed in Austin's group, but there is no direct evidence of this.[71]

We have seen how Oakeshott published a prolegomenon to the philosophization of jurisprudence, though one which does not appear to have had any influence on Hart, or indeed on anyone else. Winch's book is a work of the same character; indeed it is the only other such work which has, so far as I know, ever seen the light of day. It is true that Winch was concerned to develop a role for philosophy in relation to social science, or social studies, not jurisprudence, but in a broad sense Hart's *The Concept of Law* can be seen either as an essay in social science, or as an attempt to provide a philosophical analysis of the conceptual tools of social science. Winch's argument was directed at what he called the 'peripheral' philosophical disciplines; the examples he gave were 'the philosophies of science, art, politics etc'.[72] So it is reasonable to take the view that he would have applied his ideas to jurisprudence if he had some reason for doing so, but he had no interest in law. He did not elaborate his views in relation to political science either.

Central to Winch's theory was firstly a view as to the proper methodology of the social sciences, and secondly a view as to the role of philosophy. I shall briefly attempt to explain what these views were.

As to the first, one view, associated particularly with Emile Durkheim,[73] was that it was the task of the social sciences to explain and understand social life without taking into account the views, beliefs and attitudes of the human actors involved. Their ideas were as irrelevant as the views of

68. CL 289 note to CL 55, citations to Winch at 57–65 and 84–94.
69. CL 297, with citation to 24–33 and 91–3. See Lacey 230 The context is a discussion of whether Hart's ideas were derivative of Max Weber, and whether Hart was evasive about this, an issue I discuss below.
70. Wittgenstein's friend and literary executor; he taught at Swansea.
71. There is no mention of Winch in JL Austin's collected papers.
72. 8.
73. There is a citation to Durkheim's review of A Labiola, *Essais sur la conception materialiste de l'histoire* in *Revue Philosophique* December 1897.

Galapagos finches on evolution.[74] Winch however insisted that understanding social life and interaction was only possible if the opposing view was adopted. He gives the example of monks, whose social relations, both within and outside the monastery, will be conditioned by religious beliefs.[75] Hence if we are to understand them we have to take on board their perceptions.[76] In another passage he wrote:

> A historian of art must have some aesthetic sense if he is to understand the problems confronting the artists of his period; and without this he will have left out of his account precisely what would have made it a history of art, as opposed to a rather puzzling external account of certain motions which certain people have been perceived to go through.[77]

As to the second point, Winch rejected two contrasting views as to the role of philosophy. One he called the 'underlabourer conception of philosophy'.[78] According to this it was the role of philosophy merely to clear away linguistic confusions, the source of supposed philosophical problems. Once the job was done there would be no philosophical problems left to worry about. Ideas of this kind certainly were as we have seen current in Oxford circles in the post war period, and are reflected, for example, in Ryle's *The Concept of Mind*. They were also associated with Wittgenstein. The celebrated incident of the poker arose, according to one version, because Karl Popper had come to Cambridge to argue that there were *real* philosophical *problems*, in opposition to Wittgenstein's view that there were only *puzzles*, which appropriate analysis would consign to the trash heap.[79] Winch did not think that the underlabourer task of philosophy was valueless—it was good to clear away rubbish. His point was that it was not the only task. One long standing concern of philosophy has been with what are called epistemological issues—put simply issues as to how we can have knowledge, especially knowledge of the external world. How can we be sure that the light in the fridge really goes out when we shut the door? Well if it really matters get an electrician to check, but that will not generate a philosophical puzzle.

74. 22.
75. I suppose that if one wanted to do a Wittgenstein, one might say that the monks were engaged in a 'religious life game'.
76. 22.
77. 83.
78. See 3 and ff.
79. For Popper's account see his *Unended Quest: An Intellectual Biography* (1992) at 140–144.

The other conception of philosophy he called 'the master scientist' conception of philosophy, according to which philosophy was in direct competition with the natural sciences in relation to epistemological issues, whose conclusions as to the nature of reality, and the existence of the external world, could be refuted by *a priori* reasoning.[80] Nobody in Winch's time believed this, but, he argued, it had been wrongly concluded from its demise that there did not remain a more modest job for philosophers to undertake, and one which did address epistemological issues.[81] Only if either epistemological or metaphysical issues were addressed was a theory philosophical.[82]

Winch used a variety of expressions in an attempt to explain what this more modest job was. At the risk of oversimplifying, his basic idea was that it was the task of philosophy to 'elucidate'—here we have elucidation again—or 'make intelligible', or 'understand' both the conceptions and language we employ in studying social life, and the relationships between actors in that world. For Winch:

> . . . the social relations between men and the ideas that men's actions embody are really the same thing considered from different points of view.[83] So far as the 'peripheral' branches of philosophy are concerned, such as the philosophy of politics, 'elucidation', 'making intelligible' and 'understanding' will here be concerned with 'the peculiar forms that "understanding" [or whatever] takes in particular kinds of context'.[84]

All this could of course be applied to the philosophy of law. But Winch does not himself address legal matters except in one brief and rather confused passage dealing with the operation of the doctrine of precedent, where he argues that following precedents involves following rules, without showing any awareness of the problematic nature of this claim.[85]

Winch then goes on to argue for the central importance of the conception of following a rule (to be contrasted with simply following or conforming to a habit[86]) in the understanding of social behaviour. The starting point is Wittgenstein's discussion of language games, but Winch's emphasis is not so much on the significance of following rules for the understanding

80. 7. 81. See in particular at 10 and ff and 17–23.
82. For present purposes we can mercifully forget about metaphysics.
83. 113 and ff.
84. 39.
85. 57–58 with sloppy citations to R Pound, *Introduction to the Philosophy of Law*, M Oakeshott, *Rationalism in Politics* (1962), and E Levi, *An Introduction to Legal Reasoning* (1949).
86. 54 and ff.

of speech and language, but rather for the understanding of social behaviour and interaction.[87] Thus, for example, he argues that following rules is central to the notion of meaningful behaviour,[88] to the establishment of the identity or sameness of particular forms of social activity,[89] and to the conception of forms of social activity which commit the actor to particular conduct in the future, the obvious example being promising.[90] I do not propose to attempt to summarize his arguments, which are not always easy to follow.

Hart's citation does not explicitly refer to passages in Winch's book where he makes the point that people's social relations with other people are conditioned by their beliefs, values, and perceptions of reality. This general idea is, however, reflected at various points in *The Concept of Law*—for example in the development of the notion of the internal point of view,[91] and in the argument that rules of law conferring powers should be looked at 'from the point of view of those who exercise them'.[92]

Again Winch argued that to understand the concept of following a rule you have to take into account:

> ... not only of the actions of the person whose behaviour is in question as a candidate for the category or rule following, but also the reactions of other people to what he does. More specifically, it is only in situations in which it makes sense to suppose that somebody else could in principle discover the rule which I am following that I can intelligibly be said to follow a rule at all.[93]

Nowhere in *The Concept of Law* does Hart make precisely the same point, but his account of the internal point of view seems to me to echo Winch's ideas.[94] I think a case could be made for saying that Hart's thinking was much influenced by Winch, and that his claim that *The Concept of Law* could be understood as 'an essay in descriptive sociology' may owe something to him. And Hart himself frankly acknowledged Winch's influence.

Derivations from Max Weber?

It has been suggested both that Hart's conception of the internal aspect of rules was derivative of passages in *Max Weber on Law in Economy and Society*, and that Hart was in some way evasive about this.[95] The source of these

87. 42–3. 88. 48ff. 89. 29, 34. 90. 47. 91. CL 56.
92. CL 41. 93. 28. 94. eg CL 90, 103. 95. Lacey 230–231.

claims is John Finnis, who consulted Hart's own, heavily annotated, copy of Weber's book, which had been given to the Hebrew University, and took the view that these annotations provided clear evidence of the influence of Weber. When however he asked Hart about this, Hart

> ...denied that any such influence existed, ascribing the origins of the idea instead to Peter Winch's *The Idea of a Social Science*. Finnis felt unable to respond to this denial by saying that he had seen the counter-evidence in his own copy.[96]

En passant it is perhaps worth noting that Winch's book does contain a discussion of some of Weber's ideas, but not of ideas relevant in any way to the internal aspect of rules; one passage is however relevant to what Hart would call the external point of view.[97] Finch's discussion is not based on *Max Weber on Law in Economy and Society*, but on a work published back in 1922.[98]

Quite why Hart, who was willing to acknowledge Winch's influence, would want to deny Weber's influence, is left unexplained. One explanation could be that it is commonplace in academia for scholars to become forgetful or confused over the pedigree of ideas which they espouse. One of the crosses I have had to bear on numerous occasions in my academic career has been to sit in judgement of students accused of plagiarism, or on committees charged with defining what it is. It always comes to sound much like scholarship, more especially because few academics or students ever produce wholly original ideas, and if they do these ideas are almost always rubbish.

Hart was fluent in German and could well have read Weber in the original, but I do not know of any evidence that he did so. *Max Weber on Law in Economy and Society* was published by the Harvard University Press in 1954 as Volume VI in the 20th Century Legal Philosophy Series. This was sponsored by the Association of American Law Schools, but this particular volume was a by-product of the University of Chicago's Committee on Social Thought, an interdisciplinary organization set up there in the 1940s under President Robert Maynard Hutchins to supervise doctoral work on the fundamentals of social thought, whatever they were thought to be. It comprised a translation of parts of Part I of the second 1925 edition of

96. Lacey 230. 97. Finch 104–112.
98. *Gesammele Aufsätze zur Wissenschaftslehre* cited Winch 130.

Weber's *Wirtschaft und Gesellschaft*, the translation being principally the work of Edward Shils,[99] together with an introduction by that great scholar Max Rheinstein,[100] along with his elaborate annotations. There already existed in English a translation of the entire Part I of Weber's book, which had been published back in 1947, but this translation differed from that published in 1954.[101]

We do not know when Hart acquired his copy—I myself acquired one in Blackwell's in 1958 not through putting in an order, but simply because a copy appeared on the shelves; I cannot recall when I actually read it. Possibly Hart picked up a copy when he visited Harvard in 1956–7. We just do not know when he carefully read and annotated his copy. Correspondence with John Finnis makes it clear that he now takes the view that the chronology is critical and uncertain, and tells me that Neil MacCormick, long after *The Concept of Law* was written, told him that he was reading Weber for the first time.

I also think however that there is another good reason for thinking that he did this after *The Concept of Law* was written. It seems to me to be inconceivable that Hart, if he had carefully studied Weber before completing *The Concept of Law*, could have described his book in the form in which it was published as 'an essay in descriptive sociology'. To make good this claim once he had read Weber, Hart would have realized that his text required radical revision, and there would surely have been a need to give references to Weber in the notes, if nowhere else. This is a general point, and its plausibility has to depend on a broad view of the matter. To be more specific there are numerous passages in Weber which would, on any reading, have raised in Hart's mind serious doubts about the methodology of *The Concept of Law*. I shall mention just one, to which I shall return later. Hart's book purports to analyse *the* concept of law, without ever considering the possibility that there might exist different concepts of law, associated perhaps with different legal traditions; different legal traditions simply play no part whatever in *The Concept of Law*. His analysis is related to the claim that '. . . in almost every part of the world which is thought of as a separate

99. Professor of Sociology at Chicago.

100. Professor of Comparative Law at the Chicago Law School.

101. Translated by Alexander M Henderson and Talcott Parsons, and published as *Max Weber: The Theory of Social and Economic Organization*. I have not seen a copy of this. Talcott Parsons was the well known Harvard sociologist, who also published a translation of Weber's *The Protestant Ethic and the Spirit of Capitalism* (1905) in 1930. I have no idea who Henderson was.

"country" there are legal systems which are broadly similar in structure in spite of important differences'.[102] He used the expression 'the standard case' to capture this idea.[103] It seems to me impossible that anyone could take this line, after reading Weber's Chapter VIII, 'Formal and Substantive Rationalization in the Law',[104] without appreciating that there were serious difficulties with it. At the least they would need to have been addressed. But there is no hint of this in *The Concept of Law*. My conclusion therefore is that Hart worked on his copy of Weber after *The Concept of Law* was completed. We know he never revised the text, and his fragmentary *Postscript*, which was intended as a response to his critics, has of course nothing to say on Weber who, having died in 1920, had never had a chance to join that particular club. Nicola Lacey's biography does contain a passage which suggests the possibility that it was Jean Floud who encouraged Hart to read the classic sociologists, Max Weber, Emile Durkheim, and Talcott Parsons. Quite when is unclear, but certainly after the publication of *The Concept of Law*. In the 1988 interview Hart did not mention Weber but conceded that he found sociological books difficult to read and was suspicious of their empirical basis; he also conceded that he was 'terribly distrustful of sociology in general. That's an Oxford disease'.

Hans Kelsen

If you are impressed by labels Hans Kelsen would normally be classified as a jurist rather than a philosopher, notwithstanding his extensive writings on legal philosophy. He was a professor of public and administrative law in Vienna from 1919, and drafted the Austrian Constitution of 1919, which came into force in 1920; he was in consequence appointed for life to the Austrian Constitutional Court, but was removed for political reasons in 1930. My Oxford colleague, the composer and musicologist Egon Wellesz, Arnold Schoenberg's pupil, once told me that he had lived next door to Kelsen, adding enigmatically, as was his custom:

> They did not like Kelsen. He abolished the state.

102. CL 3.
103. CL 4. At 3 he lists the salient features of the standard case.
104. 224–255.

The reference may be to Kelsen's invention of constitutional review, which reins in the power of the state, or to Kelsen's identification of the state with the personification of the structure of norms which constitute the legal order. I was unable to get this clear. So far as I am aware Kelsen had no association whatsoever with the Vienna circle of philosophers.

There is no doubt that Hart was fascinated by Kelsen and there are, as we have seen, many references to his work in his writings; he also gave lectures and classes in Oxford on Kelsen. Thus in Hilary Term 1953 he gave a seminar on 'The Nature of the Basic Norm'. He maintained his interest in Kelsen after the publication of *The Concept of Law;* thus in Trinity 1961, and again in 1963, he lectured on 'Problems in Kelsen's General Theory'. No text of these has survived.[105] The version of Kelsen's legal theory which seems to have been used by Hart was Kelsen's *General Theory of Law and the State,* which was the first volume published in the 20th century Legal Philosophy Series in 1945.[106] Hart's account of the structure of a legal system as a body of rules identified by a rule of recognition has obvious similarities with Kelsen's model of a system of law as a body of norms whose validity (meaning existence as norms of the system) is derived from a *grundnorm*, and it is obvious that Hart's account owed something to Kelsen.[107] This is no doubt why Hart was anxious to make it very clear that his theory differed from Kelsen's in important ways.[108] Kelsen's underlying philosophical ideas were in fact radically different from those espoused by Hart, and Lacey gives an extremely lucid account of the difference, which there is no need for me to repeat.[109] In 1961 Hart and Kelsen engaged in face to face debate in Berkeley, in the course of which Hart fell off his chair and Kelsen shouted 'Norms, norms'.[110] Out of this came two publications.[111] But though the encounter seems to have led Hart to have some doubts about the position he had adopted in *The Concept of Law* it came too late to affect the text.

105. Lacey 168, 260.
106. This is the only work of Kelsen's cited in CL apart from 'Sanctions in International Law Under the Charter of the U.N.' (1946) 31 *Iowa LR* and his *Principles of International Law.*
107. Lacey takes this view; see 250.
108. See in particular 2 (and note at 277), 35–42, 292–5, 294–5, 302.
109. 250.
110. Lacey 249–53.
111. 'Kelsen Visited' UCLALR (1962) 10:709 and 'Kelsen's Doctrine of the Unity of Law' in Munitz and Kiefer (eds), *Ethics and Social Justice: Contemporary Political Thought* (1968) vol 4: 171.

Salmond on Primary and Secondary Rules

In *The Concept of Law* Hart refers in a note to what he calls Salmond's 'insufficiently elaborated conception of "ultimate legal principles"'.[112] Sir John Salmond, a New Zealander, was the author of two treatises on jurisprudence, *The First Principles of Jurisprudence* (1893), and *Jurisprudence or the Theory of Law* (1902). He conceived of the law as comprising:

> ... a principle or rule recognized and acted upon by the State in the administration of justice. The aggregate of such principles or rules constitute the law.[113]

He came up with an idea that some legal rules were *about* other legal rules. In *Principles* Salmond called these rules secondary rules, as opposed to primary rules.[114] He argued that such secondary rules related either to the existence of a primary rule, its application, or its interpretation.[115] So far as secondary rules of the first kind are concerned he thought that some such rules were ultimate in the sense that they do not depend upon any further rule or principle. He gave as examples the proposition that all principles contained in an Act of Parliament are the law, or the rule that local custom has the force of law, or that precedents are a source of law.[116] Salmond combined this with the notion that legal rules normally had legal sources, such sources being the reason why a particular rule counted as a legal rule. We, influenced by Kelsen and Hart, would say a reason for *validity*, but this term was not used by him. Salmond explained:

> In other words, though the majority of legal rules may be traced to a source, there must be some self-existent rule or rules without legally recognised source, cause or origin, being, so far as legal theory goes, self caused and self-existent; otherwise any investigation of the sources of law would lead to infinity.[117]

In *Jurisprudence* the passage distinguishing primary and secondary rules is not reproduced. Instead the rules described as secondary in *Principles* now feature in a chapter on 'The Divisions of the Law' in which Salmond offers a general scheme for the arrangement of the law, presumably one which could be used

112. CL 292 with a reference to the 11th edition of Salmond *On Jurisprudence*.
113. *Principles* 76–7. 114. *Principles* 219–220. 115. *Principles* 220.
116. *Principles* 222–3. 117. *Principles* 222.

in drafting a code. These ultimate rules are classified as belonging to 'The Introductory Portion of the Law'. They are said to comprise:

> ... all those rules which by virtue of their preliminary character or of the generality of their application cannot be appropriately relegated to any special department.[118]

The text makes it clear that these are the secondary rules of *Principles*, though the term is not used here.[119] But a rewritten passage on fundamental legal principles is included, with the additional argument that legal systems may have one, or more than one, such principle.[120]

Salmond's idea was to some degree elaborated in an Appendix, which discussed *The Theory of Sovereignty* and argued that there was no logical reason why a constitution:

> ... the existence and observance of a definite scheme or organised structure and operation,

called a:

> *datum* and presupposition ...[121]

might make no provision for a sovereign legislature.

One needs to recognize Salmond's originality; his achievement resembled that of a mountaineer who, like Whymper in the case of the Matterhorn, makes the first ascent. For centuries the feat is viewed as impossible. Once the mountain is climbed it all seems obvious that it was always climbable, and mountaineers set about elaborating the possible and most challenging and dangerous routes, the times of year at which the climb is conceivably possible, if lunatic, and so forth. We need to respect the brilliance of the climber who was first, even if, as in the case of Whymper, four of his companions were to die on the descent. One might imagine that jurisprudence, unlike mountaineering, might never be perilous to life, but this is an error. Evgeny Pashukanis, the Soviet legal philosopher, was in all probability executed in 1937 for what were thought to be errors in his theoretical ideas.[122]

118. *Jurisprudence* 483. In the 2nd edition the chapter on the divisions of the law is relegated to Appendix IV.
119. With the addition of certain unspecified 'miscellaneous rules which are of so general an application as not to be appropriately dealt with in any special department of the legal system', *Jurisprudence* 109.
120. *Jurisprudence* 111. This appears unchanged in the 2nd edn.
121. *Jurisprudence* at 636.
122. See my BDCL.

Ideas Associated with the Indeterminacy of Language

In Hart the central concept was that of a rule, and rules, whether they be legal rules, such as the English contract rule that 'contracts require consideration', or social rules, such as the rule Hart instances that 'you must take off your hat if you enter a church', can be expressed in the form of texts. Plainly the rule is not identical with the text, and some element of judgement will be involved in constructing the text. For example the rule does not in some contexts apply to women, for whom head covering may be mandated. And what about Cardinals? He wrote:

> All rules involve recognizing or classifying particular cases as instances of general terms, and in the case of everything which we are prepared to call a rule it is possible to distinguish clear central cases, where it certainly applies and others where there are reasons both asserting and denying that it applies.[123]

He used in this context a number of different terms, most of them metaphorical, to convey his meaning: 'plain cases',[124] 'paradigm, clear cases',[125] 'a fringe of vagueness',[126] 'a core of certainty and a penumbra of doubt',[127] and 'open texture'.[128] In *The Concept of Law* 'open texture' is the favourite, whereas in the debate with Fuller the metaphor of 'the core and the penumbra' takes centre stage. It is central to understanding *The Concept of Law* that Hart is arguing that these metaphors capture an inescapable feature of *language*, one which explains, for example, uncertainty in the applicability of rules, and the necessary existence in adjudication of an element of discretion.[129] They are not presented as features of rules so much as features of the language in which rules are expressed. The expression 'open texture' is an English version of an expression coined by Waissman, *Porosität der Begriffe*.[130]

123. CL 123. 124. CL 126.
125. CL 129. 126. CL 123. 127. CL 123.
128. CL 123, 128, 130, 145, 147, 204 and note on 'Standard cases and borderline cases' at 278. Open texture also features in the *Postscript* at 252.
129. See eg 204.
130. It is used in Waismann's 1945 article 'Verifiability' PAS Supp. vol XIX 119. It has been suggested (see PMS Hacker, *Wittgenstein's Place in Twentieth-Century-Philosophy* at 164–5) that it was invented by W Kneale in his *The Development of Logic*, but since this was first

As for the core and the penumbra, this seems to originate with Hart. On June 19 1927 there was a total eclipse of the sun visible in the north of England, notably viewed from Giggleswick, where I think instruments were set up in the grounds of the school. This was after Hart had left Bradford Grammar School, though he could well have travelled north to see it. It is possible that this rare event was the ultimate source for Hart's use of the metaphor. The sense of the two metaphors plainly differs. With the core and the penumbra there are no holes in the middle, whereas open texture suggests holes all over the place, as in a fishing net. Some terms are thus radically open textured in the sense that there are no cases in which the applicability of the term may not lead to irresolvable dispute. An example would be 'art'; virtually anything can count as art. Other terms are vague only in the sense that there are possible applications of the term which can be disputed—this is the core penumbra idea—whilst there are cases which are quite clear and beyond dispute.[131] These views as to the nature of language seem to be closely related to another idea which turns up a great deal in Hart's legal theory, but which is not presented as a feature of language—the idea that there are central or paradigm instances of social phenomena or institutions—and that it is on these that attention should concentrate.

In 1959 Ernest Gellner[132] launched a comprehensive attack on linguistic analysis, as practised in Oxford; he was aided and abetted by Bertrand Russell. The book is something of a rant. It provoked an extremely hostile reaction; the sheer impertinence of it! Ryle refused to have the book reviewed in *Mind* on the ground that it was abusive, and there was an acrimonious correspondence in *The Times*.[133] In his book Gellner made much of the argument from the paradigm case. He claimed that:

> The Argument from the Paradigm Case is absolutely essential to Linguistic Philosophy: it pervades it and it is presupposed without qualification, denials notwithstanding.[134]

published in 1962 this cannot be right. See See also GP Baker and PMS Hacker, *Wittgenstein: Understanding and Meaning, Volume I of an Analytical Commentary on the Philosophical Investigations* PII paras 4–7 and Exegesis para 80.

131. Schauer in his *Playing by the Rules* makes the point that there are easy cases but these rarely feature in legal theory. Thus in the UK there is no death penalty for inconsiderate parking.
132. At the time Gellner was in the Social Anthropology Department of the London School of Economics, where he became a professor in 1962.
133. See 5 November 1959 to 24 November; also Lacey at 137–8, 143.
134. See 33–40. The argument was given its name in 1953 but I have not identified the relevant article.

Basically the argument, according to Gellner, amounts to the same thing as the reliance on ordinary usage to provide the definitive solution to philosophical problems. The argument took various forms, but one, which relates to the use of the argument to counter scepticism, for example as to the existence of real objects, is explained by Flew:

> Crudely if there is a word the meaning of which can be taught by reference to paradigm cases, then no argument whatever could prove that there are no cases whatever of whatever it is.[135]

So if one can teach the meaning of the word 'cat' by reference to a thing which is a paradigm case of a cat, or the meaning of the word 'ghost' by a paradigm case of a ghost, then that is the end of the matter. Cats and ghosts exist. I do not pretend to find this in any way convincing, and have not the least idea of what a paradigm case of a cat or a ghost would be like. Never met one. But whatever the merits or demerits of Gellner's criticisms of the argument from the paradigm case they have no real relevance to Hart's use of the idea, which had nothing to do with countering scepticism.[136] Hart uses the notion of the paradigm case in two distinct ways. One is methodological—the way to understand legal concepts or the concept of law or of a legal system is to concentrate attention on the paradigm case, the plain case, the central case:

> . . . in the analysis of concepts we need first to establish what may be called the paradigm or standard case of the use of an expression.[137]

The other, a version of the core and the penumbra, involves a theory of language—words have central or paradigm cases and if they did not, communication would be impossible. This argument was central to his views as presented in his exchange with Fuller. Otherwise Gellner's general claim that linguistic philosophy dealt in trivialities could not be plausibly said of Hart's writings.[138]

135. AGN Flew, 'Philosophy and Language' in *Essays in Conceptual Analysis* (1956).
136. At CL 4 Hart writes of 'the clear, standard case or paradigm for the use of an expression'. cf 81 where the expression used is 'central case' and 129 'paradigm clear cases' of vehicles banned from the park, the motor-car, the bus, 'the motor cycle'.
137. Reply to Bodenheimer at 968.
138. The index to Gellner's book has a mysterious reference to HLA Hart 68, but the reference does not work. Perhaps a passage attacking Hart was edited out at a late stage.

5

Cyclops, Hedgehogs, and Foxes

In Chapter 6 I propose to try to identify some problematic aspects of *The Concept of Law*, concentrating on those which have not been picked up in the subsequent literature. But before I do so I think it may be valuable to say something further of a general nature about the world in which the Oxford philosophers functioned back in the 1950s and 1960s, and then to give a general account of two contrasting approaches to legal scholarship.

The World of the Cyclops

As a young schoolboy I was forced to read Dickens, with the consequence that I still react to him much as if I was in Evelyn Waugh's *A Handful of Dust*. I also read Homer, where the consequence was the reverse; to this day I virtually never travel without my copy of the *Iliad* and the *Odyssey* tucked in my suitcase, though I can no longer read these works in the original Greek as once I could. What quite the *Odyssey* is all about, if it makes sense to ask, is problematic, but I have long thought one thing; it is certainly about the relationships between men and women in the heroic world. There is Calypso, who offers Odysseus eternal youth, and Nausicaa, the chaste, unmarried, and dutiful daughter, and the dominatrix Circe, who turns men into pigs, which some rather like, and Anticleia, Odysseus's mother, met in Hades, whom he tries to embrace but never again can, and Eurycleia, the nurse who had breastfed him. And of course the faithful wife Penelope, such a contrast with the trophy wife Helen, who is happily back with her husband, the forgiving type, as if the Trojan War had never happened. Herodotus indeed thought she had never been involved at all.

I propose to relate my remarks on the world of the Oxford philosophers to Homer's story of Polyphemus the Cyclops, in which, unusually, women play no part. For although the Cyclops did have wives and children, Polyphemus appears to have been a bachelor.[1] In the translation in the *Loeb Classical Library* we are told of the Cyclops that collectively they have no political institutions:

> Neither assemblies for council have they, nor appointed laws, but they dwell on the peaks of lofty mountains in hollow caves, and each one is a law giver to his children and his wives, and they reck [ie wreck] nothing one of another.

The expression 'appointed laws' translates *themistes*, which really means 'adjudications'. In relation to early Anglo-Saxon laws the expression sometimes used is 'dooms'. In Homeric thought the distinction between the promulgation of general laws, and adjudication on particular issues, is not made.[2] The depiction of the Cyclops, who are shepherds, came to life for me when I first visited Greece in the early 1960s, and walked over to old Pylos where there was, and I suppose still is, a large cave, which must have been used as shelter for many centuries by shepherds. It was many feet deep in their droppings. In those days one would also meet them high in the mountains of the Peloponnese, accompanied by ferocious guard dogs, apparently recking nothing of their neighbours. The correct technique if attacked was to lie on the ground and expose your throat in a gesture of submission; the dog, it was said, would then merely urinate on you. I never tried.

The basic point Homer is making is that outside the family (and Polyphemus has no family) the Cyclops are a lawless lot who take no notice of each other, and they lack any system of social organization which provides a forum for adjudications over disputes arising between different family groups. Theirs is what has been called by the anthropologists an acephalous society. And, given a little pushing and shoving, this description seems to me to capture some of the character of the Oxford philosophy tutors of the period in which we are interested.

We can think of their pupils as in much the same position as the wives of the Cyclops who did have families, subservient to the unprincipled *themistes* of their tutors, as were those bullied by Austin, or sometimes to the weird

1. The story is in Book IX 105–566.
2. Maine, in Chapter I of *Ancient Law* sets out an account of the *themistes*, based on G Grote's *A History of Greece; from the earliest period to the close of the generation contemporary with Alexander the Great* (1846–1856).

eccentricities which others inflicted on their pupils. They were indeed a lawless lot.

Over their pupils their power could be arbitrary, for back in those days there were no institutional arrangements for challenging them. Thus I recall an incident in which Hart's own college expelled a student a short time before he was due to sit his final examinations without giving him any hearing. I was so outraged by this that I attempted to get the victim moved to Lincoln, but this proved impossible. This was because of the Statute *De Migratione* which required the consent of both colleges.[3] Hart in a passage not published in the 1988 interview was asked his view of the merits of the tutorial system and replied:

> If it can be sustained, it is valuable, so long as the tutorials run properly and people attend twice a week, and have a good tutor, and read two essays a week . . . of course it has its dangers. *If you get locked in with a mad tutor it is hell* [emphasis added].

There were certainly some mad tutors about, and nothing much could be done about them.

One of my friends back at this time went for tutorials to a philosophy don whose room was festooned with owls—stuffed owls, ceramic owls, wooden owls—and who would respond to a knock on the door with a cry of 'Enter!'. But on entry he was not to be seen, for he would hide, sometimes in his bedroom, sometimes in a cupboard, sometimes merely under the table.[4] The weirdest of all was perhaps Donald MacKinnon of Keble College, about whom endless stories circulated in my time. He taught Iris Murdoch who greatly admired him, and it has been claimed that the character of John Robert Rozanoff in *The Philosopher's Pupil* is in some distorted way based upon him. Murdoch herself rejected the idea that any of her characters were in any sense depictions of her acquaintances. No doubt incidental detail sometimes was.[5] The real MacKinnon sometimes conducted tutorials from his bath, or rolled up in a carpet, or with his dentures

3. See Lacey 289.
4. I am virtually certain that this was Paul Grice of St John's; Mackinnon was not an owls man.
5. One game that can be played with Murdoch's *The Bell* is to attempt, from the text, to construct a map of the area. In fact the topography is based on a real place, Malling Abbey, where there is an Anglican Benedictine community. See PJ Conradi, *Iris Murdoch: A Life* (2001) 125 note, 250, 437–442.

sticking out, which pupils tried to catch if they fell out completely. Somewhat strangely, and indicative of how the academic world has changed, Iris Murdoch was not in the least put off by all this, and greatly admired him. In the novel, Rozanoff is changed into a don who oppresses his pupils. In Hart's terms he was indeed a mad tutor.

At one point I became involved in remedial work over tutorials given by John Barton to an undergraduate from Merton; Barton, accompanied by his poodle, Montague Burton, a somewhat unreliable animal which sometimes bit his pupils, would devote the time to readings from classical texts of the canon law, the relevance of which to the forthcoming elementary examination in Roman Law escaped the unfortunate young man involved. Direct violence was not unknown. When I was Junior Research Fellow at St Edmund Hall, one of my colleagues there was known to have hit pupils with a riding crop in response to arrogant remarks. And the classical scholar Sir Kenneth Dover, who was Principal of Corpus Christi College from 1976–86, cheerfully recorded in his autobiography a plan to drive his colleague Trevor Aston, whose behaviour had become disruptive of college life, to suicide, though in the event Aston solved the problem by killing himself when his wife began divorce proceedings against him. In Magdalen the ancient historian Edward Stevens, who taught my friend Gerry Fowler, slept and indeed taught in the cloisters, having established that this was counted as 'living out' so that he could claim an addition to salary. He rewarded pupils with sherry for intelligent remarks, and hit them for stupid ones. In my own college the English tutor, Wallace Robson, once sent an American B Litt student away for the whole of her first term. He told her to return the following term, when she had read more English literature. She was puzzled as to why she was expected to pay substantial fees for this. Attempts to challenge this fell on deaf ears, though the undergraduate college magazine, *The Imp*, featured WF Yeames' painting, *And When Did You Last See Your Father?*, with Father changed to Tutor. Wallace Robson was outraged, a victim of an irresponsible and cruel attack, and *The Imp* was promptly suppressed.

The total lack of concern for other Cyclops was also mirrored in the world of the Oxford philosophers. They operated in their little self-contained groups, paying virtually no attention to anything in the nature of interdisciplinary work. In Modern Greats, or PPE, the philosophers, the political scientists, and the economists, with rare exceptions, practised their esoteric trades all in their hollow caves in total isolation from each other.

Again one might imagine that the Oxford linguistic analysis practitioners would have had some contact with linguists and lexicographers, and have invited them to join in the discussions, but nothing of the sort ever seems to have happened. The lexicographers worked away to produce the best dictionary ever produced for any language, and the philosophers built their castles in the sky on the nature of language, about which their knowledge and understanding was extremely limited.

The analogy with the world of the Cyclops can be developed in another way. The colleges were another cave which they inhabited. It would be difficult to overstate the amount of time and energy which was soaked up in the administration of the colleges. In my college the fellows met weekly for two or more hours, to discuss everything from the purchase of farms for investment to the colour of the paint to be used in the fellows' loo. Proceedings were enlivened by Sir John Beazley, who would sit there with his hearing aid turned off and from time to time break into snatches of opera, or say 'I agree' in a firm voice.[6]

The high point would come when it was necessary to elect a new head of the college, and there are hilarious accounts of the very fully documented skulduggery surrounding the All Souls elections of 1951 and 1952.[7] The successful candidate promptly had a stroke and died within a year, so that the battles could resume. The conduct of college business, and intriguing over appointments, made serious inroads into time which might have been devoted to scholarship, and Hart himself was a dedicated intriguer. And the nature of the colleges, with fellows in a wide range of subjects, isolated academics in particular disciplines from each other unless they made some special effort to meet. There was no faculty building or common room. The natural scientists however met in their laboratories.

I shall give other illustrations of the Cyclops phenomenon, which still persists in academia, and has perhaps grown somewhat worse with the rise of specialism.

6. Sir John Beazley (1885–1970) was a classical archaeologist specializing in Greek pottery. His personal archive survives in the form of the Classical Art Research Centre in Oxford.

7. H Trevor-Roper, *Letters from Oxford to Bernard Berenson* (2006) at 66–71, J Lowe, *The Warden* (1998) Chapter VI, AL Rowse, *All Souls in My Time* (1993), Isaiah Berlin was at one time a candidate; see H Hardy and J Holmes (eds), *Isaiah Berlin. Enlightening Letters 1946–1960* 231–9, 275–7, 289. At the time of writing I have been reading Adam Sisman's recent life of Hugh Trevor-Roper, which gives hilarious accounts of the goings-on in Peterhouse College Cambridge.

The Hedgehog and the Fox

I now wish to contrast two different approaches to legal scholarship, and at the outset I have to say that the use of the contrast between the hedgehog and the fox has become common and something of a bore, but I cannot help that and will ignore this fact, for which I am not responsible.

In a celebrated *Essay on Tolstoy's View of History* Isaiah Berlin made use of a profoundly obscure remark by the archaic Greek lyric poet, Archilochus, who was once to lyric poetry what Homer was and is to epic poetry.[8] Unfortunately only a few scraps of his work have survived, though there is always hope that some more will turn up in Egyptian papyri.

As quoted by Berlin the poet said:

> The fox knows many things. The hedgehog knows one big thing.[9]

One rather obvious and possible way to understand this is that it refers to the fact that hedgehogs curl up in a ball when threatened, whereas foxes employ lots of tricks and stratagems, but there is no way of telling if this is correct or not. Apparently hedgehogs do make use of a number of different protective mechanisms, and curling up into a ball does not always work, but that is another story and I cannot claim any extensive knowledge of the habits of these endearing creatures. I did know one which lived behind the Aga cooker in a friend's house at Marshside in Kent. It seems to have known more than one thing, and would emerge every evening for a dish of milk before setting out to catch slugs.

Berlin used the remark to contrast two different types of thinkers. On the one hand there are those who:

> ... relate everything to a single central vision, one system, less or more coherent or articulate, in terms of which they understand think and feel—a single, universal, organizing principle it terms of which all that they are and say has significance ...

8. Archilochus' dates are not known but he was probably seventh century BC. Berlin's essay can be found in H Hardy and N Annan (eds), Isaiah Berlin, *The Proper Study of Mankind: An Anthology of Essays* (1998).
9. There are other possible renderings of the text; see G Davenport, *Carmina Archilochi: The Fragments of Archilochus* (1964).

Whilst on the other side, there are:

> ...those who pursue many ends, often unrelated, and even contradictory, connected if at all, only in some *de facto* way, or some psychological or physiological cause, related to no moral or aesthetic principle.

I propose to use the hedgehog and the fox in a slightly different way to contrast two approaches to the study of law and legal institutions. One, which generates both theories of legal development and philosophical theories of law, sees simplicity concealed beneath apparent complexity, whether it takes the form of a pattern of development, or a single structure such as that offered by Hart. This is the way, hedgehogs suppose, to understand law and legal institutions. Sometimes this one idea is presented as empirically based, but more commonly it is not, but is based on some form of logical necessity, or on a necessary assumption.

The other, very commonly adopted by historians of the law, rejects this approach, and seeks understanding of law and legal institutions through empirical scholarship which emphasizes complexity, and the profound difficulty in generalization or simplification in the face of the evidence. To be sure these two approaches to legal scholarship may not in practice be clearly distinct; some hedgehogs may claim to know one big but nevertheless complicated thing. Sometimes it may be difficult or even impossible to classify a scholar as hedgehog or fox, and sometimes a scholar may be a hedgehog at one moment and a fox at the other.

So far as I personally am concerned Bill Twining got there first, describing me correctly as a fox in the *festchrift* published in 2000.[10] I am happy to be a fox.

Toynbee and Fisher: Joining the Foxes

Back in my schooldays at Oakham, when I was studying history under the tutelage of Bob Duesbury, I read an abridgement of the first six volumes of Arnold Toynbee's *A Study of History*, a twelve volume work published between 1934 and 1961; I may have read some of the six volumes in an unabridged form, but I very much doubt this. Toynbee, an immensely learned man, set out to give an account of the birth, development, and

10. K O'Donovan and GR Rubin, *Human Rights and Legal History: Essays in Honour of Brian Simpson* (2000) at 150.

decay of civilizations; my recollection as I write this was that there were supposed to be twenty one of them, but a check reveals that he actually covered twenty three, and dealt in addition with seven which, as it were, never really got going. So we have thirty in all. He claimed that it was possible to see a uniform pattern in the rise and decay of civilizations, a thesis he developed with great elaboration. I was fascinated by all this, but came to the conclusion, rightly or wrongly, that the process whereby he made the evidence conform to the theory was wholly arbitrary.[11] Another work I read back in those days was HAL Fisher's *A History of Europe* (1935), which contains a much quoted passage:

> Men wiser and more learned than I have discerned in history a plot, a rhythm, a predetermined pattern. These harmonies are concealed from me. I can see only one emergency following upon another as wave follows upon wave, only one great fact with respect to which, since it is unique, there can be no generalizations; only one safe rule for the historian; that he should recognize in the development of human destinies the play of the contingent and the unforeseeable.[12]

Elsewhere he combined this view with a deep pessimism, whereby history, European history in particular, not only did not conform to some pattern, but was a record of the crimes and follies of mankind. Plainly Toynbee counted as a hedgehog, though to call his theory merely *one* big thing is going too far. Fisher was a pessimistic fox.

So far what has been considered is the claim that there are simple patterns of historical development. There have been many such claims—Adam Smith, for example, thought that there was first the age of the hunters, then that of the shepherds, then that of the agriculturalists, and finally the age of commerce. Such schemes can be related to particular legal institutions; amongst the shepherds there will be some form of ownership of the sheep.[13] What relevance, however, has this to general theories of law, for

11. Later volumes, which I did not then read, or indeed have ever read, produced a strange work. There is a brief Wikipedia article which gives some information on criticisms etc, but does not refer to a violent attack by Trevor-Roper, 'Arnold Toynbee's Millenium' *Encounter* (1958) VIII: 14.
12. Preface at p 5.
13. Attempts to synthesize the work of anthropologists and give an account of the evolution of law rely on schemes of the changing economic basis of human societies. An example is A S Diamond's *Primitive Law*, originally published in 1935 and 1950 substantially unchanged, and then in a revised form in 1971. We begin with the Food Gatherers and then go on to the Early Hunters, Agriculturalists and Pastoralists, and so on. For this see the Bibliography.

example those of Austin, Kelsen, and Hart? I think that those who develop such theories can be classified as hedgehogs, whereas those who are deeply suspicious of their merits and explanatory power are foxes. And if ever there was a hedgehog it was Adam Smith. By way of contrast, a classic example of the foxy attitude is to be found in Maitland's dismissal of John Austin:

J. A. = 0[14]

My understanding of this is not that Maitland was concerned over internal defects in Austin's analysis, but was much more radical. Suppose law really did consist in the orders backed by threats of the uncommanded commander, as Austin claimed, so what? What help was this to understanding, for example, the establishment of the common law system in the twelfth and thirteenth centuries? Suppose the bulk of the then population obeyed the commands of the sovereign, etc (and how on earth could one ever tell?), where did this get you? For the dedicated fox, nowhere. And carried to its ultimate conclusion hedgehog-inspired legal theory, according to this view, is just bunk.

Take Kelsen's hierarchy of legal norms, at the top of which sat the Constitution, which for Kelsen would comprise an elaborate text.[15] The validity of any norm, as a norm of the legal system, was derivative of a superior norm, and ultimately from the Constitution. But that did not count as a satisfactory explanation, I suppose the problem was that constitutions comprise a number of distinct norms. So accordingly there had to be the single proposition, the 'Grundnorm': 'That the Constitution (whatever it happened to be), Must be Observed,' reminiscent of John Mortimer's Rumpole, and She Who Must be Obeyed. If you wanted to join the game, that is participate in the operation of the legal system, you had to *presuppose* its validity, together with the general efficacy of the system. In another version there was only one Global Grundnorm.[16]

How did it come about that this profoundly learned and experienced legal scholar—he had indeed drafted the Austrian constitution, and invented the European model of a constitutional court—came up with something which seems at least like the ultimate *ridiculus mus*. He was a hedgehog, and

14. CHS Fifoot, *The Letters of Frederic William Maitland* (1965) 235.

15. Hart used his *General Theory of Law and the State* (1949) and Kelsen's 'The Pure Theory of Law and Analytical Jurisprudence' (1941) 55 HLR 44. *The Pure Theory of Law* was not published in English until 1967.

16. Also discussed and partially developed in *General Theory* at 350 and ff.

if you are looking for one big thing, a single Global Grundnorm is about as good as you are ever going to get. But for the foxes the problem is to see how it can possibly contribute to an enhanced understanding of the multifarious legal systems of the complex world we inhabit, and whose complexity the hedgehogs seem determined to deny. And what is the function of this analysis? Surely not a scheme for empirical research, but perhaps a set of analytical conceptions applicable to the products of research? For a scholar such as Maitland are we to suppose that after he has devoted many, many hours working through the archives which survive from the late Anglo-Saxon period and the post-conquest material, he should turn to Kelsen and appreciate the significance of it all in terms of the postulated Grundnorm? The idea, put like that, seems bizarre.

Grant Gilmore and the Death of Contract

By way of illustration I shall use Grant Gilmore as a paradigm case of a hedgehog. He was a distinguished contract law scholar, who was invited to give some lectures in Ohio State University in 1970. These were published in 1974 under the title *The Death Of Contract*. No monograph can have had such a reception since the publication of Holmes' *The Common Law* back in 1881, and Gilmore's book, unlike Holmes, was highly readable. It was very widely reviewed, not at all the usual practice in the USA.[17] Gilmore's basic thesis was that those general abstract principles of contract law, whereby the purchase of a can of coca cola is governed by the same principles as those governing the purchase of an airliner, no longer served any useful function. In this sense contract was dead. The notion of death here is borrowed from the idea that perhaps God is dead. For assuming that God is all knowing, all powerful, and all benevolent, or even I suppose benevolent some of the time, how does one explain the current grisly state of the world? For this problem there are a number of possible 'solutions'. For example that God moves in a mysterious way. One other solution is to suppose that God is dead. Gilmore's book keeps clear of such mysteries.

17. R Danzig in his 'The Death of Contract and the Life of the Profession: Observations on the Intellectual State of Legal Academia' [1977] *Stanford LR* 1125 has a list of reviews but it is incomplete. Another example of a monograph which had been widely reviewed was Lon Fuller's *The Law in Quest of Itself* (1940), but not on the same scale.

Gilmore noticed that the nineteenth century saw a striking rise in the volume, and supposed significance, of abstract principles of contract law, and that this phenomenon was connected with strengthening control over jury discretion. He also noticed that their elaboration was something which primarily engaged treatise writers, and early legal academics, rather than the courts, and was connected in some way with the practices followed in legal education. These were good points. But he then went on to claim that these principles had simply been invented by Christopher Columbus Langdell, the patron saint of the Harvard Law School where he was Dean from 1870, in order to have something to teach his students by his new case system of instruction. Langdell's *Summary of the Law of Contract*, which purported to say what the principles were, was published in the second edition of his *Cases on the Law of Contract* (1879). Whether Gilmore was intending to make a joke, or whether not, is impossible to say. But there is no evidence that Gilmore had the least knowledge of their long history in the civil law tradition, or of the mechanisms whereby they were in part received into the common law in the nineteenth century. To be fair to him the subject was, in 1970, largely unexplored.[18]

In the course of expounding all this, Gilmore unleashed himself on the case of the two ships *Peerless: Raffles v Wichelhaus and Busch* (1864), which had long featured in legal education as a peg on which to hang discussions of contract theory. A week's work or so would have suggested to anyone, even someone with little or no knowledge of nineteenth century history, that the case had both a maritime and a commercial background, associated with the effect of the American civil war on the Lancashire cotton industry. Working out exactly what that association was, as I can say from experience, would have been a much more lengthy and tedious business.[19] Gilmore seems never to have even glanced at the extensive published materials, or if he did he must have rapidly decided to forget about them. One might imagine that simple curiosity would have led him at least into finding out, for example, how ships at this period were named and identified. But no.[20] Instead he set

18. In Michel Lobban's account of contract law in Volume XII of the new *Oxford History of the Laws of England* neither Gilmore nor the case of the *Peerless* is mentioned. But this is a piece of serious and foxy historical scholarship.

19. Thus the complexities of cotton grading, explained in excruciating detail in the original version of my article on the case, was cut from the version published in *Leading Cases*.

20. Here a word should be said about the conduct of research in US law schools. Equipped as they are with skilled research librarians, who do half the work for the faculty themselves, and able by the use of loans to obtain copies of virtually anything ever published, they provide

about ridiculing the judges who had been involved in the case, claiming that they had failed to grasp that the identity of the carrying ship had been, from a commercial point of view, wholly irrelevant. Absolutely everything he said about the case is wrong; in this his account is something of a *tour de force*. He brought to the subject the confidence not simply of a hedgehog, but of an arrogant, happy, and ignorant hedgehog, and that was the end of the matter. Empirical investigation would have got in the way—To Hell With Evidence. His later publication, *The Ages of American Law* (1977), though purporting to be an essay in legal history, exhibits a similar and profound ignorance, but I guess that in reality to view it as such misunderstands the appeal of the building of such castles in the sky, whose function it is to entertain rather than to illuminate. The whole history of American law is laid bare in a form which can be assimilated on a short haul flight. Or as a bedside book, providing an alternative to desperate recourse to the Gideon Bible, or to the pornographic movies tastefully provided by American hotels, but not specified on the bill because of give-away titles such as *Snow White and the Seven Perverts*, some of which we sat through when on the UK Pornography Committee back in the 1970s.[21] Or there is always the contents of the mini-bar, and alcoholic oblivion.

Elsewhere in my publications there will be found other examples of surprisingly defective scholarship, to be blamed at least in part on hedgehog-like attitudes. Sometimes however the explanation may be a little different. If, for example, your interest is in the history of tort law and accidents, and you track some aspect of this body of law back into the nineteenth century or earlier, but do not have a general broad knowledge of the social and legal arrangements which then existed, you can wholly fail to grasp the fact that there existed other mechanisms, typically the Poor Law, which were far more significant.[22] Incursions into legal history are perilous without some sort of map. This is called path dependence, a concept well

conditions hardly conceivable on my side of the Atlantic. Furthermore the academics, though forever grumbling, have by comparison modest teaching loads, and generous provision for leave. There are research assistants and financial support. For Gilmore, it appears, the law library was a prison, and it would have contained nothing which shed light on such matters.

21. Known as the Williams Committee, chaired by Bernard Williams; I was his deputy and wrote an account, published as *Pornography and Politics*. The publishers, purely from incompetence, made no attempt to sell this book and copies are now rare.

22. This point is illustrated by Chapter5 of my *Leading Cases*.

understood in Ireland, where, if you ask the way to Skibbereen you may elicit the reply:

> Well if you're going to Skibbereeen you shouldn't be starting from here.

There are also in the writings of some hedgehogs, who have seen the truth, other irritating bad habits. One is a failure to address or even mention critical articles written by scholars who are not members of the hedgehog club involved. Another is not directly addressing the phenomenon or institution in which they are supposed to be interested, but confining attention to what they and other hedgehogs have written about it. A third is to present their arguments in the form of attacks on straw men, who are made to put forward silly views, easy to demolish.

Scholarship of the Foxes: A Brief Autobiographical Account

I shall use my own writings to illustrate the approach to scholarship of the foxes, though it would be easy enough to give other examples. For throughout my career as an academic I have always been a fox.

My first book, *An Introduction to the History of the Land Law* (1961), was written in the summer of 1960 as a simple student text. It was a book which avoided complexity, whilst always making it clear that the picture presented glossed over the fact that the history of the land law was extremely complex and to a considerable degree uninvestigated. In the second edition of this book I spelled this out:

> I have attempted to pursue the same modest aim: to write a short simple book which will introduce its readers to the history of a very complicated subject, and provide guidance to the literature.[23]

Since then various distinguished studies of aspects of the history of the land law have been published, but nobody is ever going to be able to write a comprehensive general doctrinal history, let alone one which explores its social significance, though I suppose that some multi-volume and collaborative work might be conceivable. My second book, *A History of the Common Law of Contract*, was published in 1975 as the first volume of a

23. *A History of the Land Law* (1986).

two volume work, never completed; I confined my writings on the later history of contract law to periodical articles and book reviews. I was acutely aware of the book's limitations—for example it was based virtually exclusively on printed sources. But, whatever its defects, it provides a comprehensive analysis of the evolution of legal doctrine in a particular field of the common law world. And it certainly made no attempt to downplay the complexity of the legal culture, which we can only try to understand, always inadequately, from the opacity of the sources. It belongs to a genre which had become unfashionable, and proceeds on the assumption that law can legitimately be studied as an autonomous discipline. It developed no general theory of the evolution of contract doctrine.

Since then I have, through my publications, become associated with contextual studies of leading cases and with other related work, often based on archival material. This is how it first came about. In 1979 I arrived in Chicago on a visit at the height of a major blizzard, and it was only with difficulty and the offer of a huge tip that I reached the Quadrangle Club in Hyde Park, where I was both privileged and doomed to live. This was built in a version of the Scottish baronial crofter's cottage style. It provided excellent meals, but ill heated and unattractive living accommodation. In cold Chicago weather, survival was only possible through using towels to block the cracks around the lead frame windows. But there was hot water. It was when I was lying in a bath trying to get warm that it occurred to me that the celebrated case of *Rylands v Fletcher* must have had as its background some major reservoir failure, a hypothesis I soon found to be true from a short trip to the Regenstein Library.[24] This bathing experience generated an article which appeared in the Chicago *Journal of Legal Studies* in 1986, and was my first essay in the contextual study of a leading case. Some of the article was devoted to rubbishing writings in which ridiculous empirical claims were made, such as that there were not many reservoirs in England; the idea that the home of the industrial revolution would not have generated a need for the storage of water is simply incredible. Here the problem is simply pathetic standards of scholarship. Some passages criticized writers who had tried to explain the decision in terms of general theories of tort law; here the objection is to the approach of the hedgehog, for whom

24. The library was built on the site of the one-time football field, a fact that once in my experience reduced an elderly former coach to floods of tears. Excellence in football was not what Chicago was about, and the game had been ditched some many years earlier.

empirical evidence is neither needed, nor sought. It just gets in the way. To my mind it was the context which explained the decision, and the context could only be established by empirical work. This was not the first attempt to study a leading case in its social and political context; the pioneer was Richard Danzig, who had in 1975 published an article of this character on the contract case of *Hadley v Baxendale* (1854).

My next such study dealt with the case of *R v Dudley and Stephens* (1884) and the outcome was a book-length study, *Cannibalism and the Common Law* (1984). It has been described by William Twining with some justification as 'a magnificent failure' and as lacking 'focus'. The point was that the real subject matter of the book—the conflicts for example between middle class morality and the practices of seamen, the conflict between notions of the survival of the fittest, supposedly derived from Darwin, and the Christian value of the sanctity of human life, the conflict between the rule of law and of necessity, the complexities of the interaction between lawyers, courts, politicians, and elite and working class public opinion—failed to make much in the way of intellectual impact within the world of academic law. The claim that the book lacked 'focus' meant that I did not spell out what the book was about, but left this to the intelligence of the reader. There was no attempt to overlay the story with theory, or point out the moral; that is not what foxes do. Be that as it may I came to be viewed as something of a pioneer in what some have called 'legal archaeology'. *Cannibalism and the Common Law* involved work in the National Archives, and I came to be fascinated by archival research into relatively modern legal history. Extensive use had been made of archives by medievalists and the editors of texts for the legal historical *Selden Society*, but virtually no use had been made of them for the study of modern legal history. The regular historians were nervous of anything connected with the law, as they still are, and the lawyers were not interested in archival research, which involves tedious work, and does not produce rapid results.

My next project was suggested by a conversation I had with a Canadian scholar, De Lloyd Guth, who told me that he and Robert Heuston had discovered that Robert Liversidge, the litigant in *Liversidge v Anderson* (1942), was still alive, and living in the Vancouver area with his nth wife (who subsequently kicked him out to a hotel). Out of this came my book, *In the Highest Degree Odious: Detention Without Trial in Wartime Britain* (1992). Based on a very wide range of sources, including interviews with former members of the British Union of Fascists and members of the Security

Service (MI5), and many telephone conversations with Robert Liversidge, it explored the interaction between the military, the security service, the police, the civil servants, internal governmental committees, the lawyers, the courts, members of Parliament, and the media on the one hand, and the motley crew of detainees and their families on the other. It was a study of the working of the British governmental machine in times of stress. Like *Cannibalism and the Common Law* its publication had only a limited impact on the teaching or study of law and legal institutions, and it has been largely ignored by the political scientists. One of the anonymous readers for the OUP, some hedgehog or other, criticized the draft on the ground that it lacked theoretical analysis, and I therefore stitched on a final chapter which I wrote, with distaste, in two days. Especially in legal academia the moral of the story has to be spelled out, so that even the dimmest person can see what it might be about. It seemed to be as if Homer had been expected to append to the Odyssey an explanation of what his work, if it was his work, was all about: perhaps the attractions and hazards of travel in the Mediterranean.[25]

My next major project was my *Human Rights and the End of Empire: Britain and the Genesis of the European Convention* (2001). This was a large book, which, arguably, might have been more prudently published in two volumes. It is known in the family as *The Monstrous Book*, or *The Beetle Crusher*. This book, whatever its merits or demerits, represents the most comprehensive study ever attempted into the genesis of a multilateral treaty. It was however based largely on UK archives; to have embarked on an investigation into all the archives of all the negotiating states would have been impracticable. So the complete story, which will probably never be told, would have been even more complicated. Essentially it develops in another field the interests and approach which produced *Cannibalism and the Common Law* and *In the Highest Degree Odious*. It seeks of course to explain and make sense of the negotiations, developing a range of conceptions intended to achieve this, some encapsulated in expressions such as 'The Export Theory of Human Right', 'The Barbarians at the Gates', 'Dishing the Russians', 'The Wild and Woolly Body', 'Not In My Back Yard (hardly original)', 'Hypocrisy and Human Rights', but it does not develop any overarching general theory. Foxes do not do that.

My *Leading Cases in the Common Law* was published in 1995. After an introduction discussing the conception and invention of the idea of a

25. I have already made another suggestion at p 119 above.

leading case, and its relationship to nineteenth century legal education, and to theories of legal science, it provides, in the nine following chapters, extremely detailed contextual studies of nine cases. Three chapters provide revised versions of the article which had been published earlier.[26] Perhaps the strangest story which is told in this collection is that of *Shelley's Case* (1581).[27] This profoundly obscure case generated one of the 'rules' of the common law, which continues to have a sort of twilight existence in some jurisdictions today, though nobody is very clear as to which they are. When teaching property law in Michigan we still, right up to the time I retired, 'did' the rule, and when I studied law in Oxford we studied it although it had been abolished back in 1926, the argument being that unless we knew what the rule was we would not know what had been abolished.[28] The rule had long fascinated me. Was its origin medieval? If so what had been its point? Given the laconic reports of the case, for at this time the judges did not follow a practice of giving much in the way of explanation as to why they had decided a case this way or that, was the rule in reality laid down by the judges? Or did Sir Edward Coke invent it? What was the litigation really all about? Why was it of interest to the government of the day? The Shelley family was prominent and wealthy, and Justice William Shelley (c. 1479–1548) had been a friend of Henry VIII. Rich and prominent families and their doings generate records, so there existed a mass of material which can be used to answer such questions as these; by contrast the poor turn up in early sources mainly as criminals, so we know little about them as individuals. It was possible to give an explanation of the family disputes which came to a head in the case, and which reflected a religious conflict between the side of the family which embraced the Elizabethan religious settlement, and the side of the family which retained fidelity to the Roman Catholic faith. So although the case was certainly about property law, it was about much more than that. And if anyone thinks that the idea that the law consists of rules is unproblematic they need to know something about the bizarre later history of the celebrated Rule in *Shelley's Case*.

In more recent times there has developed in the US legal academic world a story-telling movement, and my work may have had some part in

26. Chapter 6 dealing with *Raffles v Wichelhaus and Busch* (1964) is a revised version of an article which had appeared in Cardozo LR 11: 287 (1989), Chapter 8 contains a revised version of my 1984 article on *Rylands v Fletcher* (1868), and Chapter 10 on *Carlill and the Carbolic Smoke Ball* (1893) is a revised version of an article published in JLS 14: 345 (1985).

27. Chapter 2.

28. It could still affect titles.

encouraging this development. Articles of mine have been included in *Property Law Stories* (ed Korngold and Morris, 2004) and *Contract Stories* (ed Baird, 2007), recent examples of this type of writing about the law. The former includes my 'The Story of *Sturges v Bridgman*: The Resolution of Land Use Disputes Between Neighbours' which sets out criticisms of views advanced by Ronald Coase, originally put forward in the Chicago *Journal of Legal Studies*.[29] No serious response has yet been made to the arguments there presented; devotees of law and economics pretend the piece does not exist. Other articles of mine have continued to emphasize complexity. Thus I contributed an article on 'The Origins of Futures Trading in the Liverpool Cotton Market' to a *festchrift* for Patrick Atiyah, published in 1991.[30]

Some of my publications have related to international law. One example is my Maccabean Lecture in Jurisprudence of 2003, 'The Rule of Law in International Affairs'.[31] In it I set out to investigate the influence of international law on the conduct of states in the use of force. There is a very considerable literature on this subject, much of a theoretical character, but the lecture did not attempt to consider it. Instead I set out to investigate, in the light of the archival and other evidence, the role and influence, if any, played by international law in relation to two specific incidents, which took place on 16 February and 8 April 1940. The first was the boarding of the German vessel the *Altmark* in Jössingfiord, within Norwegian territorial waters. The *Altmark* had on board a number of British seamen captured by the German battlecruiser *Graf Spee*. The second was the laying of mines in the Vestfiord, the aim being to block the approach to Narvik. At this time Norway was strenuously maintaining the neutrality it had enjoyed since 1814. There is no doubt that international law did play a role in the disputes with Norway over all this, but it was a very complicated role, and on some matters the evidence simply does not reveal precisely what that role was. This is foxy scholarship, and the lecture concludes by indicating the way on

29. 'Coase v Pigou Reexamined' (1996) XXV JLS 53, with cross-reply by Coase and my response to it.

30. *En passant* this collection of essays seems to me to provide an outstanding example of top quality legal scholarship. I can pass no objective judgement on my own contribution, but record that it is one of my writings which continues to please me, which is unusual. At the time of writing I was unaware of the fact that in seventeenth century Japan and the Netherlands there had existed rudimentary forms of futures trading.

31. (2004) PBA 125:211. The British actions were thought by some to present an embarrassing problem for the Nuremberg trials after the war, but I do not of course discuss this issue.

which research into these two incidents throws up a range of further questions for investigation:

> One function [of international law] I have been able to illustrate is that it provides a resource for argumentative justification of government action... Why is so much energy and importance attached to attempts to produce plausible and convincing justifications? To what audiences are these justifications addressed?... To what extent are these justifications properly considered to be legal at all? Are they at bottom ethical in nature? Or is it, in this field, not really possible to separate the legal from the ethical or the merely commonsensical?

The lecture concludes by contrasting the position in domestic law, whereby the conception of what counts as law is parasitic on judicial decisions, with that in international law, where the International Court of Justice and its predecessor, the Permanent Court of International Justice, has only dealt with a very small number of cases:

> Their relationship to international law is the reverse of that which obtains domestically; their very existence has been parasitic on the existence of international law. I cannot but wonder whether the forms and functions of justification in the international arena have been and always will be affected by this different relationship, so long as it continues. It all needs further study.

It would be tedious for me to go through the list of other periodical publications in order merely to reinforce the point that complexity and the importance of empirical evidence is what they are all about. There is a comprehensive bibliography by Jules Winterton in the *festchrift* of 2000. Richard Helmholz in his contribution to it makes the point that in my writings, even those that appear polemical, there has been an 'even-handedness', criticisms being directed both at those of a left wing persuasion,[32] and those who espouse the law and economics movement, associated loosely with the right. Others must judge, but this is certainly what I should like to believe.

I have to confess also to a somewhat ill-analysed hostility to the enthusiasm with which academic lawyers, especially in the USA, conjure up explanatory legal theory without attending to what I am predisposed to think is the only legitimate function of such theory, which is to explain or

32. The reference is to my 'The Horwitz Thesis and the History of Contracts' (1979) UCLR 46: 533. The criticisms are directed only at one part of Horwitz's work.

make sense of the empirical world, or provide guidance as to what further investigation might be fruitful. This hostility has I suspect been aggravated by the hours I have spent in my time listening, in common with those of my colleagues who also listened, to presentations by young candidates for appointments who, poor things, are more or less driven to spinning webs in the sky by the system. I shall avoid at this point dragging in a discussion of Thomas Kuhn's *The Structure of Scientific Revolutions* (1962), or of the writings of Michael Polyani, except to say that Kuhn did attempt to provide an analysis of what the function of theory was and what, to put it simply, counted as a good or fruitful theory.[33] For law we have nothing of this kind. We have lots of legal theory, but often we do not know what it is supposed to be about, or how to judge it. Perhaps this explains the popularity of theories developed outside the legal culture, for example those derived from economics, or game theory.

Hart as Hedgehog

We have seen how Hart based his analysis on what he called the standard or paradigm case of a legal system. Did he nevertheless base his analysis on any particular legal systems? There is no clear evidence in the text of *The Concept of Law*, but the only two legal systems he appears to have known much about at the time when the book was written were the British and American legal systems. His own direct experience of legal practice was confined to the Chancery Division of the High Court, presided over by a tiny handful of judges, with the work shared between a very small number of practitioners. Given the nature of the work in which he was then engaged, Hart would have had little occasion to develop expertise outside the fields of tax law and trusts; the Chancery division was not the place to be to broaden your general legal education or provide one if you had never had one. And within the tiny legal community in which he worked I should have thought that there were very many issues on which that community viewed the law as quite settled and beyond argument, and a very formalistic mode of interpreting legislation, for example in tax law, was the order of the day. I suspect this affected Hart's attitude to the law.

33. *The Essential Tension: Selected Studies in Scientific Tradition and Change* (1977) at 320–9.

Later, and I base this on personal recollection, he developed a considerable interest in the Israeli legal system. Like virtually all my Jewish friends and acquaintances he came, as Nicola Lacey points out, to feel he had to think out his attitude to the State of Israel, and an interest in its legal system may have been as it were a route into this. My recollection is that he first raised the matter in the Hart Group in relation to citizenship laws.

His analysis of the structure of a legal system as a set of rules, identified by a master rule, the rule or rules of recognition, claims to locate a single and fundamentally simple structure in legal systems which appear at first sight to be extremely complex. The American legal system was a federal system, with both federal and state law, legislatures and courts; American law applied to a variety of territories, for example, Guam, which were not parts of the union. In addition to federal and state legislatures there were hundreds if not thousands of other law-making institutions with law making and adjudicative powers. As for the British legal system it was, in 1961, of mind boggling complexity. Not only did it operate within the United Kingdom itself—with a separate legislature for Northern Ireland and a distinct legal culture and profession in Scotland, not to mention the Channel Islands and the Isle of Man—but it also applied to the vast British colonial empire, which at this time embraced around thirty five distinct colonial territories,[34] inhabited by something like 70,000,000 people. And in addition to colonies, not all conforming to a single legal model, there were protectorates, and protected states, and *condominiums*, and territories whose precise status remained mysterious. We can be reasonably sure that Hart would have a reasonably good knowledge of the legal constitutional arrangements which applied in the United Kingdom itself, though he can rarely, if ever, have needed to know much about them for practice at the Chancery bar. But we can be equally sure that he would have only had a limited knowledge about the constitutional structure of the British Commonwealth and Colonial Empire. Such knowledge was indeed largely confined to Colonial and Foreign Office officials, and to colonial law officers, and it was not until 1966, with the publication of K Roberts-Wray's massive *Commonwealth and Colonial Law*, that the full complexities were revealed. Hart was however fully aware of the existence of problematic relationships between independent and dependent territorial units; the

34. Administrative units of the colonial empire could comprise distinct territories and dependencies.

subject turns up, rather surprisingly, in the chapter of *The Concept of Law* dealing not with municipal legal systems, but with international law.[35] By way of contrast Roberts-Wray was hardly concerned with international law at all.

Hart's general analysis of the structure of a legal system was not based on a prolonged study of complex legal arrangements, with a dawning awareness that beneath complexity there could be discerned simplicity—the Darwin phenomenon. Instead the simplicity he discerned existed in the very nature of things; given the fact, if that is what you call it, that the USA has a legal system, it follows that its legal system conforms to Hart's simple model. This plainly identifies Hart as a hedgehog.

Radical Doubts

It is inevitable perhaps that someone who is a fox will from time to time have radical doubts about the value of the work of the hedgehogs, and sometimes these radical doubts seem to me to be justified. Much of their work is so unrelated to the real world as to be rubbish, but the same may be said of much academic work, and if you want the good stuff you just have to accept this. So I think one has to resist too cynical an attitude, and there are occasions on which one can have an entertaining time by joining the game. Many years ago, I and a distinguished professor of jurisprudence in Oxford had to examine a doctoral candidate. He was a dedicated conservationist. His excellent thesis explored a range of practical legal issues associated with wildlife protection; I can no longer recall details, but for example he was interested in what legal regimes would reconcile the protection of wild animals in Africa with the needs and problems of Africans whose crops might be devastated by elephants, or their cattle killed by lions. My colleague was an able lawyer, but not the sort of person who would be either competent nor indeed interested in distinguishing a wildebeest from a kudu, and his knowledge of Africa, or indeed anywhere in the third world, was somewhere between minimal and non-existent. So within a few moments he had moved the discussion onto an issue in which the candidate had not the remotest interest, and one which was not discussed at all in his thesis, *Do animals have rights?* We were now safely concerned with matters of high

35. CL 221–3.

philosophical theory. The plains of Africa, the baobab trees, the lions and the hyaenas, the vultures fighting over the entrails, the Masai, splendid fellows if ever there were any, the Ngorogoro crater, all faded away. We could concern ourselves with such issues too as to whether giraffes should have standing to litigate to protect their rights, an entertaining idea which runs into some practical difficulties to which philosophy provides no guidance. How do you get a giraffe into court? Or does he appear through his best friend? How do you tell who that is? Can a giraffe instruct counsel? And, if we are in one of the relics of the British Empire, does a giraffe have to wear a wig? Before long we were into less cuddly creatures such as cockroaches, and even tapeworms, at which point I decided to raise the intellectual stakes by suggesting that if animals had rights *surely they must have duties too*. This belief had, as I pointed out, been integral to a notable form of literature, the medieval bestiary, and was still held by the English country gentry, hand in hand with the belief that they in their turn had an obligation to start and industriously pursue the slaughter of the game birds at the appropriate time—12 August for the grouse, 1 September for the partridges, 31 October for the pheasants. The time passed agreeably for my colleague always had interesting things to say, and the candidate, who listened nervously, but with growing interest, was in due course awarded his degree on our recommendation.

There are no prizes for identifying my colleague.

6

Where Homer Nodded?

In this chapter, which may at first sight seem negative in tone, I shall try to identify what seem to me to be defects, for example omissions and ideas not fully worked out, in *The Concept of Law*. I shall not include any extended discussion of matters which Hart wholly excluded from his book, such as Marxist theories of law.[1] Neither shall I devote much space to matters which have been discussed by other commentators. What is principally of interest are issues which he does discuss, if only in a limited way, or issues which, though not explicitly mentioned, must have been known by him to raise problems. Both here and in the final chapter of this book I shall offer some explanations, but in this chapter the main concern is simply to identify them.

Drake's Prayer and the Hart Paradox

The basic ideas around which Hart developed his theory of law were that law comprised rules,[2] and that there existed two different types of rule, primary rules (which impose duties or obligations) and secondary rules (which confer powers). A rule of the second type, the rule of recognition, makes a regime of merely primary rules form a legal system, as contrasted with a mere set of rules. The existence of the rule of recognition in the case of a putative legal system is a question of fact.

What is to me paradoxical is that in *The Concept of Law* these basic ideas were never fully developed; it is as if Hart, having sketched them out,

1. But see below for a brief discussion.
2. His teacher CAW Manning at 233 called this 'the hoary assumption that law is a mere aggregate of rules'.

fought shy of working them out in any detail. Back in 1587 Sir Francis Drake wrote:

> There must be a begynning of any great matter, but the contynuing unto the end untyle it be thoroughly fynished yieldeth the true glory.

Later in the 1940s this was given a religious character by being converted into the well-known Drake's Prayer. Hart does not seem to have been much influenced by the sentiment expressed. Many years after *The Concept of Law* was published, in 1973, Colin Tapper published 'Powers and Secondary Rules of Change'[3] and *inter alia* made the point that the distinction between Hart's primary and secondary rules involved a number of different contrasts, which had not been fully analysed. I shall not do more than mention this except to say that his reaction to Hart's text was in some respects similar to my own. There are indeed other problematic issues lurking in *The Concept of Law*. For instance, is it that there are two different *types* of rule, or is it that one rule can have different *functions*? A rule which permits a policeman to arrest me, for example, (power conferring) imposes on me a duty to come quietly (duty imposing). And what counts as a rule, as contrasted with part of a larger rule? This is nowhere explained, though Hart hints at the idea that the identity of rules is determined by ordinary usage. And what are we to make of the fact that we lawyers use a much more extensive vocabulary to talk about the law, with its definitions, principles, exceptions, policies, doctrines, etcetera. Why adopt so impoverished a vocabulary when ordinary usage provides such riches?

The Rule of Recognition

Some of the issues I wish to raise concern the rule of recognition.

The first is the sheer oddity of the expression. It does not occur in such of Hart's writings as precede *The Concept of Law,* and we have become so used to it that we have ceased to notice what a strange term it is to use. My own favourite rule of recognition dates from around the late 1950s, and concerns AL Rowse. As a schoolboy I greatly admired his work on Cornish history, and indeed I was given a collection of his essays as a school history prize back in 1949.[4] Soon after I became a don I was invited to dinner in All Souls, and

3. *Oxford Essays in Jurisprudence (Second Series)* 242.
4. AL Rowse, *The End of An Epoch* (1948).

enquired of my colleague Harold Cox how I would recognize Rowse, whom I was anxious to meet. He told me this was simple: he would be the most unpleasant person in the room. This rule of recognition worked perfectly, and later I passed it on to an American friend who was dining there; he was rather shocked, but after meeting the awful Rowse, as he had by now become, was shocked no more.

But if, for example, one was taking a friend to see the English Court of Appeal, or the American Supreme Court, in session, and wanted to explain what was going on, it would be quite inconceivable that it would be described as the activity of recognizing, presumably amongst candidates, those rules which belonged to the system, from those which did not, rather as one might, when out birdwatching, apply the simple rule of recognition: if the bird hovers it's bound to be a kestrel.

Why Hart hit on the term *recognition* is not easy to explain, and perhaps does not much matter, but it is just possible that it came from JL Austin, for it turns up a number of times in his rambling article 'Other Minds'. On my count the word appears 12 times, and perhaps it was a term which Austin used in discussions with Hart, but this is very speculative indeed. I have not come across any other earlier writer who uses the term in a similar context. Birds, such as the goldcrest and goldfinch, feature in the discussion, but not the bittern with which we begin his article. There is a rule of recognition for bitterns: they boom. I think they are the only British bird which does this. Austin however does not mention their booming. In Austin's article we do have a partial explanation of what is involved in recognizing a goldfinch[5] and a mention of what are called 'the problems of recognition'.[6] He supposes there to be a linguistic convention within a linguistic community which establishes a concept of what counts as a goldfinch; there is no mention of the birdwatching guides which enthusiasts rely upon, much less on how they are produced and why. He also discusses the problem of the exploding goldfinch (echoes today of Inspector Clouseau and the exploding kind of Burmb?). We are to suppose that a goldfinch suddenly explodes: we would not know what to say, since no such convention exists. Personally my inclination would be some expletive or other—a performative. But it would all depend on a context we are not given. Is the bird being hand held for ringing? Some time back I was looking into my garden and a collared dove exploded; my neighbour dislikes them and had shot it with a

5. At 84. 6. At 96.

powerful rifle, but the report of this weapon had been muffled. Once I worked it all out I knew exactly what to say: not in my back yard, please. In the real world there are or were many disagreeable exploding things—dead bodies, and rats as used by agents in France in the war.

The second is the use of the concept of 'validity', which is again curious and alien to the language of English lawyers. Rules identified by the rule of recognition count as *valid* rules of the system. As normally used by English lawyers the conception of 'validity' is not applied to laws or legal rules, but to actions or transactions of one kind or another which are in some way defective; an example would be an invalid exercise of a power of appointment, or a will which, though otherwise properly executed, but had not fully conformed to the requirements of the Wills Act. But in the manner in which Hart employs it there is no such contrast; what would an invalid law or invalid rule of law be like? I suppose that in principle their number would be infinite. The use of this term seems clearly to have been derivative of Kelsen.

The third is that Hart sometimes writes in the singular of *a rule of recognition*, and sometimes in the plural of *rules of recognition*, specifying the system's criteria of validity, and its *rules of change* and *adjudication*, as if they were distinct.[7] Perhaps the idea is that it is possible to conceive of a body of law which is static—the Laws of the Medes and Persians—and has no rules of change, and in which adjudication is not required since disputes as to what the law is just do not arise. I doubt this. It sounds suspiciously like a regime comprising primary rules only, which lacks the rule of recognition of Hart's scheme. A related obscurity is that in modern legal systems the rule of recognition, the law which purports to tell you how to discover what the law is, is extremely complicated. A massive literature, some of it highly controversial, exists on the subject for every modern legal system. To present it all as just one rule encapsulates the attitude of a nervous hedgehog, who prefers to know just one big thing rather than worry over the complexities of life. Lon Fuller in his exchange with Hart wrote:

> It will be noted that Kelsen speaks, not as Professor Hart does, of 'fundamental rules' that regulate the making of law, but of a single rule or norm. Of course there is no such single rule in any modern society. The notion of the basic norm is admittedly a symbol, not a fact. It is a symbol which embodies the positivist quest for some clear and unambiguous test of law, for some clean

7. CL 118.

> sharp line that will divide the rules which owe their validity to their source and those which owe their validity to acceptance and intrinsic appeal.[8]

In reading this celebrated exchange the basic point to note at the outset is that the combatants differed in one fundamental respect: Fuller was fascinated by and dedicated to trying to understand law as a social institution. That is he was both seriously interested in law and a skilled legal practitioner and educator, though something of a bully.[9] Hart, as he frankly explained, was not fascinated or even much interested in law, and he had never regularly taught law, though he did develop some interest in the criminal law.

The fourth concerns the supposed philosophical problem of deriving an 'Ought' from an 'Is'. There is a very considerable philosophical literature which deals with the thesis, associated with Hume, that it is a fundamental error to suppose that a proposition as to what ought to be done (normally with some kind of moral or ethical significance) can be derived, or made to logically follow, from a proposition as to what is in fact the case. Needless to say some writers, for example John Searle, have argued that this can be done, but such a view is controversial.[10] For present purposes it is important merely to be aware of this thesis. Now it is central to Hart's theory of law, and one of the points which, as he emphasizes, distinguishes his theory from that of Kelsen, that the existence of a legal system is in principle a matter of fact. Hart concedes that there may be problems in particular cases as to whether the necessary facts exist—for example whether the primary rules are sufficiently generally obeyed. In Kelsen's theory you have to *presuppose* the validity of the basic norm, a sort of act of faith, and this, Hart insists, is a mistake. Hart summarizes his view thus:

> There are therefore two minimum conditions necessary and sufficient for the existence of a legal system. On the one hand those rules of behaviour which are valid according to the system's ultimate criteria must be generally obeyed, and, on the other hand, its rules of recognition specifying the criteria of legal

8. HFE 641.
9. I once sat in on one of his classes in Harvard. A student announced he was unprepared, and we all had to sit there for some twenty minutes for the student to correct this. There is an excellent study of Fuller by RB Summers, *Lon L. Fuller* in the series *Jurists: Profiles in Legal Theory* (1984).
10. 'How to Derive "Ought" from "Is"' (1964) *Philosophical Review* 73: 43. Searle uses the making of a promise as his basic example.

> validity and its rules of change and adjudication must be effectively accepted as common public standards of official behaviour by its officials.[11]

Whether these conditions have been or are satisfied is an 'empirical though complex, question of fact'.[12] Now according to the theory the primary rules impose duties, legal duties or obligations, on those subject to them. So on the face of things propositions as to what *ought*, or perhaps we should say *legally ought* to be done, or statements that there is a legal obligation to do this or that, are being made to follow from the statements of fact which establish the existence of the legal system. And this is at odds with the thesis, widely accepted, that you cannot do this. What is surprising is that Hart, in *The Concept of Law*, does not address the matter at all, or at least indicate the existence of a difficulty. This is the more surprising since in his exchange with Lon Fuller the claim is discussed at some length.[13] The point Hart made in that exchange is that even if one concedes the claim that you cannot get 'ought' from 'is', this does not undermine the positivist theory he espouses. It merely affects how one can justify this or that claim as to what the law ought to be. So it does not address the undiscussed problem in *The Concept of Law*.

It is perfectly conceivable that there is some way of getting around the problem—perhaps legal 'oughts' are special, and can be derived from statements of what is the case. Or perhaps legal 'oughts' are best understood as stating the means to a chosen end, analogous to such a statement as 'You ought to hit him harder than that if you have any hope of killing him'. Plainly such problems are intimately connected with the analysis of the nature of legal duties and obligations. Perhaps it was Hart's view that in his Harvard lecture, with its distinguished audience which would have included philosophers, problems associated with non-cognitive theories of ethics needed to be mentioned, but in the type of book he was writing, which was likely to be read mainly by law students, it was best not to enter these deep waters. Here however I merely draw attention to the issue.

The fifth issue concerns the relationship between Hart's rule of recognition and the conventions of legal argument. For underlying Hart's discussion, though never made explicit, is surely Hart's own knowledge and experience of the conventional practice of appellate courts in Britain, and

11. CL 116. 12. CL 292. 13. 624–627.

to a lesser extent the USA.[14] There is nowhere any indication that Hart looked outside his own legal world, for example, to the civil law world, to see what their conventional practices were. In legal argument reasons are given to support this or that putative proposition of law, and much reliance is placed on reasons related to the concept of authority:

> ... [lawyers] try to provide reasons for the correctness of the view they put forward ... Judges, who decide the matter, also offer reasons, by way of justification for their decision, aiming thereby to persuade the legal community that they have decided aright. They do not simply give judgements like oracles ... this is why the law is a rational science: reasons are offered, or at least are supposed to exist where they are not offered, for saying that this or that proposition is correct ... reasons which depend on the concept of authority may refer to some earlier statement of the law, made by a person, or institution, whose statements as to what the law is are regarded as either a conclusive or a very persuasive argument that such a statement is correct. ... Or they may involve reference to an earlier court decision in which the same view was acted on by a judge.

Elaborate attempts have been made to set out what the conventions are, and they feature in standard introductory books for law students, and in more sophisticated fox-inspired treatises. But one trouble is that they are forever changing. And it is worse than that:

> ... the conventions of the legal profession and the courts do not restrict arguments solely to those that can be supported by authority. Confronted with a difficult case courts are prepared to listen to arguments not by authority, but by reason, and what this means is that arguments which appeal to what we may loosely call common sense can be offered to a court; part of the skill of counsel is to have a feeling for when this can be a good move, and when not. 'Common sense' is used here as an embracing term to cover a range of ideas which form part of our shared culture, or the culture of the legal community, and which are regarded as providing good reasons for actions. It would be quite hopeless to attempt to provide a catalogue of such ideas, but they include moral and ethical ideas, ideas of fairness and justice, notions of practical convenience, generalizations about human behaviour or about the world we live in, as well as ideas about the role of courts in society and the limitations under which they should operate. There is therefore no closed list of the sorts of argument that can be addressed to a court. ... The looseness of conventions as to the use of legal authorities, together with the open ended nature of legal

14. Some of the passages which follow are amended versions of a lengthy discussion in my *Invitation to Law*.

argument, and its use of common sense rationality... has this result, that it is not possible to state, in the form of a set of rules, comprehensive reliable tests for telling what the law is.

This means that the law is inherently to some degree uncertain, and that the process of judicial decision cannot ever perfectly conform to the ideal of the rule of law.

Many people, including some lawyers, find this a puzzling and indeed intellectually unacceptable state of affairs; in consequence they have sought to develop theories of law which either minimize the problem, or claim that it does not really exist. Some have argued that unless such tests exist it hardly makes sense to talk of law at all. A prominent writer in this tradition is Ronald Dworkin, who ducks the difficulties by inventing a mythical super judge, Hercules, who sets about the task of finding, lurking coyly in the legal tradition, *The Right Answer To All Legal Problems*. Hercules is an odd choice indeed if you consider some of the labours he undertook, for it is rather difficult to find the equivalent of those stables in the world of the law, though I guess the US system of criminal justice would be a candidate.

Hercules is indeed the jurisprudential equivalent of that great Hollywood invention, Superman, renamed presumably out of deference to the classical tradition. Dworkin's account of how it is done, developed with analogies from literary criticism, and the writing of chain novels, is great reading. Thus there has long been discussion of how many children Lady Macbeth had, and it has been thought that the answer is somehow latent in the text. This idea it is argued can be applied to legal materials so as to tease out the best possible interpretation of them. But you can look in vain in the Shakespearean text for an answer to the question whether Macbeth suffered from athletes' foot. It all gives about as much practical guidance as an invocation to pray for divine guidance and eat nourishing meals, and has not the least connection with anything which goes on in American appellate courts or even in the US Supreme Court. Hedgehogs who write about the process of judicial decision, virtually always confining their attention to familiar appellate courts, share with Hart a reluctance to engage in detailed examination of the actual practices which are followed in them—the kind of work engaged in by CK Allen in his *Law in the Making*. The leading hedgehog whose writings can be used to illustrate this is, indeed, Dworkin. It would be a departure from the basic plan of this book to discuss his views in any detail, but any reader who is interested in this point can see it illustrated in his contribution to the *festchrift* published for Hart's seventieth birthday, 'No Right Answer?'. This contains not a single reference of an empirical character; the discussion takes place entirely in terms of abstract theory.[15] And although Hart insists that his own theory is empirically based he does not anywhere relate this claim to an analysis of the conventional practices which I have described. And this cannot but raise the question whether the existence of Hart's rule of recognition is itself a dogmatic assumption, not wholly dissimilar to Kelsen's *presupposition* of the validity of the grundnorm. He is like someone who is quite certain there is a toad in his garden; he looks everywhere until the only hiding place left is a flat wet stone. He does not lift the flat wet stone to see if the toad is hiding under it; he knows it is there and does not need to look.

The sixth concerns the relationship between the conventions of adjudication which are adopted when appellate courts are confronted with what has come to be called a 'hard' case, meaning a case which is in some way hard to decide.[16] This will involve some limited account of what has been called 'legal science', a legal theory associated with nineteenth century ideas.[17] As I have written elsewhere:

> Doctrinal study and exposition of the law, for example in legal treatises, proceeds on the working assumption, or if you like presupposition, that the law can be set out in the form of a consistent body of principle, rules, definitions, exceptions, etcetera, which can be applied to factual situations so as to generate a single legally correct answer to any problem presented for decision. So the law is all embracing; there are no legal questions, however weird, to which there are no legal answers. Is it a crime to hate hamsters? No. In addition the law must always be consistent; it cannot both be a crime and not a crime to hate hamsters. A further curious assumption is that legal propositions are timeless just as moral propositions are timeless; if it is murder today then it is murder tomorrow. But this assumption has to be modified insofar as arrangements exist for altering the law.... All doctrinal legal reasoning is carried out as if the assumptions of legal science are correct. In

15. PMS Hacker and J Raz (eds), *Law Morality and Society: Essays in Honour of H.L.A. Hart,* Chapter 3. In *Taking Rights Seriously* (1977) the index lists 25 cases cited, all but two of them American. In only one case does the author actually quote what was said in a case.
16. The term comes from the expression 'hard cases make bad law', and in this sense the point being made is that it can be a mistake to make exceptions or qualifications to a law or legal rule simply because in a particular case it leads to a harsh result. Fuller in his exchange with Hart at 661 uses the expression 'hard case' to mean a case which is difficult to decide, and I guess this was normal American usage at this time.
17. For an account see my *Leading Cases* at 4–8 and 96–7.

> an appellate court barristers do not ever get up and tell the court that the problem involved in their case is one to which the law provides no answer, so that they have nothing useful to say and might as well sit down.[18]

As Hart himself put it many years later in his *Postscript:*

> It is true that when particular statues or precedents prove indeterminate, or when the existing law is silent,[19] judges do not just push away their law books . . .[20]

This appears in the context of a discussion by Hart of how seriously the assumptions of legal science are to be taken. *En passant* there is no direct evidence that Hart himself was familiar with nineteenth century theories of legal science; the expression does not appear in any of his writings and I never recall him using it. He does not use it in this passage.

Many people think that the assumptions of legal science are myths, things we pretend to be true, although we know they are not, which assumes that the notions of truth and falsehood can be applied here. They think that the law does not really provide one single correct answer to every question, or alternatively that there is no real way of showing whether it does or does not. Even if this scepticism is justified it is difficult to see how doctrinal legal argument could possibly be conducted unless the assumptions of legal science were accepted at least as conventions as to how we argue about the law. How could one conduct such an argument on the basis that both sides could be right at the same time? Or on the basis that the first question to settle was whether there was a correct answer, and the second would then be to settle the form which a non-legal answer would take. So if these assumptions are myths, they are useful myths, that make law and legal argument and adjudication possible, and similar assumptions underlie many other forms of practical rationality and social interaction, in which, for example, there is an important role for white lies. In the political world the legitimacy of democratic government is to a considerable degree based on myths. As for wars, how could you ever conduct them without myths?[21]

18. From my *Invitation to Law*.
19. It is obscure what this metaphor means. If the law could be silent we should surely have silent lawyers in appellate courts, and who has ever known such a thing?
20. *Postscript* at 273.
21. In Wittgensteinian thought doctrinal legal argument could be characterized as an example of a 'language game', in which you can only participate by adopting the rules of the game. But Hart does not anywhere apply this notion to his discussion of legal reasoning, and Wittgenstein had virtually nothing of interest to say which might be applied to the law.

Central to Hart's theory is the claim that in at least some instances (if you like, paradigm cases) there is indeed a correct answer to a legal question, determined by a rule identified by the rule of recognition, and interpreted in the light of established conventions of meaning. This means that his theory accepts, with qualification, the assumptions of legal science, as being true in a limited number of instances. In his exchange with Lon Fuller, which appeared in the *Harvard Law Review* in 1958, that is at about the time he was writing *The Concept of Law,* his view and Fuller's criticisms of it were more fully developed in a conflict in which neither side won on points, though my own inclination would be to say that Fuller's case was more convincingly presented.[22] Discussion turns on a legislative text using the term 'vehicle' and banning them from parks, and Hart wrote:

> If we are to communicate with each other at all . . . then the general terms we use . . . must have some instances in which no doubts are felt about its application. There must be a core of settled meaning, but there will be, as well, a penumbra of debatable cases in which words are neither clearly applicable nor obviously ruled out.[23]

The use of the expression 'no doubts exist' is curious in that it suggests a psychological test. In another passage he argues that 'the central element of actual law' is to be found in the core cases.[24] In the penumbral cases the judge has 'a choice left open uncontrolled by linguistic conventions'.[25] Essentially, as Fuller points out, Hart's point is that the core meaning, which he presents, with wanton perversity, in relation to the single word 'vehicle', and not in relation to the legislative provision as a whole, is unaffected by either purpose or context.[26] Some objects just jolly well are vehicles, and that's an end of it, their identification as vehicles being determined by the 'common usage' of Oxford linguistic analysis; Fuller briefly cast doubt on this conception, praying in aid Wittgenstein, Russell, and Whitehead.[27]

It is difficult not to suspect that the central claim in Hart's theory is itself no more than a dogmatic presupposition, the toad which must be under the stone, based on an ill-developed theory of language and communication,

22. HFE. And see CL 207–212.
23. HFE 607.
24. HFE 615.
25. HFE 610.
26. See eg HFE at 663.
27. HFE 669. There is an obscure footnote 40 on 668–9; I think the word used in a wholly novel sense must be 'swim'.

which played down the contextual. Perhaps it was derivative of his association with JL Austin and the other Oxford philosophers who sang the praises of ordinary usage. Certainly he does not in *The Concept of Law* offer any empirical or detailed support for his claim, nor is it possible to think of what form that could possibly take. Nor does he provide detailed illustrations; the 'vehicle' is not mentioned. More surprisingly, given Fuller's criticisms, he did not address them in the text of *The Concept of Law;* the exchange is only mentioned in a footnote.[28] Perhaps he felt that he had said what he wanted to say and readers of *The Concept of Law* could if they wished read it all in the *Harvard Law Review*.

The seventh issue concerns Hart's use of the conception of 'the general efficacy of the system'.[29] In the Austinian theory there has to be a general habit of obedience; Hart's theory is similar:

> ... those rules of behaviour which are valid according to the system's ultimate criteria must be generally obeyed ...[30]

Hart has a great deal to say about the notion that legal systems can be viewed rather like living entities, which go through processes analogous to birth, maturity and death. But he never engages in an analysis of what is meant by general obedience to rules of behaviour, which is the state of affairs which satisfies the requirement of general efficacy.[31] Furthermore he does not relate the concept of efficacy to power conferring rules; what is the relevance of the fact that business associates register companies in conformity with the law's requirements? This is a lacuna of some considerable importance. At a commonsense and practical level the world is littered with what are supposed to be independent countries in which it is difficult to say whether they possess legal systems which satisfy the concept of general efficacy or not; it may all depend on which part of the country you happen to have in mind, or what aspect of the law you are interested in, or the level of corruption with which the law is applied. Or is it perhaps enough if there is no rioting in the streets? We lack any conceptual scheme within which to consider the matter. But one wonders whether, if we did, it would be of much help to the officials in the Foreign Office or State Department in offering advice to those travelling abroad.

28. CL 208. 29. CL 105, CL 112. 30. CL 113.
31. What follows is derivative of my *Invitation to Law*, Chapter I.

In the sort of society in which we live it would be thought eccentric to deny that there is a legal system which satisfies the requirement of general efficacy. Notwithstanding areas, such as drug control, when it seems not effective at all, law is pervasive. Thus we have laws to promote racial harmony, and good sex education, and equality between the sexes, and safety at work. Hardly a day passes without a call for new laws to stamp out this or that. Law, like the air we breathe, is all around us; it is with us from the cradle to the grave. But it is with law as it is with air; most of us know very little about the stuff. There is something paradoxical about this phenomenon: a society dominated by laws, populated by individuals who have only the sketchiest knowledge or understanding of the institution which pervades their lives. How can this be?

Part of the explanation is the high degree of specialization in modern society. Take sewage disposal. The participation in sewage disposal by most of us is confined to use, flushing and the occasional employment of the lavatory brush. Where it all goes and how it gets there are mysteries over which we do not trouble our heads. If there is a problem we call in a plumber. It is much the same with the law. When a company is being established company law experts may well be consulted, or their books read, to make sure that the legal requirements are satisfied; once the company is operating recourse to experts will be occasional, when for example some dispute has arisen. And expert knowledge is not confined to a class of professional lawyers. It filters down to many others, to tax consultants, to civil servants, to police officers, to social workers, to doctors, to electricians, and even to professional criminals. Similarly with cooking there is, mercifully, a diffusion of expert knowledge; excellent meals are to be had in private homes. But exceptional cooking does not, except very rarely, originate in private homes. It comes from experts, like the pioneering Elizabeth David, or from professional chefs. Like chefs, lawyers are expert people who devote their working lives to acquiring and selling their expertise to the public, or, as is the case with the judges at the apex of the system, to the state. And, like chefs, they also to some extent create what they sell, and do not simply reproduce what has gone before. In doing so they make the law both more complex and, ideally at least, better. What is puzzling is that even in branches of the law which have been mulled over for many years they never seem to become any clearer, but rather more complicated.

Part of the explanation lies in the fact that much conduct seems to be unaffected by legal rules. Take homicide by way of example. Common sense would suggest that the vast majority of people refrain from homicide for reasons which have nothing to do with the law. They never feel the urge, or feel squeamish, or think it morally wrong, or believe they will go to hell when they die if they have taken a human life.[32] For law is only one of the mechanisms of social control; how we behave is dictated by habits, by traditions, by inherited or instilled inhibitions, by ideals and values, by moral and religious beliefs, by fear of social disapproval, by the desire to be approved and loved. The heavy hand of the criminal law seems to operate only at the margins of social life. Suppose there is a society in which, for the sorts of reason I have listed, the homicide rate is near to zero: does this fact count in some way towards an assessment of the efficacy of the legal system? Or is it just that the legal system is irrelevant?

Part of the explanation may also lie in the fact that, in the sort of society which we think of as being 'law abiding', the passage of laws generates habits and practices, and individuals may conform to such habits and practices, but with little idea of the legal basis for them. Entering Britain regularly through Heathrow or Gatwick I knew what to do—join the correct line, present my passport, smile, refrain from irritating the person in the desk by asking him why he was sitting in front of a notice which claims to be the UK frontier, which seems plainly rubbish, since surely the aircraft from which I have just emerged was not parked in some foreign country. As for the intricacies of immigration law, which presumably underpins what goes on at immigration control, I know, for all practical purposes, nothing. But I know what I used to have to do minimize the horrors of a long, long, day. Again in some of my time in Oxford, the statutes governing the University were kept in Latin, lest anyone be silly enough to be tempted to read them; most academics, and I guess virtually all students, neither knew nor cared about them. All they needed to know about was the derivative practices which applied to them: how to apply for admission, where to turn up for examinations, how to obtain admission to the Bodleian Library by swearing the oath to kindle neither fire nor flame, and obtain a ticket, and so forth. When, in the name of progress, they were translated into English in about 1968 I guess they remained unread much as before.

There is another phenomenon which is relevant here, but one in relation to which we lack any sort of analysis; I shall give it a name, *economical simplification*. Understandably it is one which Hart does not address at all.

32. See below Chapter 7 at 204.

Professionalized law, the sort of law which is the subject of legal argument, for example, in the House of Lords, or now the Supreme Court, is extremely complex, and contentious. Quite recently an essentially trivial dispute in the London Jewish community over the criteria for admission to a faith school occupied the attention of no less than seventeen counsel, days of court time, and heaven knows how much paper. The cost of such a case must have been huge. But 'the law' which is applied and acted upon lower down in the system is quite different. It has got to be simplified and made much cheaper to operate. Cases like the one I have mentioned are only for the wealthy.

I was for many years a lay magistrate, first for Oxford City, then in the Bullingdon Bench in Oxfordshire. I have always claimed it to have been the last true home of the common law; there the gravest of crimes was conceived to be the shooting of a pheasant, destined for death, two days out of season. In a commonsensical way we applied legal conceptions like that of *mens rea*. Did the accused mean to put the bacon in the shopping trolley? But we did not do complex criminal law, with citation of cases; I do not recall ever having seen a law report produced, and the court office probably did not possess any. If that was what anyone wanted they needed to use one of the procedures, such as an appeal by way of case stated, which moved the case to a higher court. Except in very unusual circumstances the law applied by the magistrates was whatever it said in the annually revised multi volume *Stone's Justices Manual*, and that was that. So in a sense the rule of recognition for me and my colleagues was Stone.

Comparative Law

The points I have raised so far all, one way or another, concern the rule of recognition. I shall now move on to some quite different issues. Hart's theory is presented as universal in its application, though this point is only clearly stated in the *Postscript*:

> My aim in this book was to provide a theory of what law is which is both general and descriptive. It is *general* in that it is not tied to any particular legal system or legal culture.[33]

33. At 239.

A striking *lacuna* in *The Concept of Law* is its failure to address the possible relevance to the analysis of the work of the comparative lawyers.

Comparative law as an academic subject is usually said to have begun life in 1900, the date of the first International Congress for Comparative Law in Paris. Apparently the only common lawyer who attended was Pollock. So far as the common law world was concerned the subject had for all practical purposes been invented by Maine; as a branch of general jurisprudence it lurked in the job description of the Corpus Chair from the outset. But none of Maine's successors, apart from Pollock, had exhibited the least interest in the subject. He did devote his farewell lecture to 'The History of Comparative Jurisprudence', but his own contribution to the subject was, as Duxbury has shown, virtually nil.[34] From time to time other scholars did publish books on foreign systems of law, such as Sir William Markby's *Introduction to Hindu and Mohammedan Law* (1906), but Markby was not a comparativist.[35] It was not until 1948 that the Oxford Law Faculty took a positive step towards the development of the subject when Harry Lawson, then a fellow of Merton, was appointed to a newly created chair of comparative law. Lawson was a scholar of great originality and unbounded enthusiasm.[36] Originally educated as a historian, in which he obtained a first in 1921, he switched to the law school and obtained a second first in 1922. He was expert in British constitutional law, and for many years ran a seminar on the drafting of an English constitution which I used to attend, much to my profit. He was also expert in civil law systems and in Byzantine law, and he had a considerable international reputation, both in Europe and the USA. His interests concentrated on legal doctrine; when I first knew him I was working on a doctorate in the history of law reporting, an activity he regarded as a waste of time, and which he urged me to abandon. It was in part under his influence that I embarked on a doctrinal history of contract law. But in Oxford, at least in my time, he failed to establish a significant following of graduate or indeed undergraduate students. Indeed it was outside Oxford, both in the USA or in Europe, where he became prominent. He had been a supporter of Hart's appointment, and in 1953 Hart wrote appreciatively of one of his books, *The Rational Strength of English*

34. See Duxbury 110–116.
35. Also for example RW Lee, *An Introduction to Roman Dutch Law* (1915).
36. There is a charming obituary notice in the OJLS 4:153 (1984); see also ODNB.

Law (1951).[37] Nor did he become seriously engaged in what was to become a major concern of comparative lawyers: the development of schemes which divided up the world's legal systems into distinct families of laws.[38] Here the most influential pioneer so far as the common law world was concerned was probably the French scholar, René David, though in the same year in which he originally published his scheme, a rival scheme was published by Pierre Arminjon, Boris Nolde, and Martin Wolff.[39]

David's *Major Legal Systems in the World Today* was first published in France in 1964, after the publication of *The Concept of Law*; an English version with translation by JEC Brierly appeared in 1968. David had however developed the idea of legal families much earlier than this in his *Traité élémentaire de droit civil comparé* of 1950. Initially he claimed there were five such families: Western Systems, Socialist Systems, Islamic Law, Hindu Law, and Chinese Law. Later he changed his view and decided there were four families: the Romano-Germanic, Socialist Laws, the Common Law and a vague fourth category (essentially 'the rest') of Religious and Traditional Laws, comprising Muslim Law, Hindu Law, the Law of the Far East, including Japanese and Chinese Law and African, and Malagasy Law.[40] His fourth category seems faintly comical. Other scholars have gone, for example, for six or seven.[41]

One such distinct tradition, on whose distinctness almost everyone seems to agree, is Islamic Law, intimately associated with the Islamic faith, though once at the annual conference of the American Society of International Law, at which strange things tended to happen, I listened to a speaker who claimed that there was no such thing as Islamic Law, the notion being a western myth. It was very early in the morning. Islamic law in one form or another is dominant or influential in many parts of the world—for example in Pakistan, Malaysia, Northern Nigeria, Saudi Arabia, and Iraq. And just as there exist differing Islamic religious traditions, so the Islamic legal culture is not everywhere the same, nor of the same importance. Scholars steeped in Islamic learning would tend to emphasize the varied aspects of this tradition,

37. See 'Philosophy and Law and Jurisprudence in Britain (1945–1952)' at 363.
38. He did publish an article on this topic in *Hastings International and Comparative LR* 6:85 (1982).
39. See however K Zweigert and H Kotz, *An Introduction to Comparative Law* (3rd edn 1998) at 65; I do not claim any expertise in the history of the subject.
40. See his *Les Grands Systèmes de droit contemporaines* (9th edn 1988), differing from his *Traité élémentaire de droit civil comparé* of 1950.
41. Thus K Zweigert and H Kötz has six: the Romanistic, the Germanic, the Anglo-American, the Nordic, Law in the Far East, and Religious. I make that six but the authors give a figure of seven.

whilst scholars raised in other traditions may tend to overstate its homogeneity; indeed comparative lawyers are themselves inevitably to some degree prisoners of their own legal culture. But in spite of such potential for disagreement there exists in the world of the Islamic legal tradition a certain and important degree of cohesion of thought. For example it has come to be a basic feature of Western European legal traditions that law and religion belong to separate though perhaps interrelated aspects of culture. Under the Islamic legal tradition this separateness is denied.

So far as *The Concept of Law* is concerned comparative law might as well have never been invented. The idea that perhaps there might exist in the world different concepts of law, associated with different legal traditions, or that one analysis of the structure of a legal system might not be appropriate for all legal systems, is simply never mentioned. A case can be made for saying that Hart's analysis is indeed presented as an example of one size fitting all, but a scholar with the slightest familiarity with the writings of comparative lawyers would surely at least have addressed the point. Hart did not do so, and nothing in his writings suggests he ever developed the least interest in comparative law. And so far as I am aware he never established any working relationship with Lawson, though he did of course establish such a relationship with Tony Honoré, who was very familiar with the diversity of legal traditions. So the silence of *The Concept of Law* is the more surprising.

Yet I have to note that in my time at Michigan we were well provided with comparativists and visitors from China and Japan, but when I tried on a number of occasions to persuade my colleagues to make some serious effort to recruit someone who was expert in Islamic law I made no progress at all. So even those who are in general supportive of comparative law may be somewhat selective.

Hart on Positivism

Hart always identified himself as a positivist and in his exchange with Fuller he insisted on the separation of law as it is and law as it ought to be. He quoted John Austin:

> The existence of law is one thing; its merit or demerit is another.[42]

42. HFE 596.

In the course of his lecture he distinguished five meanings of 'positivism' which he said were 'bandied about in contemporary jurisprudence . . . '.[43] In the text of *The Concept of Law* the conception of positivism is principally discussed in the ninth chapter, 'Law and Morals', where he states that:

> Here we take Legal Positivism to mean the simple contention that it is in no sense a necessary truth that laws reproduce or satisfy certain demands of morality, though they have often done so.[44]

The main drift of this chapter is the argument that legal positivism, as espoused by Hart and earlier by Bentham and Austin, provides a better way of thinking about situations when there are wicked laws. It also develops an idea, presented as 'The Minimum Content of Natural Law'. This argues that certain facts about human beings,[45] together with facts about the world they live in, such as limited resources, *explain* the development of mechanisms of social control, for example the development of systems of sanctions to deal with individuals (with limited altruism) who free ride on the system. If I understand the argument it is that systems of social control which respond to the contingent facts about the human condition can be viewed as conforming to some loosely defined conception of what is natural for human beings. At one point he uses the expression 'natural necessity'. But all this depends on purely contingent facts, and so I suppose is not to be viewed as in any way a logical necessity. There is a curiosity in the structure of the book in that the discussion of the minimum content of natural law might just as well, and perhaps more naturally, have been located in the chapter on 'Law as the Union of Primary and Secondary Rules' in the section 'The Elements of Law'.[46] There is indeed some duplication. Hart's and other writers' accounts of natural law generated a response from John Finnis, whose *Natural Law and Natural Rights* (1980) has been one of the most successful contributions to The Clarendon Law Series.[47]

In the notes to Chapter IX five propositions designated by the expression 'positivism' are reproduced, together with a statement of which of these views is or was held by Bentham, Austin, and Kelsen, or by nobody. Hart

43. HFE 601–2 note 25. 44. CL 185–6.

45. Listed as human vulnerability (for example that they can kill each other), approximate equality (even the strong have to sleep), limited altruism, accompanied by limited understanding and strength of will, and the fact that they share the aim of survival.

46. CL 92.

47. Finnis was a graduate student of Hart, but his doctorate was on aspects of the Australian federal system. He became a fellow of University College in 1966.

thus did not work this analysis into the text of *The Concept of Law*.[48] This is puzzling, but one possibility is that to have done so would have caused him problems over the general structure of his book, and earlier over the structure of his lectures. Another possibility is that after his encounter with Fuller he had begun to have anxieties over the views he had set out in his exchange with him.

One serious defect, as it seems to me, is that Hart nowhere explained the curious sense of positivism which is to be found in Austin's *The Province of Jurisprudence Determined*. It does not appear in his list of the senses of positivism set out either in his exchange with Fuller, or in the notes to *The Concept of Law*. Austin wrote that:

> A law, in the most general and comprehensive acceptation in which the term, in its literal meaning, is employed, may be said to be a rule laid down for the guidance of an intelligent being by an intelligent being having power over him.[49]

He went on to explain, using language which now seems archaic, that the aggregate of laws laid down by political superiors:

> ... is frequently styled *positive* law, or law existing by *position*.[50]

Position here means the action of laying down a law. Austin also thought that what he called *positive morality*, was law by position. Positive morality comprised:

> laws *not* established by political superiors, or are *not* established by political superiors in that capacity or character... [together with] rules set and enforced by mere opinion.[51]

This view involved him in using the notion of *law by position* in an extended way, and the essential underlying idea is that both positive law in the narrow Austinian sense, and positive morality, are the product of human actions (for example a formal act of legislation or a practice of conducting duels in a

48. CL 302. They are: '(1) that laws are commands of human beings; (2) that there is no necessary connection between law and morality, or law as it is and law as it ought to be; (3) that the analysis or study of meanings of legal concepts is an important study to be distinguished from (though in no way hostile to) historical inquiries, sociological inquiries, and the critical appraisal of law in terms of morals, social aims, functions, &c.; (4) that a legal system is a "closed legal system" in which correct decisions can be deduced from predetermined legal rules by logical means alone; (5) that moral judgments cannot be established, as statements of fact can, by rational argument, evidence or proof ("non–cognitivism" in ethics).'

49. Austin (Hart ed) 20. 50. Austin at 12. 51. Austin 11–12.

particular way) and his argument was that since men may be devils or angels it follows that the existence of a law, or the existence of a rule of positive morality, does not entail any view as to its rightness or wrongness. Austin never however developed any sort of analysis of how it could be said that rules of positive morality could be said to have been 'set' or 'laid down' or 'posited'. Or to put it another way he did not try to investigate such issues as the criteria that had to be satisfied before a rule of positive morality could be said to exist as a social rule. Is there for example a social rule in Britain today which requires adolescents to drink to excess on Saturday nights? Nor does he have anything to say on how such rules came into existence.

I have explored the basic assumptions of positivism more fully in my 'The Common Law and Legal Theory', explaining how writers as diverse as Blackstone, Gray, Cross, and Kelsen all subscribed to the idea that all laws owe their status to having been laid down.[52] My essay develops the idea that not all law is the product of actions of laying down the law.

Law and Coercion

That the law and legal institutions have got some connection with coercion seems obvious, and in his account of the salient features of a legal system Hart mentions penalties, compensation, and punishment.[53] The place of coercion in the law is discussed by Hart wholly in terms of the notion of a sanction, a simple example being a liability to punishment for breach of the criminal law. Consequently Hart never gave even the simplest account of the way in which the legal order is supported by coercive force. This support is provided through contract law, through defences to criminal and civil proceedings, and exceptions. If, for example, you are sentenced to a term of imprisonment—a sanction—and decline to go there, prison officers or policemen will drag you there. These state agents of coercion are paid for the work, and given training in subduing prisoners. They are also given suitable equipment, such as stun guns, tasers, or sandbags. A lawyer who, like Hart, practised in the Chancery Division, could well in the

52. 362. Originally published in *Oxford Essays in Jurisprudence*, 2nd Series, 77–99. I am happy to call attention to the fact that Brian Leiter of the Chicago Law School, in his Legal Philosophy Blog, 1 August 2007, notes how he was struck, on re-reading the piece, by 'what a bad paper it is and puzzled, accordingly, by why it is cited so often'. Life is full of mysteries.

53. CL 3.

whole of his career have never seen the use of coercive violence to support the rule of law. Punch-ups are just not a common or even occasional occurrence in the world of the discretionary trust. Persons like myself, with experience as magistrates, only occasionally have had the experience, being present when the panic button is pressed, and mayhem breaks out.

The distinction between sanctions, and the use of coercive force to secure submission to the law, was most dramatically illustrated when Britain still employed capital punishment for murder. Execution was the sanction, and most of those condemned to death submitted without resistance, aware that resistance was useless, or wholly bemused by the horrors of their lot, and by the rituals employed to secure their cooperation. But occasionally the condemned individual fought back—this happened during the Second World War in November 1941 in the case of a German spy, Karel Richter. An account is given by Albert Pierrepoint, the executioner, in his memoirs.[54] After a violent struggle Richter was executed, being overpowered and dragged to the gallows. The Home Office euphemism for such an event was 'mishap', frustrating the normal procedures, designed, at least, to make the process rapid and painless. Now if you or I dragged somebody to a gallows and hanged them we should be in some serious legal trouble, but not Albert and his assistants, for a complicated system of defences and exceptions to legal rules put them in the clear. And in modern legal systems the law does not normally specify with any precision what form and degree of coercive force is permissible over and above providing that it must conform to a test of reasonable necessity, or not be excessive, or something similar. In practice more or less anything goes, and it is rare indeed that any official is punished for the use of excessive force.[55] The limitations are imposed either by political prudence (thus in the Northern Ireland 'troubles' machine guns were never used against rioting crowds, even on Bloody Sunday), or by public opinion, or by accepted ethical considerations. The use of coercive force is typical in riot control, for example when the security forces use baton charges, or rubber bullets, or sometimes real bullets, or tear gas, or water cannon, to disperse crowds; from time to time people die in consequence. This is nothing to do with sanctions.

54. A Pierrepoint, *Executioner Pierrepoint* (1974) 138, 179, FH Hinsley and CAG Simkins, *British Intelligence in the Second World War* (1990) vol IV 97 n.

55. In present day Britain the police may and do kill members of the public and be for practical purposes certain that they will escape a criminal trial, much less a conviction.

The complex and controversial martial law is all very relevant to this.[56] In my military career martial law was no longer relevant, but I received something like twenty minutes instruction during my officer training on how to suppress a riot; mercifully in my time in Nigeria, where I served my national service, there were no riots to suppress. The rule was to issue a warning to disperse, and then select and shoot dead the ringleader, the job being entrusted to a reliable rifle shot. Who amongst my merry men should I have chosen? This proposed killing was not a punishment for disobedience, or for a crime carrying the death penalty, but a mechanism for intimidating the crowd and depriving it of leadership. It had nothing to do with sanctions. Elsewhere I have published a detailed account of the use of coercive violence—shooting with buckshot—to prevent prisoners escaping from working parties outside prison, and of the legal and administrative history of this practice.[57] Death or mutilation was not the sanction provided for escaping, which was a crime with its own less draconian sanction. If the convict in the course of escaping injured a prison guard the sanction might include flogging. It is often said that the modern state monopolizes the use of force, which is quite wrong, as anyone can see who watches a game of rugby football. What it perhaps monopolizes is the ability to differentiate between permissible and impermissible force. Indeed a case could be made for saying that this is a defining characteristic of a legal system as we normally conceive of one. Be that as it may a general theory of law surely needs to provide some satisfactory analysis of the role of coercion, and neither Hart, nor for that matter Kelsen, does so. The explanation may be that we find it uncomfortable to associate law, which is all about order and the control of violence, with the brutish violence which is employed when the going becomes rough.

The Absence of the Common Law

One body of law with which Hart was of course very familiar was the English common law, together with its partner, equity. But the very expressions 'common law' and 'equity' do not ever appear in Hart's text

56. See HREE 58–75.
57. 'Shooting Felons: Law, Practice, Official Culture and Perceptions of Morality' (2005) 32 *Journal of Law and Society* 241.

of *The Concept of Law*, though the word does appear in a quotation from Hume.[58] At the beginning of the chapter on Formalism and Rule-Scepticism there is a very brief account of the distinction between communication of standards by authoritative examples, and communication by 'explicit general forms of language'.[59] Later in the same chapter there is an extremely brief discussion of the use of precedent in English law.[60] So far as equity is concerned, which institutionalized a separation between legal rules, and exceptions and modifications to such rules, it is not very obvious where it could have been mentioned except in the chapter on Laws and Morals,[61] but it does not appear there. For the failure to mention equity I have no firm explanation. Hart may have felt that since it was now governed by rules it required no separate treatment and that its exclusion was deliberate, but there is no way of telling.

The strange failure to engage in any significant discussion of the common law is something I explored in 'The Common Law and Legal Theory', first published in 1973. It can be explained in the following way.[62] Hart conceived of the law as comprising a body of rules identified by a rule of recognition. Throughout *The Concept of Law* he slips into modes of analysis which presuppose that legal rules have authentic texts, or texts whose form is determined by ordinary linguistic usage. He never gives a clear account of how this is supposed to be, and I find the thesis, never explicitly stated, obscure. In his criticism of Kelsen, who had argued that the substance of all laws could be expressed as instructions to officials to apply sanctions in specified circumstances, Hart argues that what he calls the 'recasting'[63] distorts the social function of different kinds of laws or legal rules. But you cannot recast something unless it has already been cast in some textual form or other, and this simply does not work for the common law. Again, throughout *The Concept of Law* Hart discusses uncertainty and the existence of judicial discretion in terms of the interpretation of *texts*, making use of such concepts as 'open texture', 'the core and the penumbra'. He concentrates his attention on supposed features of language, and their relevance to issues of interpretation. None of this works for the common law. Thus in an appellate case raising some common law issue argument does not, except in

58. CL 191. 59. CL Ch VII. 60. CL 134–5. Also see 97.
61. CL Ch IX. 62. *Oxford Essays in Jurisprudence* 2nd Series 77. 63. CL 38–9.

very unusual circumstances where a canonical text has been established,[64] turn on how to interpret the text of a common law rule, but on what the rule is, and what precisely its extension is, and whether it is subject to exceptions, and so forth.

The situation is similar to that which applies, for example, to social rules of polite behaviour. As I have written elsewhere:

> . . . there is in English middle class circles a rule, and one widely respected, that when you are invited out to dinner you arrive bearing a bottle of wine. Not uncommonly the issue arises—what bottle will do? Must it be French? Or will Chilean be acceptable, White or red? Pinot Noir or Merlot? How expensive? Should the bottle be wrapped? If white must it be transported chilled for immediate consumption? Or does this indicate an ungenerous desire to drink some of it oneself? Can one simply return the bottle that one's friends presented last time they were invited to dinner? Surely not. Is a bunch of flowers an acceptable substitute? Or is the rule perhaps not a rule about wine at all, but about gifts more generally; perhaps a box of chocolates would satisfy its requirements. What is the point of the convention anyway, and what guidance does it provide? These problems over the requirements of a social convention have nothing whatever to do with the open texture of language, nor are they solved by attending to the text of a rule, for there is no text, and any pre-prandial discussion is not directed towards establishing a text of a rule, but towards deciding what is to be done to satisfy, in a particular context, the requirements of courtesy and good manners.[65]

Common law adjudication is often like that.

It is noticeable that in spite of the assumption that the rule of recognition can be expressed as a text, coyness is met with over what this text is. Thus Hart comes up with the statement that:

> . . . in the overwhelming majority of cases the formula 'Whatever the Queen in Parliament enacts is law' is an adequate expression of the rule as to the legal competence of Parliament, and is accepted as the ultimate criterion for the identification of law, however open the rules thus identified may be at the periphery.[66]

So an 'adequate' expression is the best we can do. Yet when, to pursue the metaphor, in real life we really need a rule of recognition, for example when we have just eaten a mushroom but suddenly wonder if it was a death cap,

64. For example the rule in *Rylands v Fletcher*, or *Shelley's Case*, the rule against perpetuities.
65. (2006) MichLR 104:1437. I have amended the text.
66. CL 148–153.

we do not need a statement of a rule which is normally adequate, but one that works now. And in cases which raise serious problems over whether something is a law it becomes very complex.

As I have written:

> ... the book [ie *The Concept of Law*] devotes virtually no attention whatever to the working of the common law tradition ... Had he attended to it, Hart might have seen that his central concept, that of a rule of recognition, is an aspirational and idealized way of referring to the fluid conventions of legal argument and justification, one that concentrates on appellate courts, not a description of some kind of metaphysical reality. Common law adjudication has no rules of recognition, written or unwritten. All it has is a set of conventional practices used to demonstrate propositions about what the law is, and the forlorn hope that these propositions may be frozen and encapsulated in some definitive text. And the uncertainties and disagreements as to how one argues the law are not problems about the open texture of the rule or rules of recognition; they are not problems about language. Hart never engaged in any form of empirical study as to how, in the common law tradition, law emerges out of the process of argument and adjudication.[67]

Hart was a hedgehog, not a fox.

Adjudication and the Ideal of the Rule of Law

Most of those who will read this book will have no conception of what a world without the rule of law can be like. Let me give an illustration. One night in the dormitories of my house at Oakham School a number of the younger boys were woken up and beaten with a bamboo cane by one of the prefects, by name 'Murker' Meakin. One was a friend of mine, and he retired back to bed without enquiring why he had been subjected to this painful experience. In fact what had happened was that the hot water for baths had run out, and Meakin had been unable to enjoy one. He blamed the earlier bathers. But what was the use of this information? No school or house rule or even convention existed on the matter; this had never happened before and might never happen again, and one might be woken up and beaten next week for something else entirely. That was life in a world not governed by the rule of law. That was what life was like for many

67. (2006) MichLR 104:1437, 1456–7.

in Hitler's Germany, and it is what life is like for many people in the contemporary world.

In *The Concept of Law* the ideal of the rule of law, under that name, does not ever get mentioned. Theories of judicial decision which claim that it is at least in principle possible to come up with a right answer represent attempts to show that the ideal of the rule of law is attainable, even if this does not happen in every case. Hart's discussion of the rule of recognition is not related to the notion of idealism. This is perhaps unfortunate, since the motivation for theories of this kind is surely to demonstrate that the ideal of the rule of law is *in principle* an attainable ideal in every case, even if in practice it does not always happen. This seems to me to involve two serious mistakes.

The first involves a misunderstanding of the nature of ideals. Ideals may not be in principle attainable; athletes can seek to run faster without supposing that they will in the end achieve the speed of light.

The second involves a complete misunderstanding of the nature of rationality in decision-taking, rationality in decision-taking being entailed by respect for the rule of law. This all belongs in the practical world, in which there are never any conclusive reasons for doing anything at all. Life is like that; no conclusive reasons, though some seem better than others, and others seem bad, and some may seem more or less conclusive. They never in fact are. It all depends on what you know, and what you anticipate, and where you are coming from.

Hart's discussion of all this turns up in the chapter of *The Concept of Law* on 'Formalism and Rule Scepticism', which indicates he was aware of the kind of difficulties I have sketched. Having outlined some of the conundrums surrounding the doctrine of Parliamentary sovereignty he suggests that perhaps one day the courts—presumably he meant the House of Lords—will rule on them:

> The courts will have made determinate at this point the ultimate rule by which valid law is identified.

We now appear to be in a circular argument. What Hart seems to have conceded is not simply that the *meaning* of the rule of recognition, conceived as a text, may, because of open texture and the core and the penumbra, be uncertain, but that *the rule itself*, whatever that means, may be fuzzy at the edges. Making determinate here means crisping up the edges. I do not find this at all easy to follow. What is the difference between crisping up the edges of a rule and saying what the rule is? It's the edges surely that matter. And as for the idea that a court can settle the issue surely the institution of a court and its conventions are themselves creatures of the law.

Hart and Kelsen

There is no doubt that Hart was much aware of the similarities between his theory and that of Kelsen, and he was indeed fascinated by Kelsen. But in *The Concept of Law* discussion of Kelsen is brief[68] and much of it appears in the notes.[69] It is as if Hart did not structure his book, and the lectures on which it was based, in a way which allocated adequate space to the subject. A more basic reason is perhaps the fact that Kelsen's legal theory, though presented as universal, belongs to the civil law tradition, and is for this reason alien to the common law tradition to which Hart belonged. For Kelsen the source of law was always legislation; in the common law world it is not—a fact that would have influenced Hart even though he never developed a theoretical understanding of the common law system. The basic enterprise on which Kelsen embarked was quite different from Hart's. It was to develop a theory which showed that an objective legal science, purified of all subjective and ideological elements, was possible. In Vienna, where he lived and worked until 1929, his ideas were exciting and controversial. But translated into a different context his work seemed less exciting. For in the common law world the possibility or even desirability of an objective legal science, in the sense understood by Kelsen, has long been as dead as the dodo. Naturally Kelsen never concerned himself with those attitudes to law which have dethroned any idea that a body of law can be pure and autonomous. In Kelsen's scheme of thought the USA does not really have law at all; unfortunately I do not think he ever explained what he did think about the legal system of his adopted country. It requires considerable intellectual effort to meet Kelsen on his own terms; I suspect he is more often praised than studied. Hart seems not to have been able to decide what quite to do about him in *The Concept of Law*. And insofar as his book was directed primarily at law students he could be pretty sure that for many,

68. CL 35–42 contains the longest discussion in the text.
69. CL 292–5 contains a long discussion in the notes.

though not all of them, Kelsen's pure theory was something which belonged to the stratosphere.

Cyclopean Attitudes: Hart on the Pre-legal World[70]

Hart offers a very brief picture of a regime of customary law, though he prefers not to use this term. Under such a regime members of the society will in general have what he calls the internal attitude to the customary rules; they will accept the rules as imposing obligations upon themselves and on other members of the society. Hart presents the transition from the pre-legal world, in which the primary rules do not form a legal system, to the legal world as involving the supplementation of a regime of primary rules with power conferring rules, comprising a secondary rule or rules of recognition, change and adjudication. Hence I offer the following piece of doggerel:

> Said the jurists those primitive fools.
> Waste their time chipping flints into tools,
> If they'd only read Hart,
> They'd abandon the art,
> And formulate secondary rules.

For this he has been criticized.

> You jurists have got it all wrong.
> We've had secondary rules all along,
> Telling Susan that Harry,
> Is OK to marry,
> So long as she doesn't wait long.

The criticisms embodied in this doggerel were first developed in relation to Hart's account by LJ Cohen, who derived them from the anthropological literature.[71] By way of example one can compare the account given of the Trobriand Island culture by Bronislaw Malinowski in his *Crime and Custom in a Savage Society* (1926) with Hart's picture of such a society.[72] Indeed if

70. CL 91–99.
71. See Cohen's review of *The Concept of Law* in *Mind* (1962) 71:395 at 410—with references to the existence of rules relating to marriage, property, and contract in early forms of society.
72. Hart does not mention the blood feud. There is so far as I know no book dealing with the feud in general. Accounts are scattered in, for example, writings such as Thesiger's *Arabian Sands*.

you do so it is difficult to believe that Hart ever read the book, or other works by him at all carefully.[73] There are basic problems with Malinowski's writings. The first is that you just have to take his account of the culture on trust. He engaged in what came to be called participant observation, but we have only the scantiest account of what he observed and how, through his book on *The Sexual Lives of Savages* apparently did involve plenty of participation. The second is that he set out his views on peoples he cheerfully categorized as 'savages', as was normal in his time, in a polemical form, as attacks on what had then been orthodoxy, summed up in the catch phrase 'custom is King, nay tyrant, in primitive society'.[74] Nobody, it was claimed, ever broke the rules. The third is that although he has much to say on the legal rules of the islanders it is wholly obscure whether he is using a concept they, who have never taken a course in jurisprudence, use, or one he imposes on the material. The fourth is that it is very difficult to use his writings in tandem with, for example, those of other anthropologists, such as Evans-Pritchard, since different anthropologists ask different questions, and use different conceptual schemes. Both writers have much to say on the law and the legal, but employ radically different conceptions of law.[75]

I do not propose to discuss the anthropological literature except to say that in terms not of rules, but of institutions, and Hart was weak on institutions, early forms of society have often been described which appear to lack anything which we would conceive of as a law-making body. There will be mechanisms for reacting to violations of customary practices, such as the feud, and for the resolution of disputes, for example song duels, but there may not exist anything which we conceive of as adjudication.[76] This was surely the point Hart was making, though perhaps it could have been better presented along the lines I have sketched. He nowhere attempted to analyse the conception of adjudication.

For Albania where the feud still exists and a start is E Durham, *High Albania. A Victorian Traveller's Balkan Odyssey* (PB 1968) and *The Unwritten Law in Albania* (1854) by M Hasluck (ed JH Hutton). The conduct of the feud is supposed to be regulated by a fifteenth century code known as the Kanun of Lek. See also I Kadare's novel *Broken April*.

73. In particular *Argonauts of the Western Pacific* (1922).
74. I have given an account of this orthodoxy in 'R. S. Rattray and Ashanti Law' in *Legal Theory and Legal History* (1987) 403 at 417–421. Derived ultimately from Maine its chief exponents at this time were RR Marett, ES Hartland, and Lord Avebury.
75. See also his *Argonauts of the Western Pacific* (1922).
76. Malinowski at 115 and 118 briefly describes the feud (*lugwa*) and its composition by payment of *lula*. He gives accounts of only two gatherings as mechanisms for the resolution of disputes; see 60 and 102–4, and seems relatively uninterested in dispute resolution.

Hart's knowledge of the anthropological literature was certainly scanty, and I never recall his discussing any such literature. In the notes to *The Concept of Law* he cites a small number of books, the citations being somewhat random, and without the provision of any context.[77] I suspect his basic source was Allen's *Law in the Making*. There is for example no indication of the radical significance of Malinowski's work. What is especially cyclopean is the reference to E Evans-Pritchard's *The Nuer*. The full title was indeed *The Nuer: a Description of the Modes of Livelihood and Political Institutions of a Nilotic People*.[78] The note suggests that he merely relied on a quotation in Gluckman, *The Judicial Process among the Barotse* (1955). *The Nuer* contains a considerable discussion of the Nuer political system, and of whether the Nuer can be said to have law. Evans-Pritchard was at this time Professor of Social Anthropology in Oxford, and a fellow of All Souls, a few moments away from University College. It is quite plain that Hart never discussed the matter with him when writing *The Concept of Law*, or in all probability ever. He lived in a different cave. I myself have to plead guilty too; I never suggested asking him to the Hart group, and only talked to him once about the Nuer over a pint of beer in the Mitre Hotel. In retrospect it seems little short of bizarre.

Yet in a roundabout way Hart's inadequate discussion led me to incorporate anthropological material in jurisprudence courses. It encouraged me to read widely in the literature and to discuss it with a friend who was familiar with much of it, and when in Ghana I became interested in the life and work of RS Rattray, and eventually published an article on him in my *Legal Theory and Legal History* (1987). And in the faculty was Gordan Woodman, expert in customary law, and Justice Ollennu, also expert in some aspects of the subject. I used material on the Nuer once as the opening material in a legal philosophy course at the Chicago Law School, and by way of making a start on the subject it could hardly be bettered. Do the Nuer have law? What was the role of the leopard skin chief, was it mediation but

77. See CL at 292–3, citing BD Malinowski, *Crime and Custom in Savage Society* (1959), AS Diamond, *Primitive Law* (1935), KN Llewellyn and EA Hoebel, *The Cheyenne Way* (1941). Karl Llewellyn never once visited the Cheyenne, adopting a common attitude amongst US law professors, who know the answers in advance. Also M Gluckman, *The Judicial Process among the Barotse of Northern Rhodesia* (1955) (published with an introduction by Goodhart) and EE Evans-Pritchard, *The Nuer* (1940).

78. Evans-Pritchard also wrote *Kinship and Marriage Among the Nuer* (1951) and *Nuer Religion* (1956).

not adjudication? What was the role of the feud?[79] Sometimes in other courses I added material on the Masai, revered by some Europeans as *Noble Savages* because of their disdain for western culture. But I needed material on a much simpler society, so I added text and film of the Netsilik Esquimaux of Pelly Bay by Asen Balikci, which recreated their earlier way of life, and material indicating that their lives then were no idyll, and could involve homicide, the wife of the victim having little option but to marry her husband's killer. Does it make sense to think of them as having simply established *practices*, such as those governing the cutting up of a seal, or *customs*, based on gender roles, or what? Does it matter? Later, to give a picture of Malinowski's savages, we watched together the hilarious documentary *Trobriand Island Cricket*, in which the islanders set out to rubbish the white man's cricket, and succeed. But by this time their indigenous culture had been radically affected by western influences.

So it was that Hart's work in the end encouraged an interest which might otherwise have never developed.

Locke and the Pre-legal World

Hart explains the supplementation of primary rules by secondary rules in terms of 'defects' in a regime of primary rules. He specifies uncertainty, the static character of the rules, and the inefficiency of social pressure to conform. He then argues that:

> ...only a small community closely knit by ties of kinship, common sentiment, and belief, and placed in a stable environment, could live successfully by such a regime of unofficial rules.[80]

Homo sapiens has been around now for something like 200,000 years, overlapping, and we are now told, interbreeding with the Neanderthals from around 150,000—35,000 BC. For virtually the whole of this time we have, so far as we know, lived under regimes of what we usually call custom, or settled practice,[81] what Hart here calls unofficial rules. And we have done just fine, notwithstanding a fair amount of homicide, surviving in almost

79. Ch IV generally but esp 150–162 (on the feud) and 162–172.
80. CL 92.
81. CL 92 for Hart's explanation of why he does not use the term 'custom'.

incredibly demanding conditions. The claim that such regimes were defective sounds like some empirical claim, but it plainly cannot be anything of the kind, and Hart offers no evidence whatever to support it. There is of course a very considerable anthropological literature on all this, with elaborate studies, for example, of Australian aboriginal peoples, but Hart makes no reference whatever to it. There is also a literature which seeks to explain how acephalous, headless societies, societies that is with no recognized central authority, develop one.[82] One is left wondering what the nature of the claim is supposed to be. It surely cannot be viewed as self-evidently true. And further to this there is something surprising about an analysis of the concept of law which so plays down regimes of custom. Of Hart's predecessors in the Oxford chair Vinogradoff was seriously interested in customary law, and Allen in *Law in the Making* has two chapters on the subject, of a largely theoretical nature.[83] In Allen's 1958 edition there is some scanty reference to anthropological literature, with a citation to Diamond's *Primitive Law*, Gluckman's *The Judical Process among the Barotse,* and some writings on Hindu Law.

Hart's picture of the nature of customary law portrays it as comprising a body of rules which have in common only the fact that they are the rules which a particular group accepts, and they will form a set of rules, lacking any further identifying mark.[84] His picture of a regime of customary law is simplistic in the extreme, since customary law is everywhere intimately associated with the culture and beliefs of the society in question; individuals do not simply do this or that because that is what everyone else does, but because there exist good reasons in their culture for conformity. Thus in Ashanti customary law it is a bad idea to have sexual intercourse out in the bush since it upsets the ancestral spirits. And it is a very bad idea to say 'I mention Thursday' or 'I mention Saturday', since this reference to a military disaster upsets them even more, and whoever did this was at risk of being attached to a log with a knife through his tongue.[85]

82. eg L Mair, *Primitive Government* (1962).
83. Chs I and II.
84. CL 92.
85. See RS Rattray, *Religion and Art in Ashanti* (1927) Ch XXII. I have mislaid my copy of his *Ashanti Law and Constitution* and no reliance should be placed on the account here given; the point is merely that customary law has its own rationality. It was this that was denied by the earlier anthropologists whose views were attacked by Malinowski; they claimed that primitive law was beset by irrationality.

To a historian a critical stage in the evolution of a form of society governed by law as we now understand it seems to involve the development not so much of rules but of institutions, which have come to be called courts, which enjoy the power of adjudication. It is out of such institutions that legislation, originally not clearly differentiated from adjudication, emerges. Back in the time of Henry II (1154–1189) there were clerks in the royal entourage who specialized, as stand-ins for the King, in managing dispute resolution. They somehow acquired a power to judge, power over litigants, not power merely derived from their consent. They were neither arbitrators, nor umpires, nor mediators. They were judges. Institutions receive little attention in Hart's legal theory, and the explanation may well lie in the fact that his knowledge of the history of the common law when he wrote *The Concept of Law* was very limited.

Peter Fitzpatrick has drawn my attention to the fact that Hart's account of the defects in the regime of the pre-legal world and the remedies for it is extremely similar to Locke's account of the transition from a state of nature to civil society in *The Second Treatise on Government*.[86] There the 'pre-legal world' appears as 'the state of nature', in which men are subject not to 'primary rules' but to 'the law of nature'. But this does not work well since many may be biased and may not know much about natural law. What they need is a system of impartial adjudication, and a system under which there is an alternative to perilous attempts to enforce the dictates of natural law by individuals. Locke could have been thinking of the feud but does not say so. What is needed is a power of enforcement organized by the community. Like Hart, Locke claims that his account is empirically based, and that men are quickly driven into the formation of civil society. This is, as I have said, an error. Locke's view is based on a view as to what, in the very nature of things, is bound to come about. The idea that early man, in an interval between bringing in the elks, decided to establish civil society, seems comical.

The similarities are so striking that it is clear that ultimately Hart's account is derivative. But I am not of course suggesting devious conduct. As I write this it is perhaps 25 years since I last read a word of Locke, and it may well be

86. Paras 124–131 of Chapter IX, in the 1966 edition by JW Gough at 63 and ff. See P Fitzpatrick, *Modernism and the Grounds of Law* (2001) esp at 98. In accordance with the plan of this book I do not discuss Fitzpatrick's incisive analysis and criticism of Hart set out in this book or in his *The Mythology of Modern Law* (1992).

that Hart had never looked at *The Second Treatise on Government* for as long. There is no reference to Locke in *The Concept of Law*. It is by no means unusual for academics to forget where they first got an idea from. There is a brief mention of Locke in *Punishment and Responsibility*, but not one relevant here, and discussion of George Paul's understanding of Locke's concept of property, presumably as set out in Chapter 4. So far as I am aware Hart never lectured or gave classes on Locke.

Cyclopean Attitudes: International Law and Human Rights

The discussion of international law in *The Concept of Law* occupies the last chapter of the book, and I have no substantive points to make about what it says. At this time the Professor of International Law was Humphrey Waldock, who, like Evans-Pritchard, was based in All Souls. He had before the war been a fellow of Brasenose, and had published a book on mortgages. During the war he became in effect the legal adviser to the Admiralty on issues of international law. In 1947 he was appointed to the Oxford chair. He went on to become a judge on the International Court of Justice (1973–81); he presided over the court from 1979. For Waldock international law was an aspect of diplomacy, summed up in a remark he once made to me:

> It's all done in the corridors you know.

I have no private information on the relationship between Hart and Waldock; they certainly would know each other fairly well, for example in relation to the work of the OUP, both being Delegates of the Press. But had their relationship been a close one academically it seems to me inconceivable that at some point or other the conversation would not have come around to discussion of the post war human rights movement, in which Waldock was much involved. *The Universal Declaration of Human Rights* had been adopted back in 1948, and the European Convention was negotiated in 1949–1950, the United Kingdom ratified in 1951, and the Convention came into force in 1953.[87] The first interstate case under the Convention

87. On what follows see HREE *passim*.

was brought by Greece in 1955 over the means used to suppress the EOKA insurrection in Cyprus. Waldock was closely involved in this, and in a second related case, as a member of the Commission established under the Convention. He later presided over the Commission[88] in the first case to come before the European Court of Human Rights, *Lawless v Ireland* (1957–1961). He was President of the European Court of Human Rights from 1971–1974. Yet in the whole corpus of Hart's writings the subject of human rights is never once explicitly mentioned, not even in Hart's 1955 article, 'Are There Any Natural Rights?'.[89] It would appear that Hart had absolutely no interest in the matter. This is not easy to explain. One possible explanation is that English professional legal culture was profoundly hostile to the whole notion of codes of legally protected natural or human rights.[90] And as I have written elsewhere:

> ...I was a law student in Oxford from 1951–1954,[91] and do not recall [the convention] ever being mentioned. Indeed up to the time I left Oxford, in 1972, there was no such thing as a course on human rights, and there was no professor of the subject until 1999. The British legal profession in general neither knew nor cared about it; it was, for many years, of no significance for legal practitioners.[92]

The first full examination question to be set explicitly on the subject, 'What progress has been made in developing international rules to protect human rights?', appeared in the international law examination paper only in 1968. However back in 1951, the year the UK ratified, an opportunity was given for candidates to write on the concept of human rights. This was probably put in by Norman Marsh. There then followed a gap of 17 years.[93]

Another possible explanation is that issues connected with the conception of human rights then surfaced as issues related to the conception of natural law; it is simply a matter of fashions in usage. Thus Finnis in his *Natural Law and Natural Rights* writes:

> Almost everything in this book is about human rights ('human rights' being a contemporary idiom for 'natural rights': I use the terms synonymously).[94]

88. He was President of the Commission 1955–62. At this time the UK did not accept the jurisdiction of the Court.
89. (1955) *Philosophical Review* 64:175.
90. For detailed discussion see HREE, esp 10–41.
91. I did not however take a course in International Law.
92. HREE 809.
93. See above Chapter 2 at p 58.
94. 198.

This seems to me first of all to neglect a significant feature of the post war European human rights movement, which pressed for the establishment of *institutions* for the juridical protection of specified rights, not merely some finite or open ended list of natural rights. This eventually led to the development of a jurisprudence of such rights. In the second place it was no doubt the case that some of those involved in the negotiations would have been influenced by ideas associated with Catholic natural law teachings, which they would learn both in their education as Catholics, or through sermons and the like. And the provision of the First Protocol on education was in part motivated by the Church's desire to preserve those divisive institutions now called faith schools. But in the course of the negotiations, and I have waded through a huge corpus of documents, I never came across a single use of the expression 'natural law' or 'natural rights'. In the third place Finnis develops in his book an elaborate theory of natural law and natural rights which I have no wish or competence to criticize, it being based in part on an analysis which involves identifying a basic form of good: knowledge, and other basic goods or values.[95] The connection between his theorizing and the European (and international) human rights movements escapes me. There is simply no evidence whatever, and I am an evidence man, that the concepts he employs were part of the intellectual baggage of the negotiators either in Europe, or in the United Nations. Perhaps they should have been, but they were not. And there is plenty of evidence from the archives of the ideas which were held by those involved. In my book on the subject I have tried to explain the ideological underpinnings of the human rights movement, principally the European movement, and it had nothing to do, for example, with concepts such as the basic forms of good, which include play and friendship.[96] So obvious is this that I am nervous lest I am missing the point. Finnis does briefly discuss the United Nations Universal Declaration, the 1966 Covenants, and the European Convention, deploying his concept of the common good, but his discussion pays no attention to evidence.[97] Perhaps the idea is that those involved were *really* motivated by the scheme of thought presented by Finnis even if they did not realize this, or should have been. And I suppose

95. Chapters III and IV.
96. HREE, but this book did not investigate, except very incidentally, the archives of other governments involved.
97. 211–15.

that in some vague sense we are all in favour of whatever furthers the common good—clean water for example, and compassion, and so forth. You cannot really openly come out in favour of the common bad, however much that is arguably your true position, one held I suppose by people like Hitler, Stalin, Chairman Mao and Kissinger, to name but a few candidates.

In addition the term 'natural rights' carries with it baggage which can differ from the baggage associated with 'human rights'; for example it can be intimately connected with religious belief, as it is in Finnis' writings. Human rights were never discussed in the Hart group, and my own interest in the subject long post-dates my leaving Oxford. My memory here may be wrong, but I do not recall Finnis ever attending and much of the focus of his work was on commonwealth law during my Oxford time.

Socialist Theories of Law

Hart's sympathies were with mildly left wing views and, even if for this reason only, one might expect that in *The Concept of Law* there would have been at least a mention of Marxist legal theory. There is not a word. Any explanation of this must be speculative. One is that in a book written primarily for Oxford law students, few of whom would have any knowledge of Marxism, this would have been inappropriate. Another possible explanation is that Hart thought that although Marxist theory claimed that in the Marxist nirvana law would simply wither away, and no longer be needed, they nevertheless meant by law, that is to say, made use of the same concept of law, as those who were not of the same persuasion.

A third possible explanation lurks in the much criticized Chapter IX, Law and Morals, where Hart develops his theory of the minimum content of natural law. Thus Hart quotes Hume:

> Human nature cannot by any means subsist without the association of individuals: and that association never could have place were not regard paid to the laws of equity and justice.[98]

Hart's argument is that given certain facts about human beings, including their general wish to survive, certain recognized rules of human conduct, for example, some general prohibition of killing, may be necessary to

98. CL 191, from Hume's *Treatise on Human Nature*.

further the aim of survival.[99] At its most abstract level the claim here must be that although particular laws may be evil, and indeed whole legal systems may take this form, law in some minimal sense is essential to:

> ... social arrangements for continued existence, not with those of a suicide club.[100]

But he goes on to argue that the protection which these rules of human conduct may not be extended to all members of the society, using the example of slave owning societies.[101] According to Hart's view law, in some minimum and unanalysed sense, to put the point crudely, A Good And Necessary Thing. And this is reflected generally in the text of *The Concept of Law*, which nowhere mentions iconoclastic views, such as the claim that it is in the very nature of law that its function is, for example, to further the interests of the dominant class, or in the global world the dominant countries, and keep the lumpen proletariat in subjection and poverty. Currently this is the end product of the American hegemony. And you have only to look around the world to see that such views cannot be rejected out of hand.

Let me give one trivial example. When I worked in Ghana the police used to run out of money towards the end of the month, so they would stop vehicles on the road, point out that they did not conform to regulations over lights, brakes, etcetera—virtually no vehicles did or indeed could, given the shortage of spare parts—and they would then take a bribe and let the vehicle proceed on its way. Was this a Good Thing or a Bad Thing? What was the function of the law? Road safety? Happy police? On one occasion a policeman tried it out on me; I was on the way to see the Chief Justice so I brought him with me to discuss the matter. On arrival he fled. But most people had no alternative but to pay up. Law here is being used as a mechanism for illegality. Some sort of fundamental contradiction there!

99. See CL 193–200.
100. CL 192.
101. CL 200. Hart's discussion of the role of law in such societies is brief and the notes make no reference to the literature, which has since then burgeoned.

7

Judging a Pioneer

It is I think generally agreed that Hart's *The Concept of Law* ranks as a 'classic' contribution to analytical jurisprudence, whatever that is supposed to mean. There have been dissenting voices, but they have been few and far between.[1] The mere fact that it is still in print and selling after all these years must I suppose tell us something. There is of course a considerable secondary literature from critics of Hart's theory of law, but these critics take the original work seriously. There are, however, many legal academics who view the enterprise on which Hart was engaged as a complete waste of time and effort. If you decide to give a paper on some aspect of this subject in a law school you at once meet the yawn factor. There are others who think both that analytical jurisprudence of the kind pursued by Hart is a waste of time, and that some form of sociological enterprise is more to the purpose. Finally there are those who, like DJ Galligan, think there is room for both.[2]

Why did Hart Write the Book?: *The Disease*

Some years ago I became embroiled in a battle with the Inland Revenue, in which they attempted to bully me by a process not far short of blackmail out of large sums of money, none of which I in fact owed to them. The technique adopted is to demand, quite arbitrarily, some vast sum (in my case around £90,000), and then haggle; eventually the sensible course is to settle when the sum has been reduced to a point at which it is no longer worth the time and expense of fighting. In my case we got it down to

1. Lacey at 232 gives entertaining examples, and the new *Oxford Companion to Law* has another.
2. See Galligan Ch I.

£11,000. There had never been any suggestion that I had been in any way dishonest. A fraught meeting took place in London at which the tax men demonstrated their complete ignorance of the tax treaties between the UK and the USA; I was accompanied by my accountant who on a similar occasion had to intervene to prevent his client from attacking the officials from the Revenue. The question arose as to why academics wrote books; were they bound by contract to do so? I explained that for many writing books, or beginning and usually never finishing books, or thinking up and working out schemes for possible books, and suggesting subjects for books to others, for example one on *The Concept of the Noble Savage*, or a novel under the title *Bitter Pith*, was a sort of illness, and one from which I suffered. Indeed at the time of writing, in addition to schemes, I have two substantial books in an unfinished state, one on *The Common Law Tradition*, and another on *The Battle of Agincourt*. Other academics actually complete books at an incredible speed, an example being my friend Richard Posner. Another example is the late AL Rowse, author of more than a hundred books; sometimes three or more would appear in a single year. For some reason my explanation reduced the tension, as did my explanation that it was wholly impossible to specify the hours which academics devoted to thinking about their subject; they wanted to determine what time I spent in England on this or that project, and what in the USA. I explained that this was potty; like monks, who spend all their waking hours in the service of God, so do serious academics never stop brooding over their subject. Hence any attempt to allocate specific hours to this or that piece of academic work was simply silly. For some reason all this reduced the tension, coffee was served, and no violence ensued. I did however consider the possibility of incinerating the offices which housed my opponents, but decided that this would be both difficult to achieve without the risk of detection, involve serious breaches of the criminal law, and be contrary to Austinian positive morality.

Hart was not a person who suffered from this illness; he only ever wrote one book, and although he worked for many years on a postscript to it, he never apparently began work on any other book. It is possible to take the view that his *Law, Liberty and Morality* (1962), a slim volume of 83 pages, counts as a book, as Lacey says.[3] It contains the text of three lectures delivered at the Stanford Law School; its genesis was not a decision to

3. 259.

write a book on the relationship between law and morals, but a decision to accept an invitation to deliver three lectures on the subject.[4] Lacey gives an account of the writing of the lectures; there is no suggestion that Hart thought he was writing a book. Two were fully written out and the third apparently only in note form. It was of course normal for prestigious lectures to be delivered from a written text.[5]

So why did he write the book in the first place? His own explanation when interviewed in 1988 was that:

> Shortly after I had been elected to the chair in 1953 the undergraduates gave me a party and we had a very jolly time. And they said, 'What we want is a book about law—telling us what law is. Why don't you write one?' So I did.[6]

This is a good story but somewhat simplistic. There surely were a number of other factors involved.

The first is that Hart had been elected to the chair on the basis of a very scanty record of publication, and an idea was then current that a professor ought to have written at least one book—we have seen how Goodhart cobbled together an offering so as to make his appointment seem respectable.[7] The second is that the publication of a book, based on his lectures, and one accessible to law students (and anyone else interested) would further the general object underlying his election and clean up what Robert Heuston called 'the slum of English jurisprudence'. The third was that having been elected to the chair he may well have felt that he needed to write a book to establish his credentials as a jurist, not simply in Oxford, but also elsewhere in Britain and the USA. Then there were his philosophy colleagues to consider too; Ryle had established his reputation through his *The Concept of Mind*. Hart's choice of title echoed this. And one cannot but suspect, although there is no direct evidence, that he may have hoped that he was going to produce 'the great book' which would firmly establish his reputation. Such books constitute the crock of gold at the end of the rainbow. But some writers are indeed motivated by this phantasy. In my own case I first fell victim when working on my *In the Highest Degree Odious*. Wrong.

4. Lacey 256.
5. I suppose a case could be made for treating *The Report of the Committee on Relations with Junior Members* (1968), much of which Hart wrote, as a sort of book. See below.
6. Interview at 281–2.
7. See above Chapter 1 at p 34.

The Clarendon Law Series

Then there was the fact that Hart, who became a delegate (rather like a director) of the OUP only in 1960, had persuaded the press to establish The Clarendon Law Series under his general editorship. At this time the law editor was the scholarly Peter Sutcliffe.[8] When the OUP ran into some serious financial problems he rang me to express horror that there were accountants loose in the building, and they were sacking the tea ladies. He would have strongly supported Hart's proposal. The credo was thus stated:

> This is a series of general introductions to different fields of law and jurisprudence designed not only for the law student but for the student of history, philosophy, or the social sciences, and the general reader interested in some aspect of the law. The aim of the series is to provide not a substitute for legal textbooks but a general perspective of legal ideas and problems which will make their detailed study more rewarding.

The first volume to appear was Lawson's *Introduction to the Law of Property* (1958) and this was followed in 1961 by PS Atiyah's *Introduction to the Law of Contract* and by Cross's *Precedent in English Law* (1961). Many have indeed been introductions to legal subjects, intelligently written and readable, displacing to some extent the traditional legal treatises; also they presented the author's personal approach to each subject, and did not simply summarize views of other writers.[9] Books, Hart thought, should have a thesis, and it should be the thesis of the author. Some were of a more theoretical nature. Having established the series Hart must have felt obliged to contribute to it, and his *The Concept of Law* was in the event the third volume to appear. Many of them were highly successful and went into numerous editions.[10]

It would be difficult to overstate the contribution which The Clarendon Law Series has made to legal education in the common law world. But not in the USA. The differences between US academic culture and that of the rest of the common law world, which explains this, is very relevant to the

8. He wrote an informal history of the OUP.
9. Hart detested such works; see his ferocious review of *Dias and Hughes on Jurisprudence* (1957) in (1958) 4 JSPT L 143.
10. For example Wade's *Administrative Law* (1971) and Nicholas' *Introduction to Roman Law* (1962). Lawson's *The Law of Property* in its second edition was edited by Bernard Rudden.

continued success of *The Concept of Law*. The authors of these works came from a highly literate tradition, in which the writing of scholarly monographs was a prestigious activity, and in which a press like the OUP was prepared to encourage and indeed if need be subsidize their publication.[11] American legal academics mainly publish articles in the multifarious law reviews, most of them student edited, and if they really want to make their mark (and if successful a lot of money) they produce casebooks. Such works contain mangled extracts from cases, articles, and books, interspersed with commentary; some come with teacher's manuals, with further commentary and explanation. Compiled by able lawyers from the top law schools there is indeed much to admire in these strange and in some ways repulsive works. But if you teach one of the main first year courses you have no choice but to use one. In the many years I taught a first year property course at Michigan I used a casebook which was originally the work of Jim Krier and the late Jesse Dukeminier.[12] Casebooks commonly do not simply provide material for class discussion, but advance some thesis or other as to how the subject should be conceived. Thus Krier is an enthusiast for the economic analysis of law. I love books, but it is difficult to fall in love with a book which is a literary monstrosity, and for my casebook I always had an ambivalent relationship as I struggled to use the material provided in it to provide my students with a legal education. And I lamented the fact that I could not require my students to read an American equivalent to The Clarendon Law Series volumes on property law, though occasionally collections of essays were available for some topics. My students were condemned to purchasing various forms of degenerate nutshells, study guides, flashcards and the like.

But some leading professors do write monographs, some of them able pieces of work, others rubbish, like Gilmore's *The Death of Contract*, others eccentric, like Richard Epstein's *Takings: Private Property and the Power of Eminent Domain* (1985). Indeed Epstein has written numerous monographs. Richard Posner is a compulsive publisher of monographs. But nobody has to date set out to publish a monograph which will displace Hart's *The Concept of Law*, which is in some ways curious. His principal critic, Dworkin, has concentrated on writing about adjudication, and whatever their merits his

11. Some volumes will have earned considerable royalties. But in general scholarly monographs can also provide a return in that they enhance the author's academic credentials and thus lead to jobs. None of the monographs I have written have earned large sums in royalties.

12. It is still going strong with an editorial team under Krier's supervision. Dukeminier was a guru on future interests and conceptual complexities.

writings have never filled the niche occupied by *The Concept of Law*, which serves principally as a punchbag.

The Casebook System of Legal Education

It is conceivable that the system of legal education adopted in American law schools has been a factor. The theory of the case book system of legal education is that it is to be the basis for cooperative and intellectually challenging class discussion, but the reality of the matter is that the professor, facing a class with as many as 90 students, talks most of the time. And if laptops are permitted they copy down whatever the professor says, unless they are whiling away the time watching movies or shopping online. Other tensions can develop; on one occasion I had to intervene to prevent a fight between two students who had come to hate each other. But fisticuffs are rare; what most of the students like is to be told what the right answer is, so that they can reproduce it in the examination; over their grades the professor has for practical purposes total control. So who can blame them? To be sure the abler students read more widely, but the time spent in classes discourages this. In the Michigan Law School, students in their first year spend about 13 hours each week in classes, and about two more with their legal writing instructor, for whom preparation is needed too. For classes they mainly prepare carefully, not wishing to look stupid if 'called on', and although precise figures are not known they are recommended to devote around 30 hours to preparation for classes each week. It all roughs out at about a 50 hour week for those who want to do well, and who are not so depressed by their first semester grades as to abandon hope and take to the bottle or, as happened in one case in Michigan, attempt to burn the law school down. Although the practice of humiliating students, as depicted in the movie *The Paper Chase*, has become relatively uncommon it still goes on.[13] In addition students form study groups in which serious discussion of rival points of view may be pursued outside the classroom. Such seriously intellectual groups are uncommon; most study groups spend their time working through class notes in preparation for the examination. Members used to bombard me with queries.

13. 1973, based on the 1970 novel by John Jay Osborn Jr.

Where courses are offered in jurisprudence, philosophy of law, or legal theory, these will normally be elective second or third year courses, often with a small enrolment. They may take the form of lecture courses, or be taught through forms of casebook. Or sometimes what is offered is informal seminars. Some academics have however always believed that it was vital to get some version of the philosophy of law into the first year curriculum. This was the idea behind Edward Levi's *Elements of Law* course in the Chicago Law School, an institution deeply committed to getting its students to think the right thoughts.[14] But such courses have shown little interest in the kind of analytical jurisprudence peddled by Hart. An attempt was made when I was at Michigan to provide some first year students with a general introduction to the various schools of thought which have been developed in the US and elsewhere—the realists, the legal process school, the economic analysis of law, and so forth—but given constraints of time analytical jurisprudence could only feature as a minor component. So against this background it is not surprising perhaps that nobody has set about the difficult task of writing a monograph which attempts to replace *The Concept of Law*, nor is it at all clear what form such a book could take. Its only rival remains Kelsen, and very few law students or law teachers read Kelsen.

Style, Presentation, and Rivals

At the time when *The Concept of Law* was published most serious Oxford law students made use of one or more of the jurisprudence text books as they were called, such as Paton, Salmond, or Friedman, or I suppose Dias and Hughes.[15] These varied in quality, but all were *surveys* discussing other named writers' views, together with the editor's own comments. Gluttons for punishment might also have relied on Julius Stone's *The Province and Function of Law: Law as Logic Justice and Social Control: A Study in Jurisprudence* (1947), all 981 pages of it, which took essentially the same survey form, but advanced a distinctive thesis. Such works abounded in footnotes. Hart, in the literary style of presentation he adopted in *The Concept of Law*, departed from the survey form. Thus in Chapters I–IV there are in all 18 footnotes, only ten of which, some mere cross references,

14. See above Chapter 2 at p 61. 15. See above Chapter 2.

are in II–IV, in which he develops criticisms of Austin and Kelsen.[16] The only names of philosophers which appear in the text are those of JL Austin (once), Aquinas (once), Aristotle (once), Bentham (four times), and Hobbes (twice). Nobody reading the book would get the impression that an extensive knowledge of philosophy was needed to follow the argument. Indeed taking the text alone there is little internal indication that it is written by a philosopher. Much fuller notes are tucked away as endnotes on pp 277–290, but they do not serve to support the main text, the function of such notes in legal treatises. They in general provide information on the writings which Hart had consulted, and which his readers might like to consult too. In a passage in his working notebook, which Lacey reproduces, he states:

> One novelty in the book is to be a refusal to draw topics of importance from named authors' theories but to look at *the* object.[17]

The consequence of all this, together with Hart's skill as a writer of straightforward prose, gave to *The Concept of Law* a character which sharply differentiated it from the other books out there in the market. It personalized the book: this was Hart, the philosopher/lawyer/professor giving *his* views and ideas. The book is highly readable, and certainly on a first reading, clear and lucid, though as we have seen this is something of a false impression. The OUP, as ever, made *The Concept of Law* look good, and soon put it into a paperback edition. The fact that it came from a prestigious academic press no doubt also helped. So against this background it is not very surprising that it received glowing reviews, and soon made a considerable impact.[18] Matters were further helped by the perception at this time that Oxford was the world's centre for serious philosophy, and by Hart's involvement in a number of those academic punch ups which always attract interest in academia and put their participants name into the limelight. In 1957 there was the roasting of the unfortunate Bodenheimer, and in the same year the exchange with Fuller.

Then in 1959 Hart became embattled with Patrick Devlin, Britain's thinking judge, over the proper scope of the criminal law.[19] Briefly the specific question was whether if some form of homosexual conduct disgusted

16. Refs to Llewellyn, Holmes, Kelsen, Austin, St Augustine, Gray, JL Austin, and one JD March. There are also references to two law cases.
17. Lacey 223. It comes on 9.
18. For the reviews, see Lacey at 223–4.
19. Lacey 256–60.

the man on the Clapham omnibus that was a good reason for criminalizing it. What was played out in the controversy was a reworking of nineteenth century disputes between Mill and Fitzjames Stephen. To set the issue up you have to take some form of conduct which is agreed to be immoral, and ask if it should also be illegal. In the Hart-Devlin debate this never happened, since Hart did not think that the conduct in question was immoral, whilst Devlin did. Once in Ghana we were studying the debate, and I asked my students to come up with a Ghanaian example of the problem. One brightly said that:

> Where I come from we normally kill a few slaves at the chief's funeral custom and bury them with him.[20]

Here the point is a little more complicated for this was certainly against the criminal law, but this application of the law never took place, since those involved thought the practice perfectly acceptable. The outcome was a chilly silence and the class returned with relief to discussion of sodomy in Britain, a subject they found bizarre, it being an article of faith in Ghana at this time that homosexuality did not exist except amongst 'been-tos', those who had visited Britain and been corrupted there.

One way and another Hart's name came to be well known as what has been called a public intellectual. In those far off days there were elitist institutions which provided a platform for such people—the BBC with its Third Programme and Brains Trust, *The Listener*, and the quality press. It was a golden era for the dons, which got even better with television. This world is brilliantly portrayed in the movie *Accident* (1967), directed by Joseph Losey, and based on a novel by Nicolas Mosley, with a script by Harold Pinter. In addition to the Devlin debate, Hart's name was also given prominence through the publication in 1966 of his Oxford *Report on Relations with Junior Members*, always known as *The Hart Report*, which I discuss below. The report was internationally influential; Michigan for example set up a new disciplinary system, replete with rights, as a result of it. I once sat on the disciplinary court, and it was clear that the proceedings would go on forever, but mercifully the student concerned, who had been fraudulently using large numbers of social security numbers, solved the problem by leaving. Given Hart's public status there was bound to be interest in and respect for his one book. In the irreverent 1960s, the Oxbridge philosophers

20. The ceremonies associated with the funeral.

were parodied in the review *Beyond the Fringe* by Jonathan Miller and Alan Bennett as comical. I saw one version of this at which the issue was why we thought we thought in our heads and not under the chair one was sitting on. The participants then peered under their chairs. But Hart did not come across as one of them; he was concerned with real problems.

The Hart Report: The Philosopher as King

From May 1968 Hart chaired a committee appointed by Council which in May 1969 produced a *Report of the Committee on Relations with Junior Members*.[21] After some uncertainty the remit of the committee included student disciplinary arrangements as operated by the university, not those of the colleges. The committee had four other members, with a registry official. Until Nicola Lacey's biography was published Hart's work on this has been largely forgotten.[22] But at the time the report was widely studied both in the UK and elsewhere, and was influential. It seems right that I should say something about it. Given the fact that the report was the work of a committee of five people, serviced by an official who would have had a hand in the drafting, it is not easy to identify which parts of the report were written by Hart himself, either in first or final draft. We can only be certain over an Appendix on Student Radicalism in Oxford which he wrote in the Villa Serbelloni (now the Grand Hotel Bellagio) on Lake Como in Italy; his visit there was funded by the Rockefeller Trust, which also paid for the attendance there of a collection of important people in the university world in a boondoggle which must have cost the earth.[23] This Appendix is by any standards an impressive piece of work. Hart claimed he drafted the first two chapters of the report itself.[24] But this claim is not to be taken literally and it is obvious that some passages would have been supplied by the secretary,[25] and others modified in the light of suggestions from his colleagues. What it must mean is that he drafted (either initially or finally) the passages of a theoretical or evaluative character. And certainly these chapters contain numerous passages which read like the work of Hart, some in his moral

21. Supp 7, *University Gazette* vol xcix.
22. Lacey deals with the report from 284–289.
23. Listed at 12. The hotel is today probably the most expensive in the world.
24. Paras 1–120t. 25. eg 5–6, 44–45, 56–61.

outrage mode.[26] The committee met on 55 occasions and it is unclear when it began to work from drafts.

At this time demonizing the proctoral system was, amongst student radicals, and others who could not be so described, the flavour of the month. The Hart report did not in general go along with this; its account of the existing system and its problems was sympathetic to the view that the proctors did their conscientious best to operate a system, which Hart and his colleagues thought was gravely flawed, which they had not invented. The report published much information on the working of the system, which had, since 1965, enabled students to appeal against disciplinary decisions to an independent appeal body.[27] A list of the seven appeals since then and their outcome was provided; unfortunately it is inaccurate, not recording a successful appeal against rustication which took place when Roberts and I were proctors. We were delighted.[28]

What the report certainly brought out was the minimal role which the proctors played in the individual discipline of students, which almost wholly took place in the colleges. Somewhere about 1 per cent of decisions were taken by the proctors. The measures which could be taken included fines, compensation orders, gating, deprivation or suspension of scholarships, rustication, and expulsion. Most were accepted, but a few were not. No college at this time had any formal system of appeal except for Lincoln, where I managed to establish one. It was possible for an aggrieved student to appeal to the visitor of the college,[29] but they were not informed of this, and the right was at this time effectively obsolete. Indeed the report never mentions the college visitors. Within the colleges proceedings were usually very informal; I recall sitting in an armchair enjoying a glass of sherry while the dean of Queens, Charles Kennedy, fined me for throwing oranges about at a party, one going through the window and hitting the Principal of St Edmund Hall.

So far as student discipline was concerned the report took the general line that what went on in the colleges was not open to serious criticism or to

26. eg 63–4.
27. A recommendation of the Williams Committee, chaired by Bill Williams, Montgomery's former intelligence officer and then Warden of Rhodes House. The report is Supp 2, *University Gazette* vol xcvi.
28. See 60. The appeals committee was chaired by Sir Kenneth Wheare (1907–1979) VC 1964–1966, Rector of Exeter College 1956–72, President of the British Academy 1967–71, a distinguished political scientist.
29. For example in the case of Lincoln, the Bishop of Lincoln.

criticism at all; this was not based on any detailed enquiry, which would have been outside the terms of reference and been a massive undertaking. A number of passages sang its praises.[30] But the proctorial system needed radical reform. As Lacey puts it:

> He voiced a swingeing critique of the concentration of legislative, executive and punitive power in the hands of just two people operating, in Herbert's memorable phrase, 'a blaze of secrecy'.

Broadly his solution was to establish a rules committee which would curb the legislative activities of the proctors, and the concept of a major university offence which could either, with consent, be tried by the proctors, with an appeal to a new Disciplinary Court, or if the student wished by the new court, which it was envisaged would operate as a pale imitation of a regular criminal court, with the production of witnesses, cross examination (a conception only intelligible to professional lawyers[31]), and if wished legal representation.[32] The burden of proof would be on the prosecution. But there would be no jury, and if convicted a written explanation of the decision would be provided. There would be no appeal from its decisions. Neither Hart nor any of his colleagues had any personal experience of the administration of the criminal law, either in magistrates' courts or in trials by jury. I did as an Oxford City magistrate; the experience had given me a somewhat jaundiced view of the criminal justice system. At the time of the report I mainly worked on the juvenile court, but also attended jury trials at Quarter Sessions, and took part in a discussion group in the Oxford prison with long sentence preventive detention prisoners. One was called 'Tizer' and had been sent down for seven years for stealing the bottle of a sort of lemonade he took with him on burglaries. Another was outraged since he had been convicted of stealing the cross from a church, being thus fitted up by the police. He had in fact stolen the candlesticks and would never have stolen the cross.

The report did not recommend radical reform because the proctors had in the past operated a sort of reign of terror, but for a combination between theoretical views on the concept of a fair trial, and a division of functions, and because of student hostility to the existing system. It took particular

30. 28, 40.
31. Non-lawyers cannot grasp the difference between cross examining and giving evidence.
32. See report at 122 (13–18); my account is simplified.

objection to the vagueness of the 'umbrella clause' under which a substantial number of decisions were taken:

> No Junior Member of the University shall engage in conduct liable to bring the name of the University or any of its members into disrepute or any conduct lacking in respect for any member, officer or servant of the University, or any conduct liable to constitute a serious impediment to the prosecution of his studies in the University.[33]

The proctors also possessed a general rule-making power.

The report strongly reflected the idea that the scope of the university discipline should be restricted as far as possible since discipline was better left to the colleges. There should be a clearly defined basic university offence:

> No Junior Member of the University shall
> 1. Engage in conduct likely to disrupt teaching or study or research or the administration of the University, or to obstruct any officer or servant of the University in the performance of his duties;
> 2. Damage or deface any property of the University or of any college, or occupy the same otherwise than in accordance with the rules or other prevision made therefore by the University or college authority concerned.[34]

Otherwise rules should in future be made by a 12 member rules committee comprising six senior and six junior members, and if they were equally divided the decision would be taken by Council.[35]

As for the trial of university offences, minor ones would continue to be dealt with by the proctors, subject to appeal to the new disciplinary court. This would, at the option of the accused, try minor offences. Some minor cases would be referred to the relevant college. Under this scheme the existing appeals committee was to be abolished.

The members of Hart's committee, though unanimous in approving a new basic offence along the lines at least of the draft I have quoted, were by no means otherwise agreed on the proper scope of university discipline.[36] But under the scheme proposed it was not necessary to reach agreement, for problematic issues would be the future concern of the rules committee.

33. App B at page 172–3. See Title XV. Hart never investigated the role of precedent and custom in interpreting this.
34. 105. This was not offered as a final draft.
35. For composition of the committee see 72–3. My account is simplified and I do not discuss offences against Bodleian Library rules.
36. See eg 53 and ff and 57.

Hence many issues were hardly touched on in the report—an example is the question of what role the university system ought to play in relation to the problem of drugs, if it was a problem.

On student participation in the running of the university, the report recommended an elaborate system but one which did not make students into members of the basic decision taking bodies, such as the Council and General Board of the Faculties. I shall not do more than mention this, except to say that I could see no strong objection to it. The report did not discuss the evaluation of teachers by students, an idea not then around.

I am said to have described the report as a dog's dinner, but I have no recollection of this.[37] However I was irritated by a passage in the report which partially quoted the text of a memorandum which Roberts and I had submitted on the merits of setting up a new court. Although we were not named it was possible for quite a number of people to identify us.[38] Hart wrote that:

> ...we cannot accept the statement made by two senior members that those who object to the concentration of Legislative, Judicial and police function are 'over impressed by a somewhat naïve belief that the current system under which criminal law is administered (in the case of adults) is an ideal to be copied.'

I thought that this personalization was quite improper, and made the worse because the whole document was not reproduced. The same paragraph referred to the restraint, humanity and special concern for the young which had '*generally*' been a feature of the exercise of proctorial power, with the obvious implication, though no example was given. I also thought the report somewhat hypocritical. About this time I was approached by a student who had been expelled from Hart's college with only a few weeks to go to his final examinations. There was no formal hearing; the decision was taken by his tutor and rubber stamped by the governing body. There was no appeal. I tried to get him moved to Lincoln but was unable to secure the needed consent of the two colleges.[39] I was in Ghana when the report appeared; Roberts frivolously cabled me 'Proctors Reproved'. After some fuming I took no action over this and I do not even recollect discussing the report with Hart on my return though I may well have done.

37. Lacey 289.
38. 64.
39. This was under the statute *De Migratione*.

The main problem which the report had to address was 'If it's not broke don't fix it'. The existing system, constantly being modified in response to criticism, and with its appeal system, did not work badly, as the report itself made clear. Hart's background as a philosopher rejected this; the system was wrong in principle. The report came in for criticism ranging from those who could see no justification for pandering to the ill informed views of the spoiled brats of Oxford, to those who sympathized with their anxieties and did not think the report went far enough.[40] But it was welcomed by many of a liberal persuasion, and did much to establish Hart's reputation even more firmly. The report was further evidence that he was a philosopher who did not spend his time splitting hairs over Wittgenstein or whoever, but instead, as he had earlier done, addressed important practical issues. Here was an example of the Platonic ideal of the philosopher as king.

The Structure of *The Concept of Law*

As anyone who has written a book knows, the main initial problem is to settle on a basic structure. As we have seen he appears to have been working on the ideas presented in the 24 lectures on 'The Concept of Law' which formed the basis for the book, from 1954 or even earlier or so onwards.[41] But until the collaborative work *Causation and the Law* (1959) had been finished, which would have been some time in 1958, he cannot have been able to devote a great deal of time to his next major project, and he allowed himself to be distracted by a developing interest in criminal law and punishment.[42] For Hart seems to have suffered from The Sock Drawer Syndrome—before I can screw myself up to doing some urgent work I really need to sort out my sock drawer. By late 1959 the final text, which was finally written up in the summer vacation of 1960, must have been in an advanced state. The book has ten chapters, divided into 33 sections, and it prints out at roughly ten pages of text for each lecture. In the Hart archives, now in New College, there is a notebook, 81 pages long, which contains Hart's working notes on *The Concept of Law*.[43] It is unclear

40. In times of student disturbances academics divide into three schools—join them, bayonet them, compromise with them . . .

41. See above Chapter 3.

42. Lacey 217–221.

43. Lacey 223–4.

when exactly this notebook was begun; probably sometime in 1959 or so.[44] Nicola Lacey is no palaeographer, why should she be, but her account overstates the difficulties in deciphering this hand written text. Compared to some sixteenth century hands, Hart's writing is not particularly difficult, and it would be perfectly possible to produce a publishable text, though it is not a job I should be competent to undertake. For I, like Lacey, am no palaeographer either. But the problem of making sense of many of the cryptic jottings would remain. What I shall do is to pick out, and in some instances reproduce, passages which seem to me to be of interest in showing Hart's developing ideas on the structure and central themes of his book. But first of all a very general point emerges from the notebook. This is that Hart was still unsure about the structure and organizing theme or themes of his book whilst he was writing it. Thus in one passage he writes gloomily:

> My scheme and ideas for this book have got lost. I find difficulty now at times in making of it (1) any kind of unity as contrasted with scattered observations about certain unnoticed certainly but unimportant so it may seem aspects of a legal... view (ii) getting with a [serious...][45] from any idea that there is a core to this concept (authority—validity—obligation—procedure—for settling question.[46]

The second is that one summer vacation is not a long period to devote to the writing of the complete text of a book such as *The Concept of Law*. No regular diary exists for this period, so we do not know what else engaged his attention during the summer, but if we bear in mind these two points they may well do something to explain any defects in the final product.

Hart's notebook does throw some light on the evolution of Hart's ideas, but it is not a clear light, and I shall not attempt to provide a full analysis. Early in the notebook, in a passage reproduced by Lacey,[47] Hart notes that he has a dim outline in mind, and that the basic structure of the book will be built around the conception of a '*standard* legal *system*'.[48] Then non-standard cases, such as international law, can be addressed, and secondly 'the relations of law with "morals" as a means of social control can be analysed'. The

44. There is a reference which indicates that it was begun after the Michaelmas Term lectures he delivered in 1959.

45. One word of text obscure.

46. At 28. The passage following seems disconnected from this.

47. Lacey 222 from 3.

48. CL 2–3.

passage then goes on to say that the 'Hard Core', (and new to English readers) would be:

> . . . an illuminating survey of 'essential' features (and neglected features of a municipal legal system. This would . . . bring out the *multiplicity* of kinds of law: *Substantive*; Crime and Private; *Jurisdiction*; *Procedure*; *Evidence;* Constitutional (Grundnorm) and drive away the obsession with Command. . . .[49]

He then sets out a scheme which had been in his mind for some time and was imperfectly controlled by the Michaelmas Term lectures. These would start with the 'Hard Core', which would 'knock away the obsession with command, should this be the presupposed substructure.' He would then:

> II Make central the institutional, authoritative identification of law (validity).
>
> III show Courts' activities as presupposing all the system.
>
> IV deal with [text obscure].

So Hart is here groping his way towards the notion of the rule of recognition, though the term is not used here.

This is followed by a scheme of Parts and Chapters.[50] First there would be a preliminary Part I with a Chapter 1 which would deal with problems of definition. For example it includes:

> Conceptual knowledge and Definition. What can be done. Characterization of standard case.

This was to become Chapter I.3 of *The Concept of Law.*[51] The subject of Chapter II is very obscurely noted and I can make little of it. Chapter III was to deal with rules generally including validity, and rules about rules, with discussion of authority, rules commands and habits, tradition, private standards and obligation.

Then Part III would deal with the place of concepts of Justice and Morality and Natural Law. It includes a reference to the Austinian separation of law and morality, and is the first incidental indication of the positivist thesis Hart was to develop, though the term itself does not appear. There is a hint that Hart was considering writing an essay on natural law—it is unclear if this was to be in the book or perhaps the reference is to his 'Are There

49. This is developed in CL Chapter III, 'The Variety of Laws'.
50. From 7–9.
51. 13–17.

Any Natural Rights' already published in 1955. Then on page 16 we have a hint of the idea which was eventually to become the rule of recognition:

> Can this be the organizing theme? The idea of an authoritative test by form not content—one [text obscure] authoritative virtue of their source.

Part IV was to deal with International Law.[52]

The rest of the notebook does not contain anything in the nature of a revised scheme.

It would be tedious, and extremely difficult, for me to attempt to give any extended account of its later content. But I shall mention some passages. Lacey incompletely[53] reproduces a passage dealing with the concept of obligation:

> . . . A. Does obligation involve all three or only one of the following,
>
> I coercion or pressure behind the rules (sanction) . . .
>
> II recognition of primacy of rule . . .
>
> III recognition of rule as giving reason for action?
>
> B. What is the proper inference from the fact that (logically) x's obligation is compatible with no chance of suffering sanction . . .[54]

From time to time appear short passages which summarize the form the theory eventually took;

> General.
> rules—system—institutional procedures
> authority
> obligations
> validity.[55]

One passage is devoted to the 'facilitative' side of law, though here as elsewhere the terms used in the final text—primary and secondary rules—do not appear. The conception of the pre-legal world appears late in the notebook, in a passage which gives no indication of sources, and which suggests, insofar as one can make sense of it, that at this stage Hart's ideas were in an embryonic state. There are no references to the idea that there were problems and inefficiencies in this pre-legal world, to be cured by secondary rules.[56] Indeed I strongly suspect that there must once have been

52. In CL as Chapter X. 53. Presumably because of difficulties in decipherment.
54. Developed in CL in a variety of passages. 55. 26. 56. 71.

further notebooks, perhaps many, now lost. It is not conceivable that Hart went from this notebook to the final text.

We have seen how Hart explained that his ideas had been influenced by Peter Winch's *The Idea of a Social Science*, and the notebook sheds some light on this.[57] Apparently Hart was still trying to master this book whilst he was working on *The Concept of Law*. At 22 there is the following passage:

> Last chapter of W's book made me think that the idea of 'ethically neutral' acceptance of authority (complex practice of a social group—differentiated from Austin's habit of obedience not by moral obligation but by contents of rules never habit—must be in some way require modification for statement of an abstraction useful for legal purposes (sorting out law from non law). But I am not sure what W's point is on this yet. [text obscure] My problem is that his complex practice is a sufficient condition and the [one word obscure] of moral obligation.

But, typically, this does not get us very far.

It is noticeable that at this stage the terminology employed in *The Concept of Law*—the use of expressions such as primary and secondary rules, the rule of recognition, *etcetera*, had not been developed. The general impression which the notebook gives is that of Hart holding a conversation with himself, as he struggled to get his ideas into some order.

A Mystery of Chronology

I now have to raise a problem over chronology to which I can provide no satisfactory solution. In 1958 the University of Washington Press published a collection of essays under the title *Essays in Moral Philosophy*. The editor was one AI Melden, who taught philosophy there. One essay had been previously published, but the others were written specially and in effect commissioned by Melden. Hart contributed one entitled *Legal and Moral Obligation*.[58] According to Lacey, and I have no reason to doubt this, Hart's essay had been written in 1956. Lacey also records that Hart had visited Seattle during 1956 and gave lectures there and elsewhere; I assume that he delivered some version of the essay there and perhaps at other universities.[59]

57. See above Chapter 4 at pp 105–9.
58. There is a brief review by A Phillips Griffiths in (1961) *Philosophy* 36:237.
59. Lacey 191–193. This was before cheap air travel and Hart would visit the northwest by train.

Now this essay both contains the criticisms of Austin which were to feature in *The Concept of Law*, virtually as they appear there, and the essentials of Hart's general theory as set out in his book. There are only trivial differences—for example the expressions 'primary' and 'secondary rules' are not used. All this being so it is extremely odd that Hart's notebook, which dates from some considerable if uncertain time later, gives the clear impression that Hart is still struggling to decide what the basic thesis of his book should be. The Melden essay does not include a scheme for a book, but Hart's anxieties went well beyond this. Perhaps the explanation simply is that this is yet another example of Hart's sense of insecurity. Furthermore Hart's basic legal theory is also found in another piece, published in 1959, 'Scandinavian Realism'.[60]

The Replacement of Austin

Manning said in his lecture and article back in 1932 that:

> What seems to me, however, to estop us, as it were, from speaking slightingly of Austin today is not any supposed perfection in the results of his efforts, but our own comparative failure to put anything more satisfactory in their place.[61]

Hart had, through the publication of his edition on Austin's *Province of Jurisprudence Determined* and *The Uses of the Study of Jurisprudence* (1954) made Austin's work more accessible, but so far as the common law world is concerned *The Concept of Law* soon replaced Austin as the starting point for those interested in analytical jurisprudence. Austin's theory was set out in a lucid form, analysed in detail, and criticized in Chapters II, III and IV of *The Concept of Law*.[62] In the same chapters of his book, and in the endnotes, Hart also put forward criticisms of Kelsen.[63] Later in the notes to Chapter VI Hart develops other criticisms of Kelsen, but these are not spelled out in the main text.[64] But the book does not take the discussion of Kelsen very far, or explain the conceptual background to his thinking, or give any account of the notion of a pure theory of law, and the impression given is that Hart did not quite know where to put his discussion, whilst being anxious to make it

60. (1959) CLJ 33. 61. 224. 62. CL 18–78.
63. CL 35–42, 286. 64. CL 292–5.

clear that his theory was distinguishable. In the final text the problem may have been to keep the size of the book down; there was no room for Kelsen. In the planning stage perhaps the problem was that he was nervous or unsure of writing up a detailed criticism. So far as the civil law world is concerned *The Concept of Law* has never replaced Kelsen. And back in Oxford and indeed elsewhere even in the common law world there remained those who thought of Kelsen as the greatest analytical jurist of the century; I recall, for example, Peter Carter of Wadham being of this persuasion, and so too was Tony Honoré. So Kelsen still featured in what counted as jurisprudence, and this meant that some students devoted time to relevant reading, and examination questions were set which enabled them to use their knowledge. Oxford students of this period also found the concept of norms and the grundnorm faintly comical; this generated graffiti, some indecent, for example, in the Turf Tavern. The terminology belonged to a different world.

Hart as Philosopher

Nicola Lacey's biography brings out the fact that Hart himself was oppressed with doubts as to his ability as a philosopher, and it is the case that he never published any books or articles which made any contribution to the central and traditionally established problems of philosophy. Such contributions as he did make were solely confined to the philosophy of law and as we have seen *The Concept of Law* and its precursors played down the input of philosophical ideas into the text. Furthermore my own inclination would be to be surprised over the extent to which he came to express admiration for the influence of JL Austin, and his ideas on the nature of dictionary definitions of, for example, elephants, were strange indeed. But I have no idea as to how if at all it is possible to rank philosophers. Do you do this in his case for 1961 (or is philosophy an ongoing activity?), and if your work is still being written about and talked about over half a century later, and your book continues to sell, that must surely count for something.

So one way of assessing his work is to think of him as having started a dialogue, and from my own experience of working with him so many years ago he was very good at that.

The Positive Contributions of *The Concept of Law* and Related Writings

So it is now time to adopt a more sympathetic and, at the risk of appearing to be punning, positive approach to Hart's achievement, which adopts the view that philosophy is an ongoing activity.

Hart's first achievement was to rescue the positivist tradition. Is there some necessary connection between law and morality, and if so what is it? Is there a moral obligation to observe the law? Can a legal system exist unless such an obligation is accepted by at least some of those who operate the system? I shall not make a list, but questions of this kind are not going to go away. The most useful text here as a jumping off point is not that of *The Concept of Law*, but that of the Hart-Fuller Exchange, and I think it was these two scholars who revitalized discussion of the issues involved. Now a general point needs to be made about the context in which both worked—that of a very law abiding society—to be sure that observation did not apply in their time to the proletariat, regularly abused for example by the police, but neither had any contact with that world. I doubt if Hart had ever met a worker from the Cowley Factory in Oxford, and I wonder how many African Americans were known to Fuller. People like Fuller and Hart did not, except very rarely, break laws; Erwin Griswold, one time Dean of the Harvard Law School was aberrant in that he sometimes stole boundary markers. But he was an exception.

His second achievement, though this does not come from *The Concept of Law*, was to reinvigorate the earlier dispute between Mill and Fitzjames Stephen on the proper reach of the criminal law. To be sure nothing particularly new was said, but there was new life in what there was.

His third was to establish the importance, in any attempt to understand modern legal systems, of an analysis of the nature of rules, and of attitudes to rules. In particular he introduced into the currency of jurisprudence the notion that rules could be of different types, primary and secondary, and that a distinction of fundamental importance existed between the internal and the external point of view in relation to rules. In addition there is his analysis of the concept of validity and the problematic hypothesis of the rule of recognition. All this became the starting point for analysis by later critics, and at a pedagogic level for the teaching of legal philosophy. To be sure

Hart did not have a great deal to say about the concept of law in general, for his book ended up as a book about the concept of a legal system. A book exploring the various senses in which we talk of law would be entirely unlike *The Concept of Law*. A quick look at the *Oxford Dictionary* is all that is needed to see that.

The fourth was to offer an alternative, intelligible to common lawyers, to Kelsen. How successful this was, and to what extent his theory really was different, is a matter for dispute. But he made the attempt, and this I think was both bold and valuable. To this day we do not seem to have a major study of this issue.

The fifth was to give plausibility to the idea, best set out in his post-script,[65] that even if you adopted the view that the route ahead lay with some version of the sociological study of law and legal institutions, there was a need to be armed with a carefully worked out tool kit of categories and concepts. As Galligan puts it:

> . . . legal theory, in providing concepts, categories and ideas, is a good starting point for an analysis of law in society; at the same time, it is only a starting point.[66]

Whether Hart's specific contribution was valuable, as some would argue it was, is another question; here I am only drawing attention to his general thesis, which is an important one not, I think, to be found in earlier writers.

The sixth achievement, which may seem an odd point to make, is that his mistakes and defects combined with his attractive style made analytical jurisprudence enjoyable for generations of students. I base this of course on personal experience. Doing Hart was, or could be, fun. He was not alone in this; students got a lot of fun out of Hohfeld, and I even had one student who constructed a Hohfeld machine, with bulbs which lit up appropriately to indicate correlatives. But Hart was a much more significant thinker than Hohfeld, whose theories were in some ways little short of weird.

In all these respects I have mentioned Hart was a pioneer, although some of his ideas had been anticipated at least in part by earlier scholars, for example Sir John Salmond, and Peter Winch, though Winch as we have seen did not apply his ideas to law. Pioneers always get a fair amount wrong. Whymper's first ascent of the Matterhorn, or rather his descent, preceded by four of his unfortunate companions, one of whom simply vanished, is as

65. CL at 239 and ff. 66. 12.

good an illustration as any. Errors in legal philosophy are in general not so dangerous though there have been exceptions. For making mistakes as a pioneer he should not be judged too harshly.

All this sounds like damning with faint praise, but that is not what I intend. Hart's *The Concept of Law* defined and continues to define the subject of analytical jurisprudence more than half a century since it was written. None of his critics or expositors, Dworkin, Raz, McCormick, have written books which have in the least rivalled its position. And no rival work has been created out of the work of Kelsen. Hart's was an extraordinary achievement.

Bibliography with Annotations

This is not a comprehensive bibliography, but a collection of notes placed here so as not to clutter up the text, and provide guidance on further reading.

Allen, CK, *Law in the Making*. Seven editions from 1926, the last in 1965, but the one most relevant is that of 1939. At one time it was widely used in American law schools.

Austin, J, *The Province of Jurisprudence Determined* (1832) and *The Uses of the Study of Jurisprudence* (1863) with an Introduction by HLA Hart (1954). The first of these works was first published in 1832 and the second in 1863. The author John Austin (1790–1759) is not to be confused with John Langshaw Austin (1911–1960). Austin's *Lectures on Jurisprudence or the Philosophy of Positive Law* were reconstructed by his widow Sarah Austin and published in 1863. There is some suspicion that she was not above some creativity in this.

Austin, JL, *How to Do Things with Words: The William James Lectures delivered at Harvard University in 1955* (JO Urmson ed 1962). This was put together from notes after Austin's death. It is therefore not entirely clear that Austin himself would have approved of the text.

Ayer, AJ, *Language Truth and Logic* (1936). This was the book which established Ayer's reputation. It purveyed the doctrine of logical positivism, which Ayer later repudiated.

—— WC Kneale, GA Paul, DF Pears, PF Strawson, GJ Warnock, RA Wollheim, *The Revolution in Philosophy* (1960). With Introdution by Gilbert Ryle. The revolution discussed was not the post war Oxford movement but extended over the whole of the 20th century.

Baker GP and Hacker MS, *Wittgenstein: Understanding and Meaning, Volume I of an Analytical Commentary on the Philosophical Investigations.* I think there is also a volume two either now available or about to be published. I mention this as it is the latest volume to contribute to what I have called the Wittgenstein industry.

Buckland, WW, *Some Reflections on Jurisprudence* (1949). Buckland trained as an engineer and then studied law in Cambridge, becoming Regius Professor of Roman Law. His *Textbook of Roman Law* (1926) remains the most outstanding study ever to have been produced by an English scholar, and has grown in reputation. His *Reflections* was published when he was 85, but is based on some earlier lectures. It is described by Honoré in BDCL as ultra-positivist, which

I think is going a little too far, but it certainly is the case that he did adopt a positivist line. He wrote for example that 'There have been wicked laws (and it is enough for the argument that there may have been). Such things are none the less laws'. He also wrote 'To introduce goodness into the definition of law is like introducing the ability to trot into the definition of a horse. A horse that cannot trot is still a horse, but a bad horse'. It is a brilliant book, and it is surprising that nobody has brought out a modern critical edition.

Conradi, PJ, *Iris Murdoch. A Life* (2001). This remarkable book gives is own picture of the world of Cambridge and Oxford philosophy and Iris Murdoch's place in it. The author does however adopt positions which not everyone would accept, so it needs to be read both admiringly and critically.

Dancy, J, *Walter Oakeshott: A Diversity of Gifts* (1988). Oakeshott was Rector of Lincoln College throughout my time there; he became Vice-Chancellor and although not all his plans succeeded he was in my view an outstanding incumbent of the position. Some of the material in Dancy's book was provided by me.

Diamond, AS, *Primitive Law* (1935, 1950, 1971). Abraham Sigismud Diamond (1897–1978) was a Leeds grammar school boy who became senior scholar at Trinity Cambridge, and practised at the bar from 1921. He wrote a book on master and servant and eventually became a Master in the Queen's Bench 1962–9. A person of enormous industry, his work on *Primitive Law* was extensively revised in the 1971 edition. The edition of 1950 is cited by Hart. It develops a chronology which relates evolving human societies to their state of economic development, and seeks to identify the *legal* institutions of such societies. As a work of synthesis it is impressive, but it contains some errors and has no doubt been superseded. It is difficult to believe that Hart actually read it.

Dias, RWM, and Hughes, GBH, *Jurisprudence* (1957) reviewed by Hart in (1958) 4 JSPTL 143. Hughes had published a treatise *Jurisprudence*; Dias complained that it was derivative of his lectures. The book, of which I own a copy, was withdrawn under pressure, and a committee of the Cambridge Law Faculty persuaded Dias and Hughes to collaborate on a rewritten treatise, which is the book Hart reviewed. Stories circulated that Glanville Williams then complained that Dias had based his views on his lectures.

Duxbury, N, *Frederick Pollock and the English Juristic Tradition* (2004) in *Oxford Studies in Modern Legal History*. I edited this series and this was I think the first contribution which related to the history of jurisprudence.

Dworkin, RM, *Taking Rights Seriously* (1977), *A Matter of Principle* (1985), *Law's Empire* (1986), *Justice in Robes* (2006). Dworkin has also made many contributions to the *New York Review of Books*. His evolving views can be followed in these books and there is an extensive secondary literature.

Edmonds, D, and Eidinow, J, *Wittgenstein's Poker: The story of a ten–minute argument between two great philosophers* (2001). This should be read in conjunction with Karl Popper's *Unended Quest. An Intellectual Biography*. People will differ but my personal view is that it is not possible to establish just what did happen. Be that as it may the book is something of a tour de force, and gives a wonderful picture of the strange world of the philosophers.

Finnis, J, *Natural Law and Natural Rights* (1980). This has been both re-issued and revised, and is one of the most successful books to appear in the Clarendon Law Series. The author is Catholic and presumably his book is much used in Catholic circles, but its readership must be much wider than this, and the intention was never to write a sort of primer of Catholic natural law doctrines. It was originally written as I understand it because of Finnis' reaction to the picture of natural law in *The Concept of Law*, and in other writers, who were either dismissive or ill informed. Hart and Finnis were colleagues in University College, and Hart read and commented on the text; he was uneasy about the inclusion of Chapter XII, 'Nature Reason God' but did not insist on its removal. After this or indeed earlier they did not establish an ongoing working relationship. There is an extraordinary account in Lacey at 346–7 of them looking down together over the Temple Mount and the old City of Jerusalem, each with utterly different emotions, one an atheist Jew, the other a Christian, an event which induced them to hold, for the first and only time, a ten minute personal conversation. This was in 1983. Can it really be so?

Galligan, DJ, *Law in Modern Society* (2007). This is a volume in the Clarendon Law Series. The author is the Professor of Socio-Legal Studies in Oxford and directs the centre there. I include it here because it contains a very perceptive analysis of *The Concept of Law*, much of it related to the original text, and extensive discussion of the social scientific analysis of the working of social rules in society. Put at its simplest it differentiates the enterprise on which Hart was engaged from the enterprise which Galligan and other social scientist are engaged upon. It contains extremely helpful suggestions for further reading, covering relevant work published over the last half century.

Gluckman, M, *The Judicial Process Among the Barotse* (1955) is incidentally cited by Hart at 292, but it has no relevance to Hart's pre-legal world and there is no reason to believe he read it. Gluckman also wrote *The Ideas in Barotse Jurisprudence* (1965) which can be accessed on-line. Readers should be aware of the fact that under some versions of British colonialism there was thought to be a special role for government anthropologists. The function of these anthropologists was to investigate and set down accounts of customary law and institutions, which could then be used by colonial governments to establish systems of indirect rule which operated through traditional institutions. Anthropologists could also offer advice on contentious issues, as did Rattray over the desecration of the Golden Stool of Ashanti.

Goodhart, AL, *Essays in Jurisprudence and the Common Law* (1931). This includes his 'Determining the *Ratio Decidendi* of a Case' (1931) 40 *Yale LJ* 161, at one time obligatory reading both in the UK and the USA. In the USA a theory such as Goodhart's came to lose its status under the influence of the realist movement, and came to be associated with an outmoded formalism. At its most emphatic the article was telling you how to find something which either did not exist or if it did was of no relevance to the process of judicial decision. I have no idea if American law students still read it. Goodhart was also an international lawyer, and a letter written by him to *The Times* was relied on by the UK government as justifying the 1956 Suez intervention. There is no evidence I know that he was put up to this, but there have to be suspicions. Goodhart, also wrote *English Law and the Moral Law* (1953).

Hacker, PMS, *Wittgenstein's Place in Twentieth Century Analytic Philosophy* (1996). Hacker is the premier Wittgenstein scholar currently in post in the UK. See too Hacker PMS, and Raz J (eds), *Law, Morality and Society: Essays in Honour of H.L. A. Hart* (1977). This contains a valuable bibliography.

Hart, HLA, *The Concept of Law* (2nd edn 1994). This was edited by Peter Cane, Tony Honoré, and Jane Stapleton, and includes the unfinished postscript. The main text is the same as in the original edition. Page references to the first edition are not precisely the same as those in the 1994 edition, which prints out at 237 pages instead of 231. There have been numerous translations of the book, none of which I have ever seen.

Hohfeld, WN, *Fundamental Legal Conceptions* (1923). There exists no comprehensive study of Hohfeld's ideas, many of which are to be found tucked away in parts of the book nobody ever reads and in footnotes. Some of them were extremely strange. Many years ago I started work on such a study but gave it up on the ground that it was impossible to make sense of them and that the effort would prematurely drive me to drink. For a brief account see my BDCL.

Kelsen, H, 'The Pure Theory of Law and Analytical Jurisprudence' (1945) 55 *Harv LR* at 44, *General Theory of Law and the State* translated, presumably from a draft in German, by Anders Wedberg. Reprinted 1949. So far as I know there is still no study of Kelsen emanating from the common law world.

Kramer, MH, *In Defense of Legal Positivism: Law Without Trimmings* (1999). With others (eds), *The Legacy of H.L.A. Hart. Legal, Political and Moral Philosophy* (2008). This includes an excellent bibliography. The bibliography in Lacey is incomplete.

Lawson, FH, *The Oxford Law School 1850–1965* (1968). This book seems to have been produced in something of a hurry, and does not make use of much of the archival material available, but it does contain much valuable material. The reality of the matter is that it is extremely difficult to discover details of the teaching in Oxford in the pre-war world, and the earlier position is even more obscure. It is however possible to discover at least the titles of lecture courses.

MacCormick, N, *Institutions of Law: An Essay in Legal Theory* (2007), *Legal Reasoning and Legal Theory* (1978), *Rhetoric and the Rule of Law: A Theory of Legal Reasoning* (2005), *Jurists: Profiles in Legal Theory, H. L. A. Hart* (2nd edn 2008). The first edition was published in 1981. MacCormick, who was a friend of Hart, has been perhaps the most influential expounder of Hart's ideas, whilst not being in any way uncritical.

Raz, J, *Between Authority and Interpretation: On the Theory of Law and Practical Reason* (2009), *The Authority of Law: Essays on Law and Morality* (1979), *The Concept of a Legal System: An Introduction to the Theory of a Legal System* (1970), *Practical Reason and Norms* (1990). Along with MacCormick, Raz is the leading scholar who has as it were built his ideas up through a critical approach to Hart, but this is something of a simplification and his publications are very extensive. Raz discussed with Hart his attempts to write his Postscript, and two articles of his are cited in it at 254 ('Dworkin: A New Link in the Chain' (1986) 74 *Cal LR* 1103 and 'Legal Principles and the Limits of Law' (1972) 81 YLJ 823). In the latter Hart accepts Raz's point, which is related here to *Riggs v Palmer*. Apparently a similar point is made by Waluchow in (1985) 5 OJLS 5: 187 at 189 but I have not read this piece.

Riggs v Palmer (1889) 115 NY 506, 22 NE 180. This case features prominently in Dworkin's writings and it may be useful to say something about it. Briefly one Elmer Palmer had been left property by his grandfather, Francis Palmer; the residuary legatees under this will were the testator's daughters, Mrs Riggs and Mrs Preston, who had also been left small legacies. The grandfather remarried one Mrs Bresee, and Elmer thought that he was soon likely to change his will in favour of his new wife. So to prevent his grandfather executing a new will Elmer, who was 16 at the time, murdered him by poisoning him. For this he was convicted of second degree murder and sent to prison, probably imprisonment for life.

Through his guardians ad litem he started legal proceedings to recover the property under the will. His lawyers' case was that the will was a valid will, conforming to the *Wills Act* of 1837, and it said nothing to the effect that such a will was defective or invalid or unenforceable by a murderer. The decision in the case was that Elmer and his administrator be enjoined from using any of the testator's property for the benefit of Elmer, and that the provision in the will be declared ineffective to pass title to him.

The extremely complicated legal and theoretical context in which the case was litigated has been explored in an outstanding article by Kim Scheppele which I shall not attempt to summarize here. It is 'Facing Facts in Legal Interpretation' in (1990) 30 *Representations* Special Issue: Law and the Order of Culture 42–77. In particular this article explores the relevance and complexities of the doctrine that a conviction for felony has the consequence that the felon becomes for some purposes treated as if he or she were dead. I shall add a few comments.

The first is that discussion of the case tends to proceed on the assumption that the power of testamentary succession is derivative of the *Wills Act* of 1837. This is a mistake; the *Wills Act* merely regulated a power of testamentary succession which long predated it. Hart for example makes this mistake. The complexities of the history of this power are explained in my *History of the Land Law*. In a broad sense the power was conferred by the common law.

One judge, Gray, accepted the murderer's lawyers' argument. Attention has however focused on the majority opinion by Earl. It was in favour of the residuary legatees. My second comment is that modern commentary has tended to focus on the reliance in this opinion on the maxim:

> No one shall be permitted by his own fraud, or take advantage of his own wrong, or to found any claim on his own iniquity, or to acquire property by his own crime.

And in an alternative version that:

> All laws as well as contracts may be controlled in their operation and effect by general fundamental maxims of the common law. No one shall be permitted to profit by their own fraud, or take advantage of his own iniquity, or to acquire property by his own crime.

Two collections of maxims, Broom and Noy, were cited to the court.

The general fundamental maxim of the common law on which the majority relied has a long history. It is to be found in Book 50 of *Justinian's Digest* (50, 17.134.1) in the form:

nemo ex delicto meliorem suam conditionem facere potest.

I have discussed the literature and significance of maxims in my 'Rise and Fall of the Legal Treatise' in (1981) UCLR 48: 632. The propositions set out in Book 50 came to be known as the Regulae Juris, and the subject is explored by Peter Stein in his *Regulae Juris* (1966). So far as I am aware nobody has attempted to produce a study of when Ulpian's principle has been applied to control the operation of laws, or in other ways, which would be a massive undertaking.

My third comment is that counsel for the legatees presented an elaborate barrage of legal arguments, supported by citation of authority, in their favour, including one based on estoppel. And the majority opinion did not simply rely on the maxim, but also on a version of the long established doctrine of the equity of a statute. So this was not a case in which, as it was handled, it was supposed that the law was 'silent'. Convincing or not there was plenty to say.

For an account of a Canadian case, but involving a joint tenancy, raising similar problems see my discussion in *Annual Survey of Commonwealth Law* 1972 at 230 where conception of a constructive trust was employed.

Schauer, F, *Playing by the Rules: A Philosophical Examination of Rule–Bound Decision Making in Law and in Life* (1991). This needs to be read in conjunction with 'Is the Common Law Law?' (1989) *Cal LR* 77: 455. Schauer at 212–3 defends Hart's thesis that 'There are core meanings of rules (clear cases under the rules) even though they may not always be congruent with the core meaning of the ordinary language of the rule's canonical formulation. We must distinguish the conceptual possibility of literal interpretation as contrasted with its absurdity'.

Stone, J, *The Province and Function of Law: Law as Logic, Justice and Social Control. A Study in Jurisprudence* (1946, reprinted 1950). This is particularly valuable since it contains a very comprehensive bibliography and discussion of more or less everything relevant in print at this time. Chapter IV has an analysis and critique of Kelsen; it is not very good but it was all there was from the common law world at the time. Chapter XIX deals with Maine, and in his writings note should be taken of his very strange conception of customary law (in the Everyman edition reprint of 1972 at 7). Malinowski's polemics in *Crime and Custom in Savage Society* (1926) were directed against a picture of the nature of early society derived from Maine. I have explained this in my *Legal Theory and Legal History* in Chapter 17, dealing with 'R. S. Rattray and Ashanti Law at 418–421'.

Wittgenstein, L, *Philosophical Investigations* (1953). Edited by GH von Wright, R Rhees, and GEM Anscombe is the edition I have used. Note however there is now a 3rd edition of 2001 with the German text, and a revised English translation by Anscombe.

Index